The Art of Terror and Wonder

The Art of Terror and Wonder

A Novel

M. Alan Elwell

Copyright © 2024 M. Alan Elwell.

All rights reserved. No part of this book may be used or reproduced by any means, graphic, electronic, or mechanical, including photocopying, recording, taping or by any information storage retrieval system without the written permission of the author except in the case of brief quotations embodied in critical articles and reviews.

This is a work of fiction. All of the characters, names, incidents, organizations, and dialogue in this novel are either the products of the author's imagination or are used fictitiously.

CHAPTER ONE

Staring ahead as far as he can see, he watches the line of weeds along the side of the road stretch unbroken. He glances down at the odometer again: 1.3 miles since the last turn. According to the directions, he should be seeing the trail cut into the road by now.

Then he sees it, a break in the weed line up ahead. He slows the vehicle, then slows the vehicle further.

Driving up to the trailhead, he is surprised to find it isn't much of a trail at all. It's nothing more than an overgrown two-track that disappears into thick brush. This is getting a bit extreme. He's been driving dirt roads out into the middle of nowhere, and now this? Is this guy leading him on a wild goose chase? He hesitates. This is a lot to go through for a first meeting.

But this is the end of it; according to the directions, the trail dead-ends up ahead after two-tenths of a mile. He has been driving for more than three hours, and now the drive will be over. He slowly eases the SUV onto the trail.

Immediately, he becomes engulfed in greenery; branches and tall weeds scrape against the vehicle. It's like driving into a tunnel. The road is badly rutted. He is forced to slow down even further; it's a good thing he is driving a truck, not a car. What was Nate thinking, bringing him out here into something like this? Suddenly, the brush opens, and the trail smooths out. He is relieved to be traveling on slightly higher ground. On either side, tall trees rise from the brush, and there is plenty of light.

He shifts his focus to the situation ahead: he will be meeting Nate for the first time. This is the start of a new round; they could be working together for the next six months. He has started many new rounds before, but it's been a while, and he can't help but feel a bit uncertain. The challenge is to be open and responsive. He prepares himself by relaxing to connect with himself. He reminds himself again that he can't have high hopes for the encounter; his whole focus is on the opportunity to engage.

The trail ends exactly as the directions said it would. But he doesn't see another vehicle. After the long drive and having to slow down to navigate so many unexpected dirt roads, he is running a little late. He expected Nate to already be there, though he was fine with arriving first. It will give him a chance to relax and focus. It will feel good to get out of the vehicle.

Getting out of the SUV, Owen extends his arms above his head and stretches deeply, then extends the stretch through his body to the ground as he looks around. It is an interesting setting, definitely in the big woods. He appreciates Nate's effort to at least make their first meeting interesting; he takes it as an attempt to reflect the magnitude of their endeavor. Sunlight filters through the branches, and a breeze moves through the leaves. He takes a couple of deep breaths.

"Oh, here he is, the great warrior...."

Sounds of yelling crash around him from the woods beyond. "The lover of the unknown."

His instant reaction is to crouch down against the vehicle. "The explorer of consciousness...the liberator of possibility."

What is going on?

"Come to do battle with the great forces of *infinity*."

Where is the yelling coming from?

"There are worlds upon worlds before us."

Owen braces against the yelling. He recognizes the yelling as passages from the books.

"We are surrounded by unfathomable mystery." The yelling has to be Nate, but what is he doing?

"It's monstrous to think the world can ever be understood."

What comes to him is that the yelling must be some kind of ploy, an effort to take control. His next thought is that Nate must be off on some kind of indulgence, thinking he is practicing some technique from the books.

"Our lot is to learn, to be hurled into inconceivable new worlds."

Owen has experienced so many people lost to their ideas about what they think the material is about. From their emails, Nate seemed serious enough, sober enough, but he is probably just another goofball wannabe, caught up in the outrageousness of what he thinks is going on.

"The goal of life is the expansion of consciousness."

As Owen stands up from the vehicle against the force of the yelling, a huge wave of disappointment threatens to overwhelm him.

"The war is against ignorance…we are being robbed of our heritage."

Not again. He had such high hopes, worked so hard, struggled so hard. But he also finds himself in the middle of a situation. What he feels most is the force of yelling pushing against him.

"The individual self has deprived man of his power."

Owen feels the intent to hold him back. That's not what his life is about. His life is about action and moving forward, and this is the challenge before him. In an attempt to gain perspective and in reaction to the yelling, he lifts his eyes to the expanse around him. There is so much beyond; the world is immense.

"The thrust of the warrior's way is to dethrone self-importance...Life for a warrior is an exercise in strategy."

Against the magnitude, he feels the volume of his own living, and it is from that awareness that he responds. He hopes to open himself and be moved by the full power of existence; the full force of his life will proceed from this moment.

"A man goes to knowledge as he goes to war...wide-awake, with fear, with respect, and with absolute assurance."

Focusing on the yelling, Owen feels pressure against him, but his only interest is to move forward. He feels his commitment as a gathering of resolve from the volume and focus of his life and from the space around him. He next focuses on the source of the yelling as the source of the situation.

"Energy is the irreducible essence of everything."

His training has prepared him. His effort is to open to the yelling, take it in, connect with it, and be directed. The yelling fills him until it extends through him and engages with the ground, where the energy gathers and compresses, before expanding and extending back through him along the path of his focus to the yelling.

"The ultimate accomplishment of a warrior is joy."

Once established, his only choice is to follow the connection. Owen gathers himself and then starts forward. The challenge is to keep the energy moving. It is not of him and can't be him, or it will get stuck in him. He has to keep returning it as a flow; it is a life force he is keeping alive.

"Being detached from everything, a warrior becomes a part of everything."

Whatever happens is beyond him; he can only be open and connected. It is a dynamic he has exercised and trusts.

From the sound of yelling, the source isn't far, but the direction is through thick brush. Yet the path leading from where he parked his vehicle curves in that direction. His whole focus is to stay open and let the yelling fill him, and from that fullness, the energy expands and extends back to Nate. Owen follows that connection. The connection determines everything that will happen; his whole fate in the moment is to return the energy.

"A warrior considers himself already dead."

Nate keeps yelling. Owen feels the energy coming at him, but his only interest is to stay open and connected, letting the energy return through him.

"To break free from attachment and fly away on the wings of perception."

The energy has to return. If the energy doesn't return, the connection is broken, and he will be available to the energy. A lot of energy is building as it expands into a swelling pressure.

The path does turn left toward the yelling. He can see a flash of clothing through the trees, and then the sight of a guy is before him. The guy is not big, youngish, with a round face, and papers in his hands. His eyes show surprise, but there is also a look of determination as he keeps up the force of his yelling.

"Only as a warrior can one withstand the path of knowledge."

Through the yelling, Owen focuses on the center of energy. Intensity builds, with an element of compression and expansion. It drives him to focus all he is worth on taking in the energy and returning it. He has to keep receiving and returning. It's critical now. There is so much energy. If the energy's intensity gets stuck in him, it could be devastating. His whole life depends on returning the energy. As Nate draws closer, the space compresses. The energy is inside the space.

The intensity escalates to a scream. Owen focuses completely on the dynamic of opening and returning. Nate is not giving in. As the gap between them reduces, the compression between them escalates until it almost lifts Owen, but instead, it lifts his arm in the continuance of compressing and expanding, and as he reaches Nate, his arm comes down in the last instant of return on the top of Nate's head. The reaction is instant. It is like an explosion. Nate takes the full force of compressed energy; it is inside him, and immediately he begins vibrating with the power of the energy racing back and forth. The vibrating continues until Nate is convulsing. His body stiffens. His eyes roll up in his head, and his mouth is open.

Suddenly, Nate falls to the ground and convulses violently. Owen is shocked. He has never seen anything like it; he is witnessing a remarkable sight. He has no care for the outcome or conclusion. In that sense, he is in no position to control his involvement. He has fulfilled his role as a conduit for returning energy and is left only to witness. The rest is up to Nate and his involvement with the energy, so that as he convulses on the ground, he becomes aware, with a further element of wonder, that he may be witnessing the death of someone. It is unlikely Nate's body can withstand such convulsions; it seems it will shake itself to pieces. His eyes are bulging, his face is darkening, and his breathing is paralyzed. Unable to breathe, he will not survive.

Yet as he witnesses the scene, he is conscious of another awareness, as if on a horizon, but knowing that awareness is also of him, and with the same objective and dispassionate observation, he is aware of it growing, until the awareness begins to take shape and focus in the form of elements that at first remain arbitrary and passive, then grow in precedence until they gather and formulate and become personal. There will be a body. The body will be found. As the concept expands to fully form, it connects with the idea that Nate knows people and will be missed. Those connections could be traced back to his involvement, and authorities will be called. He is many things of space and time, but he is also of the particularity of this world. Directed by that particularity, an awareness coalesces until a concern begins to rise. He could be accused of causing the death of someone. For a moment longer, he remains caught between the different interpretations of the event until the ramifications against him continue to build, and he experiences something like a "Pop!" There will be a trial! He could spend the rest of his life in jail! The realization overpowers him with speed and force. He has to do something! And by the contortion and darkening color of Nate's face, there can't be much time. He steps forward, then drops to the ground. "Nate!" he yells. But nothing changes. He yells again as if trying to penetrate a barrier. "Nate!"

The energy racing back and forth inside of Nate has disconnected him from his breathing. "Breathe, Nate!" But his words aren't registering. He feels Nate is trying to look at him, but his body is thrashing about.

He could spend the rest of his life in jail!

An idea bursts into consciousness: it is whole and complete, something he remembers from the books, an almost exact situation between two apprentices. He immediately jumps on top of Nate, outlining him with his body. He inhales deeply, pushing his abdomen into Nate's. "Find my breath," he yells, his face just inches away. When he exhales and contracts his diaphragm, he hopes to feel Nate's abdomen follow, but nothing happens. He inhales again, extending his belly. "Find my breath!" he implores.

Nothing happens.

Again, he exhales and inhales deeply. "Follow my breath!"

His feeling is that Nate is at least hearing him but there isn't much time. Nate has to be on the verge of passing out. Owen has to be prepared to do everything he can to revive him. He expands his stomach into Nate's but nothing happens.

Then, after another sequence of thrusting and withdrawing his stomach, Nate's abdomen pushes back, spasms back and forth, and then he explodes in a huge gasp. Nate is suddenly gasping for air. The barrier has been broken.

Nate's breathing comes in gasps and spasms. He tries again

to get Nate to follow his breath, but it is of no use. Nate's breathing is trying too hard; he is trying to get it back all at once. Realizing he is only hindering him, he rolls off, leaving Nate to gasp on his own.

Nate continues rolling on the ground, gasping. His stomach heaves with his gasping.

His head thrashes back and forth as he struggles to breathe. Finally, he rolls on his side and pukes.

CHAPTER TWO

Owen squats off to the side, waiting for what will happen next.

Nate has gone back to rolling on the ground, gasping for breath.

His concern is for Nate, but he has no idea of his condition.

Nate's head rolls back and forth, but he isn't thrashing as much. His gasping is less intense. At least it seems Nate is going to survive. His eyes are closed, his face grimaced. The gasps become more controlled until his breaths come one after the other. Nate brings up a hand to cover his face. He then rolls onto his side and props himself up on an elbow, but the effort seems too much, and he rolls onto his back again. His body heaves with his breathing.

Owen can only watch and be ready. He has no idea what state Nate will end up in. He is also aware that something remarkable has happened; the explosion of energy is unlike anything he has ever experienced. He would like to think about it, but for the moment, he needs to stay focused on Nate.

"Keep breathing," he offers, as the need to offer something. Nate continues to breathe heavily.

Then, through the gasping comes a sputtering, and Nate's body begins to shake. Owen becomes alarmed; he doesn't know what to think.

Nate's body continues to shake. His head rolls back and forth, and gurgling noises come out of him as he gasps. His initial thought is that Nate's condition is worsening. Then, as he watches closely, a realization develops: Is Nate laughing? It is a shock to think that Nate could be laughing, and he watches closely as Nate's body sputters and shakes. Is he in pain? But a kind of giggling comes from the sputtering that makes him think Nate is actually laughing. What could he be laughing about? The guy nearly died! His immediate concern is that a lack of oxygen has damaged Nate's brain.

Nate is definitely laughing. His mouth is open, and a giggling bubbles out of him as his head rolls back and forth. "What the hell?" he then mutters through the sputtering. It is the first sound of words since the incident started. "Holy crap." The words aren't directed anywhere and mix with the escape of his laughing. But at least Nate has said something; it is a big deal. It is a further sign of possible recovery.

Nate's arms and legs continue to move about, his head rolls back and forth as he continues to laugh. His eyes are closed, but his mouth is open in something like a grimace or a grin. There has to be something wrong with him.

Nate then rolls onto his side again and props himself up with his elbow. Hair hangs over his face, and he shakes his head from side to side as if trying to clear it. "Damn," he says, and again the word isn't directed anywhere but is more speaking. The only option is to wait to assess what happens next. Nate stays looking down and shaking his head, "Man, that was weird."

Owen is sure whatever he experienced was weird, but what matters most is that Nate is connecting words. It is another sign of improvement. But in the next moment, Nate has pushed himself up further, leaning on his extended arm and looking at him through the messy hair hanging over his eyes. "So what the hell was that?" The words push at him. Is Nate really asking for an explanation? He isn't sure what Nate is referring to or how much he is even aware of what went on.

But before he has a chance to decide anything further, Nate continues speaking. "Man, you nailed me," he states, shaking his head again. There is a tone of annoyance mixed with amazement.

Nate then lifts his head and stares straight at him. "What did you do to me?"

Owen is shocked. There is no doubt now about what Nate is thinking. A moment ago, he was wondering whether Nate would even survive and had to hustle to catch up with the new direction of what was going on. Nate thinks he did something to him. He can imagine how Nate might think that, but it's not what happened. The real challenge is that he feels forced to respond. "You were the one doing the yelling," he says, dismissing the accusation directly.

Nate continues staring at him. "Oh, and that's why my head exploded?"

Owen laughs, just once. His surprise is at the force of accusation in Nate's voice; it could have felt like his head was exploding. But he doesn't want to offend Nate by making him think he is laughing at him, so he bites off the end of his laughter. "Yeah, something like that." Still, it might be too late. Nate remains staring at him. The most pressing issue is that Nate thinks he did something to him, even though he really didn't. It could seem that way; he was definitely involved and feels the need to address the issue as the next step in getting Nate to understand. "Hey, I just returned your energy."

Nate continues to glare at him through the hair hanging over his eyes. "My energy?" He seems annoyed, but he is also considering what was said. "Oh, and you didn't hit me?" Another flash of recrimination crosses his face.

Owen can see he isn't getting anywhere trying to get Nate to simply believe his explanation. But he isn't about to take on the force of recrimination, either. Because he didn't do anything on his own, Nate caused the situation. Owen feels the need to direct that truth back at him. "You pretty much did it to yourself."

Nate continues to stare at him, though for the moment he can't outright reject what Owen has said. "I did it to myself, huh?" His tone is a tangle of annoyance and sarcasm. He keeps thinking while maintaining a look of recrimination. "Well, I don't remember any of that in the books."

It is Owen's turn to laugh. He even tilts his head back, but catches himself again. Part of his laughter is the continued relief that Nate is processing thoughts and moving further toward recovery. Another part comes from the growing awareness that a ludicrous situation has settled on him. Now, Nate is trying to connect what he experienced to events in the books. It is an understandable attempt, but Owen is quick to spare Nate the trouble. "It's not in the books," he offers.

Yet as soon as he responds, he is aware that he has opened himself to further scrutiny.

"So what was it?"

Owen is now in a different situation. He knows Nate won't understand what he did, so he will only add to Nate's confusion. He doesn't want to make the effort to try to explain, and he doesn't want to seem evasive or get Nate more annoyed, so he feels he has no other choice but to be direct. "It was more a martial thing."

"Martial arts!" Nate nearly yells, pushing himself up farther on his arm. "Now we're doing martial arts!" Nate has turned his whole body to face him. "Man, I could have died!"

Owen can't help but laugh, a sudden release after taking the full force of the accusation. Yes, it's true that Nate could have died, but what's missing is any responsibility for what happened. And Owen isn't willing to have the onus put on him anymore. "Hey, what did you expect?" he says, feeling his own flare of annoyance. "You can't just go off yelling like that and expect nothing to happen. We're not playing tiddlywinks here. This is serious stuff!" It's Nate's turn to be the focus of the accusation. For the moment, he remains puffed up with indignation, but he can't sustain the posture and slowly begins to deflate. Nate continues staring at him without saying anything more, then looks down, unable to deny what he has been told. Owen's attempt to push back at him seems to have at least neutralized his momentum. But Owen's response has also caused a rise of amazement. What was Nate thinking? It's true that if Nate was going to yell like that, he had to expect something might happen. It makes him wonder. He decides to continue pressing Nate. "So what was all that yelling about?"

Nate remains looking down. He suddenly seems sheepish. He then shakes his head as if feeling forced to confess. "Obviously, something that didn't work."

Owen laughs again, this time freely. It's as he thought; Nate's yelling must have been some misguided attempt at some technique from the books.

Being able to deflect Nate's accusation and get him to see his own part in what happened has brought everything back to an even level between them. It allows Owen to shift his focus for the moment and refocus on Nate's condition. What Nate experienced had to be devastating. He is sure Nate is a whole lot better than before, but isn't convinced Nate is fully recovered. "You all right?"

Nate seems to take the inquiry seriously and, for a moment, assesses himself. "I think so," he says. There remains a tone of annoyance in his voice, but it doesn't seem directed at anything in particular. "Man, this is some crazy shit," he says as punctuation.

Owen again laughs. Of course, this is crazy. "We're dealing with *power*."

They have come to a neutral space.

Nate then sits all the way up, and after another moment, makes the effort to get to his feet. He dusts himself off and takes a couple of steps. He seems to be assessing himself further. Owen stands up as well.

Nate continues to scrutinize his condition by walking around, then stretching his arms over his head, then turning his torso from side to side. All indications are that he is OK. Owen feels further relief. After a few more moments of extending his arms and legs, then twisting around, Nate simply states, "I still don't think you had to hit me."

Owen struggles not to laugh.

Nate continues stretching, then simply asks, "So what should we do?"

Owen shrugs, not wanting to be the one to make the decision, but he is willing to make the situation clear: "We're here for a reason." Yes, they are. They are here to do the interview, and Nate nods in agreement but says nothing more, so Owen decides to push the issue. "You up for it?" Nate hesitates, then says he is, though he doesn't seem very enthused. "So what's next?" Owen asks, since Nate suggested they come out here.

"I've got a place," Nate answers. Owen figured he did.

"We'll need to go this way." Nate motions with his hand along the trail, away from where he parked. Owen says he needs to get his things. He walks to his vehicle and grabs his backpack.

When he returns, Nate turns halfway to face him. "Hey, I thought we weren't supposed to get into any kind of confrontation," he says. There is an undercurrent of recrimination in his tone, but his question seems mostly genuine. Owen knows what he is referring to because he has thought about the issue himself. The system guidelines clearly state that the two participants are not to have any physical contact. It is a safeguard against things getting out of hand. A lot of intensity can be unleashed when dealing with the material; it taps into people's deepest hopes and fears. Bullying and abuse are on one end of the spectrum of possibilities, and sexual involvement is on the other. As a warning, the consequence of a confrontation is that participants consider their involvement terminated, and each must wait to participate in the system again when the next cycle begins after another six months. There is no doubt that he and Nate had a confrontation, but Owen isn't willing to dismiss their working together so easily and has already thought of an explanation. "We hadn't started yet," he says. It's true; they hadn't yet agreed to work together, so they weren't officially involved.

After a moment, Nate nods his head. He seems satisfied with the answer. Nate simply turns and leads down the path.

CHAPTER THREE

The path through the brushy area is well-defined, then becomes less discernible as it climbs uphill into a large area of pines. The pines are spaced apart, with few lower branches, and are planted in rows; they are walking through a pine plantation. It makes Owen wonder if this is private land. Because of all the undeveloped land he had traveled through to get here, he thought the area was mostly state land, but maybe not, though it hardly mattered. He assumes Nate knows what he is doing. Beneath the trees, the ground is bare of undergrowth and covered with a blanket of yellowed pine needles. The sun blinks on and off through the canopy; otherwise, the understory is shaded and cool.

Owen is still feeling a bit unsettled after his initial encounter with Nate. What went on between them was extreme; the whole exchange was crazy. The explosion of energy was far beyond anything he had ever experienced and was a monumental moment. His initial reaction is to want to review the details, but he is hesitant to ponder what happened or try to figure anything out; there will be plenty of time for that. Now he faces another situation. They will have their interview. It will determine what else goes on between them. He wants to be ready.

Owen walks behind Nate. They are quite possibly starting another round together. It has been a while since he has been involved with the system, and he is always impressed by how it works. He emailed his interest in being included in the next round and received a contact email address. He and Nate then connected and set up their meeting. It's how it always happens. It is a simple process, though a bit mysterious. When he first encountered the system, he was talking with someone he never spoke with afterward about the don Juan books, and the guy told him about the system. The books were amazing, and he knew there were millions of other readers as impressed as he was, so it didn't surprise him that people wanted to explore and work with the material. So he decided to give the system a try. He sent an email to the system's general email address and received a contact email address in return; the rest is history.

Owen continues to follow Nate. This could be his new partner, the guy he could be working with for the next six months. And they got off to such a crazy start. He wonders who he is dealing with and takes a moment to open himself to his impressions. He already knows that Nate is young, probably in his mid-twenties, which means he isn't very experienced, though that isn't necessarily a bad thing. All Owen cares about is having someone he can engage with. Walking behind, he notices Nate's physicality: he isn't big or muscular, but he does seem athletic in a wiry way, and there is a bounce in his step that at least indicates liveliness and strong energy. Owen is reminded of the wild yelling of passages from the books and how Nate pushed back at him and even got indignant. There is at least some life in the guy. All Owen really wants in a partner is someone with exuberance and, hopefully, some staying power. So many of the people he has been involved with over the years have had a great attraction to the material, but when it comes to action, which is the essence of the practice, there just hasn't been much. Owen is looking for someone to cause action in him as well, as a kind of boost, a greater challenge, and from the way they started, Nate has at least been that. Otherwise, he doesn't want to get too detailed in his assessment of Nate and is willing to let the encounter unfold. For the moment, he allows himself the pleasure of knowing he is at least having an encounter; it's been too long since he has been working on his own. And he is in one hell of a setting. Looking around, the pines stretch tall, the air is fresh and scented, and it is good being outdoors. In that sense, he is already grateful to Nate for his effort in making the setting of their first encounter impressive. So many of his first interview meetings have been in parks and coffee shops.

The path leads gently uphill in an ascending. Then, up ahead, he sees open sky emerging beyond the pines. The landscape will change. But before they reach the opening, Nate turns left off the trail and follows one of the last rows of pine trees farther uphill. Near the top of the incline, Nate turns right.

Leaving the pines is like walking through an entrance. The expanse of blue sky and sunshine is immediately intense. Owen hesitates, trying to make sense of what he is experiencing. Before him, just above eye level, thick green foliage extends into open space.

But after taking a few more steps and encountering tightly-spaced saplings, then overlaid dead and whitened branches that litter the ground through the underbrush, he begins to understand that they have entered a massive, overgrown clear-cut. By the height of the new growth of young trees extending to over his head, the clear-cut has to be several years old.

He expects the going to become difficult, but as Nate leads decisively through the tangle of branches, his progress appears only slightly impeded, and Owen wonders if there is some path he can't see. He looks for any sign of branches being cut or moved to the side, but there isn't a defined trail.

Before going much farther, they step into a small opening in the brush. Two chairs face each other. On one sits a backpack.

So this is where they will have their interview. Owen can't help but be impressed. "Nice," he says, nodding in approval as he looks around. The space has clearly been shaped from the surrounding brush: branches have been pushed back, and some small saplings where the chairs have been placed have been cut off close to the ground. It is a fine example of Nate's effort to make their first meeting dramatic. They are out in the middle of a big expanse. Owen takes his impression as a reflection of their condition of being human, surrounded by the immensity of existence, and believes Nate probably intended the feeling as a reflection of concepts from the material. Otherwise, his feeling is of being in a pit or a nest, surrounded by walls of greenery.

Owen takes off his backpack and moves to the empty chair. They both sit and open their packs. Nate offers a bottle of water, but Owen declines, saying he has brought his own. They both take a moment to open their bottles and take a drink.

It is on to the business at hand. They both pull out notebooks with their interview sheets.

The interview, as the first step in any involvement between two new partners, is an icebreaker, a chance to get to know each other and focus on the material. It has been Owen's experience that in a very short time, he'll be able to tell a lot about what kind of person Nate will be to work with.

"Any interest in going first?" Nate asks.

It doesn't make any difference to him.

"All right," Nate says, flipping through his notebook until he finds the list of questions. "Here we go: How many years have you been involved with the system?"

Owen is ready with his answer. "Ten."

"Ten," Nate repeats and nods his head, seemingly both a bit impressed and surprised. "Well, that's a chunk."

Yes, it is a chunk, though it is obvious he is a bit older than

Nate, so it should make sense that he has been at it a while. He then returns the question.

"Three," Nate answers.

That's about what Owen expected, though he had hoped for a higher number. It suggests Nate is just getting started with the system and probably doesn't yet have a solid foundation for understanding the material. In his experience, it takes years to form a clear picture of what the books are about. Yet it hardly matters. Again, his greatest hope is that Nate will have some exuberance and staying power.

"So, how long do you think the system has been going on?" Nate asks.

Owen is surprised by the question; it's not part of the interview, and the guidelines specifically state that communication between the participants should stick to the list of questions and topics. The intent is to keep the partners focused and prevent them from getting off on tangents. Yet Owen can understand Nate's interest. He has probably never known someone who has been with the system so long, and wanting to know how long it has existed is a natural curiosity. But Owen doesn't have much of an answer for him. All he knows is that the system was in place before he got involved, and he tells him so.

"So who do you think set it up?"

Owen hesitates to answer. Again, he is concerned about getting sidetracked, but this question is obvious enough, so he answers directly. "Don't have a clue." He has never really cared to know. As far as he was concerned, the system was set up by power itself to perpetuate itself, and the people it worked through were inconsequential.

Nate looks down at his sheet while taking a moment to think.

He was obviously hoping for more information.

"So how many rounds you been through?" Owen then asks, taking the lead in moving the interview forward by asking the next question.

"This will be my fourth," Nate answers directly. That sounds about right.

"How about you?" "Fourteen."

"Fourteen!" Nate responds incredulously, not even trying to hide his surprise. "Holy smokes!"

Owen is again surprised that Nate is so surprised. He already told him he has been involved with the system for ten years, and with each year having two six-month rounds, there have been at most twenty rounds available. The fact that he has done fourteen means he has taken time off, and he has, mostly over the last few years.

"Wow!" Nate adds. A short burst of laughter punctuates his amazement. "I bet you've seen some things."

There he goes again, getting off subject. Owen doesn't bother bringing it up and gives a short answer. Yes, he's seen some things. The scope of the material is huge.

"So have you stopped the world?" Nate then asks.

What! It is Owen's turn to be incredulous. He laughs, first, because Nate is so blatantly ignoring the interview directive, and second, because what he is referring to is one of the greatest accomplishments of a warrior. Stopping the world is when the endless flow of perceptual interpretations a person makes to form an understanding of the world we call reality is brought to a halt, and the world consequently collapses. It is what a warrior strives for. When the barrier is broken, other perceptual possibilities hidden behind the façade of continuous interpretation become available. He can understand Nate thinking he might have accomplished stopping the world because he has been working at it for so long, but it also speaks to Nate's ignorance of the obstacles a warrior faces. The forces that keep a person's attention fixed on upholding a description of the everyday world of familiar perception are truly formidable.

And Owen has experienced some remarkable moments, but

he isn't interested in telling Nate about them because it's none of his business, though he also doesn't want to be evasive.

"I've had my moments."

"Are you able to shut off the internal dialogue?"

There he goes again. Is this guy incorrigible? Owen feels the need to say something. The system's directive is very clear. "Hey, we need to stay focused here."

Nate reacts as if he were being reprimanded and is also surprised by himself. He sits back in his chair and lowers his head.

Owen's only interest is to get on with the interview.

"So what techniques are you practicing?"

Nate answers directly. "I'm focused on using *death as an advisor*."

That's something. He was expecting Nate to say he was practicing *erasing personal history*, *disrupting routines*, or practicing one of the other techniques mentioned in the books, and in all the rounds he has been through, he has never had anyone say that *using death as an advisor* is the technique they were most focused on. And it's a powerful technique. Death is the great equalizer, the overriding force; the idea of death is what gives life its immediacy and flavor. Having Nate mention he is *using death as an advisor* makes Owen curious about him, and he would like to ask how he is treating the subject, but he just made a big deal about Nate sticking to the interview and doesn't want to commit the same offense. But he doesn't hesitate to let Nate know that he is impressed. "That's some powerful stuff."

"It really is," Nate answers, as if given an opening. "It really puts things in perspective. I mean, we're all just people on our way to dying, right? The idea of death tempers a warrior's spirit. How can we feel overly important if we know that death is stalking us?" Nate then sticks his finger in the air to make a point and is clearly quoting from the books. "Without a clear view of death, there is no order, no sobriety, no beauty. The knowledge of his death is what gives a warrior courage. It guides him and makes him detached and silently lusty." He gives a short laugh, seemingly impressed by the idea of being "lusty." They both smile.

The fact that Nate has quoted from the books is impressive, though Owen has known others who have quoted from the material. The real indication of someone's seriousness isn't their ability to memorize passages but their commitment to the practice, and that remains to be seen. He looks at Nate more closely and, for the first time, notices a slight upturn to his nose. His eyes seem a little wider apart than normal. His mouth is wide as well. There is an impish quality to him.

"So what techniques are you focused on?" Nate asks in return.

Owen is ready with his answer. "I'm focused on recapitulation." Nate reacts strongly. "Really? Wow, that's some serious stuff."

Yes, it is serious. Owen is glad Nate seems at least to be somewhat familiar with what he has mentioned. Recapitulation is mostly dealt with in the later books of the series.

"So you have a crate?" Nate asks.

Yes, he has a crate.

"So how long you stay in there?"

Nate is getting off on a tangent again, but he doesn't raise the issue.

"As long as I can."

"And recapitulation is the way to gain energy," Nate adds. "And energy is all we need for our path."

Owen is pleased that Nate has at least some understanding, but is anxious to move on.

They are now ready for what is considered the "awareness section" of the interview. It consists of a list of general topics the new partners are to discuss. The topics are broad in scope and, by association, can cover a large portion of the material. It is up to the partners to decide how to handle them. Nate's response will tell a lot. Owen's approach to handling the topics is to address them generally, mostly for the sake of expediency. The topics are too broad to explain fully, and it can be easy to get caught up in a volume of interpretation; there will be plenty of time for clarification later. He only wants to present a flavor.

Before getting started, the system's directive is to read an opening statement. The intent is to get participants focused on an overarching perspective. He lets Nate read it.

"Everything that surrounds us is an unfathomable mystery. We must try to unravel these mysteries, but without any hope of doing so. A warrior, aware of the unfathomable mystery that surrounds him and aware of his duty to unravel it, takes his rightful place among the mysteries and regards himself as one."

OK. On to the particulars.

"Discuss: Reality: The Nature of Perception."

Owen has a statement he prepared in the past for this moment. He looks down at his notes.

"As human beings, we are perceivers. The nature of reality is what we perceive. The world we think we see is only a view."

"All sentient beings are perceivers," Nate interjects.

He is taken aback but attributes the interruption to Nate's natural enthusiasm.

"True. And the reality we perceive is the interpretation of a description, dictated to us from the moment we are born, until our world is maintained by our endless internal talk, which leaves no room for possibility and becomes the permanent view that all human beings share."

Owen pauses to give Nate an opportunity to add to the discussion, and he does. "The world is as it looks and yet it isn't. All our lives, we develop one direction to look and keep repeating our choices until the day we die, never realizing that the reality of our perception is only a view."

Owen is pleased. Nate seems to have some understanding. He picks up the conversation.

"Yes, and if we are able to break the fixation and the constant flow of interpretation of perception from its socialized norm, a vast world of expanded perception becomes available."

"It's what we as warriors are determined to explore," Nate adds. "There is incalculable power at our fingertips. Our goal is to return to our natural state as magical beings."

That's good. Owen can't help but be a bit impressed. He has nothing more to add. It's a good place to end the discussion of the first topic. They've gotten off to a nice start working together.

On to the next subject. Nate takes the lead.

"Discuss: *Power*, the *spirit*."

Owen is ready with an answer.

"*Spirit* is the pervading force of the universe that guides men's lives and the lives of all things and is available to everyone. But only as warriors are we aware of it and work to strengthen our connection and be available to its directive."

"Eh, that's good," Nate says.

It is the effect Owen was after. He's not messing around. If they're going to bang a drum, they might as well bang a big one.

"*Spirit* is like a voice that speaks to us if we can hear. It is what we strive to polish our connection with," Nate offers. "So that we can become sensitive to its influence."

"Every act performed by warriors is either performed as a way to strengthen their link with *spirit* or as a response triggered by the link itself."

It's a good general summary.

Owen brings up the next topic. "Discuss: Self-importance."

Nate is ready. "Self-importance is what separates us from our heritage of magnitude and mystery."

Owen nods in agreement. "Self-importance is the activity that consumes the greatest amount of our energy."

"Self-importance is the force generated by the perpetuation of man's self-image," Nate adds.

Owen responds, "Self-importance requires that we spend most of our lives being offended by someone. Self-Importance is the three-thousand-headed monster," he then says, in an attempt to get them to the big picture; it is the dramatic description offered in the books.

"Every effort should be made to break the chains of self-reflection," Nate says, raising his finger again for emphasis.

They reach a crescendo, and both end up laughing. It was like leapfrogging along, and they had fun. They are both impressed with the exchange.

Owen asks the next question, giving Nate the chance to answer first. "Discuss: The Warrior's Way."

Nate looks up at him. "It's what we do as a way to get closer to the *spirit*."

Owen is ready and returns his response, "The Warrior's Way is a strategy of action, designed for maximum effect, to account for the understanding that we are surrounded by an unfathomable mystery, and our commitment to try to unravel it."

"OK. Right on," Nate says, he is impressed. He then adds something of his own. "The Warrior's Way is how we approach the condition of being human."

Owen nods his head.

"And it's a strategy for gaining energy," Nate continues before Owen has a chance to respond. It's obvious Nate has had a thought come to mind. "Because energy is what we need to go forward on our journey."

That's true. Energy is all that is needed to accomplish everything available to a warrior. Along those lines, Owen thinks of something else to add. "The Warrior's Way is also a strategy for disconnecting us from what has captured our energy and holds us in place." He then remembered a concept he had reviewed and used before when preparing for this interview. "The Warrior's

Way is designed to revamp our lives by altering our basic reactions about being alive."

Nate then jumps in, thrusting his finger into the air again as dramatic punctuation, making it clear he is going for another quote from the material. "War, for a warrior, is the total struggle against the individual self that has deprived man of his power."

Owen has to smile. Nate's response is pretty good.

His answer is a good finish to the subject. Their answers have been direct and to the point, leading to a quick back-and-forth between them. What most impresses him is that Nate doesn't hesitate; he is willing to jump in. This shows a level of effort and confidence.

So, it is on to the next topic. They should be able to get on another roll. Owen looks at his notes. "Discuss: *Controlled Folly*."

But before they start, Nate brings up another issue. "Hey, it's getting late. We probably should decide on what we're going to do for the night."

Owen is surprised. Neither of them has a watch. For Owen, not having a watch is an attempt to avoid the organizing and defining nature of time, but lifting his head, he can see above the circle of greenery that the light of the sky has become golden. The day is moving toward evening.

In their initial communication to set up the meeting, given the distance between where they each lived and the effort required to coordinate their schedules, they agreed to be available for a couple of days. In his mind, the only thing Owen committed to was the interview. He expected it to be over by now. He was a little concerned when Nate suggested meeting later in the afternoon than he would have liked, but he decided to go along with it, thinking they would still have plenty of time to finish, and if he didn't see any future in continuing with Nate, he could just leave. But their initial encounter delayed them from getting started, and Owen hadn't expected to be hiking out into the woods. Now he has a decision to make.

But things with Nate have gone decently enough; they are surely in the ballpark of what he could hope for. And heck, having a crazy experience like their initial encounter is reason enough to continue being involved. So, he is willing to move forward, and if they plan to spend the night, they probably need to prepare.

"What do you have in mind?" "I have a place to camp."

Owen figures Nate did, since he was asked to bring a sleeping bag. "Where is it?"

"Not far."

But Owen will need to get his sleeping bag from his vehicle. "I've got some extra blankets," Nate suggests. "You can use them, or you can have the sleeping bag. There's a tent, and it should stay nice tonight."

Owen hesitates, but he can't think of any reason not to go along.

With the decision made, they pack up their things. After putting on his backpack, Nate simply turns and steps into the underbrush.

CHAPTER FOUR

Owen follows Nate as he leads them farther from the direction they came, farther from his vehicle, and deeper into the clear-cut. He is again surprised that Nate isn't struggling through the saplings and tangles of scattered dead branches, and he again looks for some kind of trail. But Nate is taking his time, picking his way through the growth and debris, and seems confident in his direction. Owen is a little uncomfortable being part of someone else's initiative, but what truly unnerves him is the awareness that with each step, he knows less and less where he is. He believes he could still get out of here if he had to, but it will be dark soon, and everything will change. He is reminded that the warrior's first precept in any situation is to control the battlefield, and he has surely lost that opportunity. He wanted to make something happen and was willing to let Nate take the lead, but this is getting far beyond where he thought things would take him.

As they continue through the clear-cut, Owen notices they are beginning to move slightly downhill. Suddenly, they step into another opening. It is immediately clear that this opening has been carved out of the brush. With a cleared ground floor, the brush forms thick walls on four sides, and the opening is about the size of a small bedroom. On one side is a tent, on the other a fire pit.

But what most catches his attention is the view, the fact that there is one. The land before him falls away, and he can look out over the tops of small trees across a marvelous expanse that sweeps out to the full extent of the clear-cut, ending at a far line of trees. At a quick glance, Owen can see that some of the saplings in front of him have been trimmed to reveal the landscape. Owen is impressed. "Excellent," he says, nodding, expressing his first impression. For a moment, Nate stands next to him, looking out over the expanse.

Owen turns, takes off his backpack, and looks more closely at the site. The small fire pit on one side is lined with rocks, looks well-used, and has a small pile of kindling beside it. Behind the wood is a curious setup of two weather-worn posts sunk in the ground, with two equally trimmed, thick branches connecting them. Owen isn't quite sure what they are for. He wonders aloud to Nate, "Did you make this place?" Nate says he didn't, which makes Owen wonder who did. Are the other people involved warriors? This place definitely shows a warrior's sensibility. But he doesn't care to pursue the question now, though he will surely return to it.

Owen is again drawn to the expanse; it is truly stupendous. The sun is setting, and the golden light illuminates the sweep of greenery. What is most captivating is the feeling of great space; the view is perfect for cultivating a warrior's mood of wonder and humility. Owen is sure the place was selected and created with that in mind.

Nate moves to his backpack, takes out his notebook, then steps past the fire pit and sits on the ground. He leans back against the two crossbeams attached to the two sunken posts. Owen can now see that the branches' design serves as a backrest for sitting, which makes perfect sense. He is surprised to find that when sitting, the ground has been slightly scooped out beneath him to accommodate his hips and make sitting more comfortable.

Sitting causes a very different experience with the site. Owen is now unable to see beyond the opening at all unless he looks up at a steep angle. It makes him feel confined and is a stark contrast to what he was just feeling looking out over the expanse. He is sure the dramatic change is also intentional and cultivated by whoever chose this site. It seems a reflection of a warrior's awareness that the world is immense, while the condition of being human is contained and small.

They are ready to get back to the interview. They return to where they left off: "Discuss: *Controlled folly*."

"*Controlled folly* is a warrior's strategy of behavior," Nate begins. "For dealing with oneself and the world around him."

Owen replies. summarizing from a statement he has devised. "*Controlled folly* is an artistic way of being separated from everything while remaining an integral part of everything."

"The idea of death reduces everything to equal," Nate continues, also reading from his notes. "And with nothing being more important than everything else, and in the absence of self-importance, a warrior's only way of dealing with himself and the world around him is in terms of folly."

That's pretty good. Owen is again impressed.

"A warrior has nothing but his *controlled folly*."

The topic feels decently summed up. Time to move to the next.

"Discuss: The First Attention."

"The first attention is our everyday awareness," Nate offers. "It's everything we can possibly perceive in our normal state of endless interpretation."

"The first attention is the known," Owen states. "It's our socialized perception." There is the feeling of an effort to return to the back-and-forth dynamic that served them well.

"The first attention is the bubble of perception we live our lives in," Owen continues, in an attempt to expand the definition. "And what we witness on its round walls is our reflection."

"Good one," Nate says, then adds another description. "The first attention is just one layer of the onion. There are layers upon layers available."

Yes, and the inference that there are other layers of the onion testifies to how much lies beyond everyday perception, a lead-in to the next topic: the second attention. But there is also another side of the first attention that is not usually mentioned. "The first attention is the great organizer," Owen offers. "It makes order out of the great volume of our perception. It gives our everyday perception continuity and cohesion. Without it, we would be surrounded by chaos."

"That's true," Nate says and nods his head as if remembering the concept. "The first attention is what organizes the chaos into a cohesive and shared perception."

They are then set up for the next subject. Nate starts.

"Discuss: The Second Attention."

"Everything beyond the first attention," Owen offers. "The vast area of perception is too vast to understand, but as warriors, we choose to explore."

"The part of us that, as average men, we live with all our lives, but are never aware of. The other layers of the onion." Nate then offers something different. "The first attention is like a wave, and the second attention is the ocean."

The analogy catches Owen's attention because it feels familiar, not from the books but perhaps from Zen Buddhism. It suggests Nate's experience with spiritual paths might extend beyond the don Juan material. There might be more to this guy than he originally thought.

Owen thinks of something from the books and decides to bring it up.

"Remember how the two attentions are separated by a barrier that can't be crossed? It's a quirk of perception."

"What happens in the first can be remembered in the second, but not the other way around," Nate clarifies. He then laughs. "Remember how Carlos used to dread returning to his normal state of awareness after being in heightened awareness? He dreaded knowing the ass he was going to become and how bleak and petty his life was going to be, and don Juan had to rap him on the top of his head with his knuckles to settle him down."

Owen laughs as well. That section of the book was hilarious. Carlos Castaneda, as the author and protagonist of the books based on his involvement with his teacher, don Juan, and his world of alternate reality, experienced countless shifts in expanded perception. Much of his training was done in the second attention, yet when he returned to the first attention, none of that experience carried through. Then he broke the barrier of perception, and memories flooded him as if he had lived a whole different life.

They are ready for the next subject.

But before they continue, Owen suddenly feels resistance to moving forward. It comes from a growing awareness that the sun has gone down; twilight is upon them. He looks up to see the sky bathed in golden light. Twilight is the time of power for a warrior, when the world as it is generally known loses its definition and other forms of perception become more readily available. Owen feels the need to take advantage of the twilight in this impressive setting; he hasn't had an opportunity like this in quite a while and might not again for some time to come. If they are going to spend the night, they might as well take full advantage of what's available. The rest of the interview can wait. He tells Nate that they should take advantage of the twilight as a warrior's time of power, and Nate seems surprised by the suggestion. Owen then says they should focus on sitting quietly and turning off the internal dialogue. He is sure that turning off the internal dialogue, as the key accomplishment a warrior strives for in stopping the world, is something Nate is very much aware of.

"OK," Nate says in consent.

To further his interest, Owen gets up and moves to the edge of the opening and sits down cross-legged, staring into the wall of greenery, in an attempt to be cut off from as much outside stimuli as possible.

His next effort is to relax and open. After all the day's activity, Owen looks forward to quieting himself. He is truly in a magnificent setting. The space around him is already laced with shadow, and above the site, the sky remains thick with golden light. He hears the sporadic calls of birds as they prepare for the coming evening. Owen gazes forward and lets his eyes relax.

From a warrior's perspective, the internal dialogue is our endless talking to ourselves, a flow of perceptual interpretation that upholds our inherited description of the world, turning it into something known, solid, and defined, and keeping us confident that we understand the world around us well enough to decide how best to proceed. But when the internal dialogue stops, so does the steady stream of interpretation, and the solidity of our perception collapses, revealing extraordinary facets of ourselves as though they had been kept under wraps. In theory, turning off the internal dialogue seems simple, but it is not easy. There are powerful forces within human beings invested in upholding our inherited view and satisfying our need for control, even if it means holding us back from our true nature and potential. Owen has struggled greatly to turn off his internal dialogue, and any success he has had has come from a determined, persistent effort. There have been moments when the internal dialogue has dropped away and the immensity beyond has come forward, but they have been few. That is the pattern of progress for a warrior. After enough time and repeated effort to turn off the internal dialogue and accrue the resulting increments of inner silence, the internal dialogue collapses.

Owen slows his mind by letting his thoughts pass through like a parade. The key is not focus on any thought because it will quickly expand into a line of thinking and dominate his awareness. Owen intends to just open himself and be available. There is so much magnitude and mystery in the world. Against the backdrop of infinity, the idle chattering of his thoughts is boring and inconsequential.

At one point, Owen shifts his focus from the expanse around him to the leaves of the small trees and shrubs just in front of him at eye level. By focusing on something specific, he can capture his attention and block out the thoughts that constantly threaten to buzz into consciousness. He is also aware of the idea from the books of enlarging the world by making it smaller, by focusing on the minutest detail. His intent is to be absorbed by every facet of the leaves. There is still a greenish color to the leaves, but it is fading fast. He picks out one leaf to focus on and notices its oval but pointed shape, the pattern of veins, and traces each line of vein with his awareness. He then moves on to another leaf. There are times when he feels his attention dragged away by an intruding thought, but he simply brings his attention back to the study of leaves. It is the most important thing right now. The world is made up of an infinity of detail. There are worlds upon worlds before him.

When it grows too dark to make out the leaves in front of him, Owen shifts his focus to examining shadows. There are layers upon layers of them. It is like staring into a rich tapestry. Owen concentrates on his breathing, the steady in-and-out of inhaling and exhaling.

After a time, the strain of keeping thoughts from intruding into consciousness becomes too much. He knows it isn't good to force the matter. Turning off the internal dialogue is like water wearing away stone and has to be done gradually. He tries not to focus on his body beginning to ache from sitting cross-legged for so long.

CHAPTER FIVE

A massive silence has grown to dominate the world. The night is huge. Infinity stretches beyond. Owen is aware of an intensity in himself matched by the world around him. But his legs are becoming numb.

Suddenly, there is a small flash of flame from behind him.

Owen doesn't break his posture before shifting his body. The first thing he does is stretch out his legs.

A fire will be good. After another moment, he stands and returns to sit next to Nate, huddling over a pile of sticks. The fire catches and starts to grow.

He is very much looking forward to having a fire. The fire will be a great addition to all that he is feeling. As Nate works on the fire, Owen focuses beyond it. The night is amazing. What he feels most is the huge volume, and is content to bask in it. His interest is to continue to open himself.

But someone is sitting next to him, someone he could be working with to pursue his path. In that sense, Owen is willing to include the person in his sense of openness; he feels obligated to include Nate if he wants to include everything. In the next instant, Owen realizes they will have to speak at some point. The sound of their voices against such expanse and silence will sound like gunshots. He decides to be the first to say something.

"Quite the night," he says, in an attempt to encompass everything that he is feeling. He is almost surprised that his voice doesn't echo. "Absolutely," Nate answers, reflecting his own sense of amazement.

Looking at the fire, he is only grateful. The fire seems the perfect touch to all that he is feeling. But he would like it to be bigger, to match everything both inside and outside; he wants to take full advantage.

So, when Nate sits back to watch the growing flames, Owen takes it upon himself to reach out and take another couple of sticks from the pile and put them on the fire.

"Better be careful," Nate responds. His words suddenly compress the space between them. Then, as punctuation to what he said, Nate leans over and takes off the couple of sticks just placed. Owen can't help but feel he has been reprimanded. And there doesn't seem to be any real reason for it. The night air is still, so there isn't any wind to cause a chance of the fire getting away from them.

"You sure?" he says, feeling the need to address the issue.

"Fires are illegal," Nate says, then gives a quick laugh, aware of the obvious irony. "Hey, I'm OK with being a little illegal."

Owen struggles to make sense. He understands that fires might be illegal, but they already have one and are going to take care of it, so they're honoring the spirit of the law's intent. If they have a little fire, why not have a little bigger one? Nate's decision seems arbitrary. Is he trying to control the situation? Owen isn't willing to simply acquiesce. "Can we be a little more illegal?"

Nate hesitates before answering. "If there's too much fire, they'll spot us."

What? Owen is even more surprised. How will someone spot them? "We're out in the middle of nowhere."

"They got planes."

Airplanes! Owen's mind suddenly somersaults. Where is Nate coming from? "Who's got planes?"

"The Forest Service. They can spot a fire up to ten miles." Owen struggles to make sense. "In the dark?"

"They have infrared."

Infrared? Owen is suddenly left reeling. The image that comes to mind is of guys flying around all night, hunched over instruments. And what if they did see them? The idea of guys in battle gear fighting their way through the tangle of clear-cut, trying to find them, in the dark is ludicrous. The image makes him laugh. "They'd sure have a hell of a time finding us."

Nate answers matter-of-factly. "They'd be waiting in the morning." Owen's struggle to make sense is becoming desperate.

Nate then laughs, adding, "And your vehicle will be a lot easier to find than mine."

Owen feels his head begin to spin. What is truly unnerving is that Nate seems convinced of what he is saying. And it just doesn't make sense. Is Nate making this up? Is he delusional? Is he still suffering from being hit on the head? What then strikes him is how little he really knows about this guy; he seemed OK, but everything he knows about him is on the surface. To steady himself, Owen stares at the flames as a kind of reference, but they are weak and don't offer much.

"Have you ever been caught?" Owen then asks, in an effort to gain some clarity.

"Nope. Don't plan to."

Owen feels a swirl of intensity. There is always the chance that Nate is telling the truth. Forest fires can be devastating, so maybe the Forest Service would take such extreme measures. But the thought that suddenly expands to dominate him is that he is out in the middle of nowhere with a guy he hardly knows who could be unstable. His next thought is that he doesn't have a clue how to get himself out of there. It is an absurd situation. He is suddenly annoyed at himself for getting caught in such a predicament; a flash of agitation overtakes him, but it doesn't solve anything and leaves him feeling even more unnerved. Owen makes an effort to center himself but is surprised when he can't.

Something is going on with him. He is feeling very unsettled. The swirling inside of him begins to expand. He has never felt like this before. His vision is beginning to blur.

Something is pushing out of him! The feeling escalates until Owen feels he is only hanging on. For a moment, he feels he could fly off somewhere, and in the next instant, he thinks he is going to pass out. Is he hyperventilating? His breath comes in short bursts. He tries to control his breathing so Nate doesn't hear and realize how vulnerable he is. So when Nate says something, he is sure it is in response to his breathing, but when he hears what Nate says, he is surprised it is unrelated.

"Wow, there must be a million stars," Nate states. He has extended his feet to block out the little bit of fire in front of them, expanding the darkness. "It's like you can see forever!"

Owen doesn't want to see forever, and he isn't interested in looking up. The only thing he can think about is containing himself. He continues his quick and shallow breathing.

"This place is huge!" Nate exclaims, giving way to an escalating amazement. He then gives a quick laugh that Owen struggles to interpret. "I mean, what is this world?"

Owen doesn't want to think about it. It is everything he can do to maintain himself.

"It's like we're floating on some island!"

Owen doesn't want to go there.

"It's absolutely crazy!" Nate exclaims, continuing to push off in a direction.

Owen isn't interested in following Nate's thinking.

"It's like what the hell have we gotten ourselves into!"

Owen has no idea what he has gotten himself into.

"And we're supposed to make sense of all this?"

Owen isn't making sense of anything. He still feels like he's just hanging on. He hears the words but focuses only on what is happening to him. There is still a force trying to expand from within.

Nate then starts to laugh. A crazy laugh that Owen struggles to understand.

"I mean, this is our arena," Nate says, continuing to be excited. "You have to live a life!"

Owen's only concern is how he feels. His feet feel a long way away. His mind is separating from his body.

"Yes."

"And then there are these damn books. Holy crap! Like, where did that come from?"

Owen can tell that Nate has turned his head to look at him.

"I mean, did they spin your head around? When you first read them?"

Owen is lost. He stares into the fire. The last thing he wants is to be the focus. But he has to say something, and he struggles with a desperate need to say anything. "Yep." But it is how much effort it took to even say that that has his attention. He feels fully exposed.

But Nate is suddenly off in his own direction.

"It's like, I couldn't believe what I was reading. And it kept on going. Book after book. It's like I had entered some bizarre world, and of course I had, but it was the world I live in! And it was telling me things that made perfect sense, but things I could never have imagined!"

Nate looks at him again from the side, but only as a pause.

"It's like my mind exploded and came back together. Then it exploded again."

Owen expects the attention to turn back to him and wants to be ready with something to say.

"So did you laugh your ass off?" Nate questions.

He can tell that Nate is looking at him, but before he can manage to answer, Nate is speaking again.

"I mean, that's what really did it for me. If something can make you laugh like that it's got to be real!"

Owen feels the need to say something. It takes everything he has. "Yep."

"Those books still freak me out," Nate continues, following a momentum. "I read them over and over. And it's like I'm reading them for the first time! It's the craziest thing. From one crazy thing to another."

Owen doesn't speak.

"It's like I could be losing my mind. But the mind isn't such a big thing to lose, right? It's the thing that keeps us chained to our perception."

Owen doesn't want to think about it.

Nate then looks at him. Owen can tell he is really looking at him this time, trying to determine what is going on. "You all right?"

No, he isn't, all right. But he isn't getting worse. In the next instant, he might be feeling at least a little better. Maybe it is the need to become more solid, because Nate keeps looking at him. He grips himself. He focuses on the need to answer.

"Been a long day," he finally manages.

Nate laughs in a single outburst. Owen doesn't think he said anything funny.

"I'll say," Nate adds. "That was some crazy shit."

Owen isn't exactly sure what Nate is referring to. What he says next is a determined attempt to get himself out of the situation. He doesn't want to be sitting with Nate by the fire any longer. With great effort, he gathers himself.

"I'm gonna lie down."

Nate acts surprised. "You sure?"

Yes, he's sure.

Nate continues looking at him but doesn't question him further.

"OK. Take the tent. The sleeping bag is rolled out."

It takes everything he has to stand.

"I'm good with sleeping outside," Nate adds. "It's a beautiful night."

CHAPTER SIX

When Owen wakes, it is still dark outside. A volume grows, becoming dominated by time and space. He is in the middle of something. It is a vast universe. The challenge is to move forward and expand his consciousness.

When he wakes again, it is daylight. Owen can hear birds chirping. He hears Nate moving around the site. He thinks of last night and all that went on and is easily amazed. It was the strangest thing. He truly felt he was on the verge of breaking apart. But he's not going to dwell on it. What is most important is that he feels all right. And what happens next is more important; he has another encounter with Nate ahead of him. What gets his attention is the brightness inside the tent and the rising heat.

Owen crawls out of the tent and then gets to his feet. Nate is squatted by the fire. They greet each other. He steps into the brush and urinates.

Owen's first interest is to be sensitive to any remnants of last night. When he stretches and looks up into the sky, he notices a heaviness about himself, an odd fatigue. It can't be any surprise after what he experienced. Otherwise, he feels good. The sky is cloudy. It is a different kind of day than yesterday.

When he steps to the fire, everything seems normal between them. Nate asks if he would like some tea. A cup of tea sounds good.

As Nate sets about making the tea, Owen stands, looking out over the expanse. He is again impressed by the view, and when he turns back toward Nate, he is surrounded by greenery. The contrast catches his attention, and he is again aware that the effect was intentional. He appreciates someone's ability to make him feel this way. It only increases his curiosity. Nate mentioned he didn't create this place, and Owen wonders again who did. He is sure other warriors are involved, and Nate's involvement with the system makes it evident he is in contact with others. He would like to get more information, but remembers Nate's reluctance yesterday to be forthcoming about the site's creation and doesn't expect him to be willing to add much more.

When the water boils, Nate pours each of them a cup. After adding a tea bag, he hands Owen a cup. The warmth of the cup in his hands feels good; it is pure pleasure. Owen stands another moment, looking out over the expanse, letting the tea bag steep in the hot water.

The two of them sip their tea. After a while, Nate gets up, steps to his backpack, grabs an apple, and takes a bite. Owen moves to his backpack to grab a granola bar.

After eating, they decide to return to the interview. It is what they are here for, and there are still a few topics left they need to discuss. They get their notebooks, then return to sitting next to each other.

Owen is reminded of Nate's effort in preparing for the interview. In the light of day, Nate seems far less the lunatic than Owen thought he might be in dealing with him last night.

It's onto the next subject. It can be a big one, essential to the understanding of reality and the nature of perception. And after what happened to him last night, it seems especially relevant. What he experienced is a perfect example of the flexibility of consciousness and how awareness happens; it was that intense, that outlandish.

"Discuss: The Assemblage Point."

"It's about how perception happens," Nate answers. "It's the point on the energy body where perception is assembled. It's how reality is perceived."

Yes, it's a general description of the assemblage point, but it seems remedial, especially given his experience the previous night. He is tempted to relate his comments to what he went through, to make them personal, but he suddenly isn't sure what he would say. His impressions haven't clarified; he isn't sure exactly what happened, and he doesn't want to speculate. He decides to stick with his original approach to the topic.

Specifically, the definition of the assemblage point and its function are complex and involve the world's lines existing as energy filaments. Some of those filaments converge through a point on the energy body of every sentient being and are converted into sensory data, which is then interpreted and perceived as the world experienced.

"When the assemblage point shifts, some activated energy fibers are disconnected from their usual positions, and others become activated, until the shift moves far enough for cohesion to take place, and another view comes into focus." Owen hadn't reached the point of cohesion last night and doesn't think he came anywhere close, but he thinks it was within the realm of what was possible if his shift had continued. "Any movement of the assemblage point is like dying because everything in us gets disconnected."

Nate agrees but hesitates.

"This is tough stuff," he offers. "To keep things simple, what works for me is the idea of a radio dial. I mean, if you turn a radio dial, the station shuts off. And when the radio dial reaches another station, a whole different world becomes available."

The analogy is interesting. Owen has never heard the assemblage point described as a radio dial, and he isn't sure the description is complete, but it's an easily understandable image that still relates to what he experienced last night. The radio dial was definitely turning. He was experiencing some real static.

"And the station we're hooked into is the same one every other person is hooked into," Nate adds to further clarify. "Like the human station or something, WHUM."

Owen has to smile. The analogy is one that Nate has clearly spent time considering. Owen is willing to go along with the idea. But he also wants to stay close to what was described in the books. "The position of the assemblage point determines perception. Reality is a matter of perception, and if perception changes, so does reality."

"It's hard to believe," Nate says and shakes his head, allowing himself to be amazed. "That's all there is to us as human beings—a cluster of perception that tunes into a radio station. And every other conscious being in the universe has its own station, because it has its own position of the assemblage point,"

Owen agrees.

"And the ancient practitioners were aware of like six hundred different layers of the onion," Nate says.

Owen doesn't remember that in the books. But he's not going to doubt him.

"And all our effort is directed at loosening up the radio dial," Nate continues. "It's our whole goal as warriors. And when that happens, our whole world changes."

Yes. The shifting of the assemblage point and the ability to fixate it at different positions are the ultimate accomplishments they seek. Some of that was happening to him last night. Because of all the craziness with airplanes and Nate being a lunatic, his notions of what was real began to scramble, and his assemblage point shifted beyond its normal cohesion. The event is monumental.

But he doesn't care to think about it anymore, not now; there will be time for that. When Nate doesn't add anything further to the discussion, Owen quickly moves on to the final topic.

"Discuss: *Dreaming* and *Stalking*."

"They're the two great systems of practice for a warrior," Nate begins. He again reads from his notes. "*Stalking* is the systematic control of behavior, and deals with the first attention, the everyday world, and is a set of procedures and attitudes that enable one to get the best out of any conceivable situation, and has as its basis: *controlled folly*."

That's a good description. Nate pauses to give him a chance to pick up the explanation, and he does. "*Dreaming* deals with the second attention, expanded awareness, and is the capacity to utilize one's dreams and transform them into *controlled awareness*."

Nate agrees. "They are like the two sides of a coin. And the energy we capture and redirect from its unproductive use in the first attention is redeployed in *dreaming* to bolster our focus on accessing and enhancing our ability in the second attention."

That's pretty good. Nate has definitely made the effort to understand. The ramifications of what they are involved in are amazing.

It is then on to the last topic of the interview. "Discuss: Impeccability," Owen offers.

"Impeccability is nothing else but the proper use of our energy," Nate says. "Impeccability is to do your best in whatever you're engaged in."

"Everything else drains our power. Impeccability restores it," Owen adds.

"The key to all matters of impeccability is the sense of having or not having time. The feeling of having time is an idiocy. When you feel and act like an immortal being that has all the time in the world, you are not being impeccable."

"A life of impeccability leads to a sense of sobriety, and this in itself leads to storing enough energy to move the assemblage point."

"The only freedom warriors have is to behave impeccably."

They both nod their heads in agreement.

And that's the end of the interview. Short and sweet for the most part. The two of them spend a moment packing notebooks and pages into their backpacks.

After finishing the interview, it might be implied that they are going to go forward with working together, but Owen believes the decision needs to be a conscious choice, a line that needs to be crossed, so he asks Nate, "So are you in?"

Nate hesitates a moment, then nods his head and says it makes sense to him.

Owen states that he is willing to go forward as well.

Then it is a matter of what to do. They could start working with the material—they have the whole day ahead of them. But after thinking about it, neither of them has anything immediate come to mind, and they don't think they should do something just to do it. Maybe they are done with their first meeting. It kind of feels that way.

They should at least decide on their next step. The good thing is they live only a few hours apart. The system tries to pair people who live relatively close to each other, and it seems to be getting better at it, probably because there are more people in the pool to match from these days. In a round years ago, Owen was paired with someone who lived ten hours away, so getting together became impossible. They decide to get together again soon. Next Friday should work for both of them. Nate will have to juggle some things, but he commits to keeping the weekend open. Beyond that, they can take time to consider their next step and email each other. With nothing more to do, they pack up their few things. When asked about the tent, Nate says it can stay, though he goes inside and zips up all the windows. Owen makes sure the fire is completely covered with dirt. Nate then takes the lead and starts downhill through the clear-cut. It is a different direction from where they initially came, and immediately there is a trail or at least signs of passage. Owen remembers how unsettling it was yesterday, not knowing how Nate moved through the brush, but seeing a slight trail now makes him realize they came to the tent site from a less-used direction. Soon, they hit a main trail, and it makes even more sense to him; the trail they are on surely leads back to his vehicle. Nate must have parked somewhere else. It occurs to him that Nate was controlling the battlefield, the first precept of stalking for a warrior in any given situation. If things didn't go well between the two of them, Nate could have ditched him at any time and simply disappeared into the brush. It was a good strategy.

CHAPTER SEVEN

On the ride home, Owen lets the impressions of his meeting with Nate expand inside him until he is only impressed. Wow! That was definitely the most intense first meeting he has ever had! He thinks back to last night, when he couldn't figure out what was happening and his sense of continuity seemed to be on the verge of collapsing. A warrior spends years trying to shift his assemblage point, and he could have been on the brink of it happening! The more he thinks about it, the more it makes sense that it did happen. He was in an unfamiliar, dramatic setting that both unnerved and stimulated him, and he had focused on turning off his internal dialogue. Then that whole thing with Nate and the airplanes threw him for a loop, coupled with the sudden fear of not knowing where he was and of feeling trapped with someone who might be a lunatic. What he experienced was a total incongruence he couldn't rationally account for. A great fear and uncertainty overtook him. It's just the kind of situation that is perfect for loosening the assemblage point. He is reminded that shifting the assemblage point isn't hard to do and that illness, fear, or stress can cause it. He was surely under some stress last night. Most people would think they might be losing their minds, but to a warrior, the mind isn't very much to lose, because what is generally understood as a person's mind is just the self-reflection of man's inventory, a conglomeration of impressions and projections and half-baked inherited notions that have little to do with the true nature of reality.

Owen also reflects on his initial encounter with Nate and the explosion of energy he felt when they came together. He has never felt energy like that before, though it is something he is somewhat familiar with through his practice of tai chi chuan. He has been studying for close to fifteen years. Tai chi chuan is an ancient Chinese art of moving meditation and self-defense. It is an energy-generating system and is considered a soft martial art that focuses on yielding and receiving. He is fortunate to be part of a great lineage. Owen has found his practice of tai chi very compatible with the don Juan material, with the shared understanding that "energy is the irreducible essence of everything." In some of his martial exchanges with great teachers, he has experienced the discharge of energy, but never anything like what happened with Nate.

And what about the feeling that overtook him before he moved toward the sound of Nate's yelling? The feeling started as a determination not to be held back, as a reaction to Nate's attempt to control the situation, then became something else. It was as if he were operating from a different part of himself, beyond thinking, as if his body separated from his brain. He felt a cold indifference, combined with a certainty that left no room for doubt. He felt abandoned to action. He didn't care about the outcome or what happened to him. In fact, there wasn't even any awareness of self to care about. He is sure it was a directive of his connection to *spirit*.

Owen continues to let his impressions of events move him.

His experience was remarkable. And such a relief. After all the years of working with the material, to have something profound truly happen! It gives him confidence that he is moving in the right direction!

There is something else he can't deny, something else impressive—the feeling that something was going on between him and Nate. When he steps back and recalls their first encounter, he has to believe the spirit is involved. There was just that element of the otherworldly, as if forces were acting on and through them. And he has to give some credit to Nate. He's still not sure what to think of the guy. He's young, enthusiastic, and not very experienced, but he definitely has some understanding of the material, and the bottom line is that he can make things happen. Maybe Nate is just talented; there are incidents in the books where some warriors had a clearer connection to the spirit than others, and Nate could be one of them.

Arriving back at his house, Owen's only interest is to continue to bask in the remarkableness of his meeting. But the elements of his everyday life are also present around him. There are emails and voicemails to check and respond to. He fixes himself something to eat. One of the voice messages is from his lawyer regarding the final settlement with his former business partners. The odyssey of madness and frustration in dealing with the breakup of their partnership and the loss of their business has challenged him in ways he could never have imagined, and now the end is near. Thank goodness they were able to settle through mediation. For a while, it looked as if the only solution was to go to court, which would have taken months or years and surely would have left them all broke. There was just so much acrimony, misunderstanding, and varied perceptions and interpretations. And the three of them had been good friends! For Owen, it has been a firsthand view of human madness, and he has to include himself in that equation. Owen has struggled against his emotions as he has never struggled in his life. To say he needed to work with the don Juan material is an understatement. The material and his tai chi practice were the only things that gave him any sense of hope and sanity.

In the morning, Owen spends a long session in his recapitulation crate. His hope is that it might consolidate the gains he made in his encounter with Nate; his energy was definitely loosened. Spending time recapitulating his life is one of the techniques from the books and involves reliving it as a strategy to free up energy. According to don Juan and his lineage of practitioners, each encounter we have with someone throughout our lives is an exchange of energy. That exchange leaves energy filaments in each person. The recapitulation is the process of both expelling the energy that was left in oneself by another and retrieving one's own filaments left in the other person. Breathing, as the systematic method of inhaling and exhaling, is essential to the process. The goal is to free up every bit of energy that has ever been exchanged. It replenishes a warrior and returns them to their rightful place as an expression of energy connected to spirit. The crate itself is a simple structure of four sides, just big enough to enclose a seated person, with a lattice top for ventilation. The intent is to be shut off from distraction. The crate is symbolic of a person being isolated within themselves and cut off from their greater nature. It is said that the result of a vigorous recapitulation is that a warrior becomes as light as air. Owen hasn't achieved any great result but has felt relief from an overbearing pressure and heaviness. It has definitely changed his perspective on being alive.

After spending more than an hour in the recapitulation crate, Owen is left with the feeling of being in the middle of something huge. His only challenge is to move forward and live his fate. He hardly needs reminding that the path of exploring human awareness is endless. His gratitude is in having a path to shape his life that he truly believes in.

As he considers moving forward, he returns to the idea of working with Nate. He is still thrilled by how well their first meeting went, especially since he really had to force himself to get involved with the system again after being out of it for so long and having had so few truly positive results in the past. But he needed to engage. It's so easy to stay contained in his own world. And the effort paid off! He is anxious for the next step. He and Nate had left things open about contacting each other. He wants to push the issue and sends a simple email: "Ready?" The next time he checks his computer, he has an answer: "Yep."

The decision is what to do. And it is not something Owen wants to discuss. He wants to take the lead this time, in response to not taking the lead the first time they got together. He does have something in mind for them as their next step. The setting in the woods is a perfect opportunity. The maneuver is used for other reasons in don Juan's world, but when a warrior faces an arduous task, they draw energy from the earth by being enclosed in an earth mound. Ancient practitioners discovered that the earth was a sentient being from which they could draw energy. Nate has picked out the perfect place. Owen emails his thoughts to him and is pleased when Nate emails back his agreement. Owen then emails that he has an early-morning appointment on Friday and can't get away first thing, so, allowing for drive time, he suggests they meet at two o'clock; that should give them enough time to construct a mound before dark. Nate says he might get started early. They then go over what is needed. According to the books, the mound's frame should be constructed of sticks, and they will need a lot of dirt to cover it. The issue of dirt is easily solved when Nate says he has a friend in landscaping. He will also be able to get a couple of shovels and some five-gallon buckets.

On Friday morning, Owen is up early. The sky is clear, and the weather is projected to be warm. Since he won't be in class on Saturday, he makes sure to get in a Tai Chi workout. Afterward, he changes his clothes, packs his vehicle for his time with Nate, and arrives at his lawyer's office for a meeting. He then drops off some documents at the post office before heading out of town. The drive is much easier this time because he knows where he is going. As he gets farther from home, the land opens up, and the forest dominates the landscape.

CHAPTER EIGHT

Pulling up to the site, Owen finds a truck already parked. There is a mound of dirt in the back, so of course it is Nate. But Nate isn't there. After getting out of his vehicle and looking around, Owen calls for him and gets an immediate response from a fair distance away, in the direction of their first encounter on the trail. Owen starts walking. When he calls again, Nate answers, but from farther back in the woods, beyond where the trail turns right and leads up into the pines. He leaves the trail and walks in that direction.

Walking toward Nate, Owen finds him standing over a nearly completed framework of interwoven sticks and branches. Owen is surprised by the progress, then takes time to look over the mound's frame. It seems about right. "Looks good."

Nate steps back from the structure, obviously pleased with his handiwork. "It's getting there."

Nate must have been here a while. Owen knows how much work must have gone into the framing. He is impressed not only with the structure but also with Nate's initiative.

Owen does notice one problem, however. He almost hates to bring it up, but it's essential. He hopes Nate is open to comment.

"I think the sides might be too steep; they might not hold the dirt."

Nate nods his head and admits he thought the same thing.

And it might not be an easy fix. The curve of the mound is set by forked branches stuck in the ground on both sides, then connected along a ridge-line branch extending along the top. The only way to relax the curve without tearing the frame apart is to pull the branches out of the ground and move them back a bit. The challenge will be to keep the branches interwoven and connected at the ridge line. It will be delicate work, but they decide to give it a try. By Nate working at the bottom of the frame, pulling out the branches one at a time, moving them back before sticking them again in the ground, and Owen making sure the branch they are working on stays connected to the ridge line at the forked end, they are able to move all the main branches of the frame and relax the curve of the structure.

They both stand back and look at the mound, pleased with the results.

Glancing around, Owen takes a moment to survey the site. Being so close to the parking area and the trail is a concern, but they don't want to be too far from the vehicle when hauling dirt. Where they are standing is near the end of a short finger of land that extends and dead-ends into a low-lying area of thicker brush. The low-lying area is tough to walk through, so unless there is a specific reason to come this way, anyone entering should stay on the trail. The mound is far enough from the trail that, if people do pass by, it will be out of sight.

Owen turns his attention back to the mound itself. He thinks the opening for them to crawl into might be a bit big; it needs to be sealed when someone is inside, and in his experience, that can be difficult. It's best to start with the hole as small as possible, so he spends some time gathering a few branches and weaving them around the edge of the opening. The next question is what to cover the frame with to keep out dirt. In the books, don Juan used leaves and natural debris, and Owen is all for being as authentic as possible, but the couple of times he has done this, he has had trouble keeping dirt from falling in. Maybe he isn't skilled enough, but he feels the priority should be on function. "Warriors are endlessly pragmatic," he quotes from the books, then mentions that he brought a newspaper. He explains to Nate that they can spread newspaper over the mound, a couple of sheets at a time, then cover it with dirt.

Then it's just a matter of bringing the dirt. Together, they walk back to the vehicles.

Hauling the dirt will be an effort. Owen decides to change into shorts. Afterward, they get out the buckets and shovels. They have enough buckets for each to carry two at a time, balancing themselves as they walk. Nate fills his buckets, then starts off. After a few steps, he calls back and advises Owen to fill his buckets only halfway. Owen does so, then tucks the stack of newspapers under his arm and begins walking. In no time, he catches up to Nate, who is struggling to carry his full buckets. After reaching the mound, they work together to spread the newspaper.

The challenge is to keep the newspaper in place while they pore over the dirt. They work with the newspaper, section by section. "Hey, I'll be able to catch up on current events while staring at the ceiling," Nate jokes. Owen smiles, appreciating Nate's light attitude. Then it is a matter of repeating the process. The dirt they bring each trip doesn't go far, so they need to make plenty of trips. Fortunately, Nate has brought plenty of dirt.

Each trip hauling dirt is about a hundred yards. The day has gotten hot. They take off their shirts as the sweat begins to pour, but soon flies find them. Unable to swat away the flies while carrying their buckets, Owen and Nate wear T-shirts over their heads to protect their necks and shoulders.

At the outer edges of the mound, it is still difficult to keep the dirt from sliding off, so they stack branches at the base to build out the slope.

They are finished. Nate crawls into the mound to try it out. "So, what if you have to take a crap in here?" he seriously asks.

Geez. There surely can't be any crapping in the mound, but they should be able to piss. It's a simple enough solution. Owen suggests he take in an empty water bottle.

The only thing left is to decide how to seal the entrance. But it has to be done after someone is inside. It raises an interesting question. "So who's going first?" Nate asks. Owen has thought it through. Since they're both going to have a turn and he has done it before while Nate hasn't, it should probably be Nate who goes first. After Owen explains his reasoning, Nate agrees. They leave a pile of dirt outside and a couple of sections of newspaper for sealing the opening.

They then decide to spend some time on the outside, where the other person will keep vigil. Nate clears a bare space off to the side. "The best thing to do is to stay standing," Owen states. When Nate glances at him to see if he is serious, Owen smiles. "Standing keeps you awake." Falling asleep will be a big challenge for both the person inside the mound and the person outside. In his experience, the best place to stand for hours at a time is between two trees growing close together, so a person can sort of wedge themselves between them, and the trees can take some of the person's weight. But there aren't any trees nearby growing close together, so it looks like the person keeping vigil will have to sit. It is decided that one of the buckets turned over will be fine for a seat. Owen is already not looking forward to keeping vigil. If it were up to him, he would rather be inside the mound; keeping vigil can be tedious and boring. With nothing else to do, they walk back to their vehicles. After taking time to drink from a bottle of water, Nate mentions that there is a stream nearby and it would be good to wash off. The presence of the stream is welcome news to

Owen, and he quickly agrees. The two of them jump into his vehicle.

The stream isn't far in the other direction from where Owen pulled onto the two-track from the road. After crossing a narrow bridge over the stream, he pulls to the side and parks at the first opportunity.

It's a good-sized stream, maybe thirty feet across, and after stepping down the bank and kicking off their shoes, they wade in. The stream pools at the base of the bridge and is more than waist-deep. The water is surprisingly cool and refreshing. It feels great to sit down and dunk themselves. They take off their shirts and wring out the sweat. They rub their arms and chests and run fingers through their hair. Neither of them is interested in staying in the water long, and as soon as they are sufficiently rinsed off, they walk out of the stream and back up the bank to the vehicle. Arriving back at their site, they quickly change clothes and decide to eat; each of them has packed a small cooler. Owen has a sandwich, and Nate eats from a bowl of grain and fruit salad.

"So what exactly are we wanting to accomplish?" Nate asks while eating.

It is an obvious question. Nate has been good about following along with the mound's construction, but sooner or later, Owen knew he was going to need more details. He has thought about it enough, and it's something he has done before in previous rounds with different partners, and his explanation is straight from the books. He tells Nate that the books state that being inside the mound isolates a person from external stimuli while keeping them in direct contact with the earth. They are able to soak up the Earth's energy. But he also feels there are other opportunities. "You're going to be in a dark, enclosed space, cut off from distraction, so it's a good chance to work on turning off the internal dialogue." Owen glances at Nate to gauge his reaction, and Nate simply nods his head, as if what he has been told makes perfect sense. Owen feels the need to expound a bit more to make sure he and Nate are on the same page. "As you know, shutting off the internal dialogue and gaining inner silence is a major goal for a warrior." He again looks over at Nate, who again nods his head and continues eating.

There is one more thing he feels is available for them to practice while on the mound. "You remember from the books, the calling of intent?" This time, Nate looks at him quizzically. Owen thinks the reference might not register because it is from one of the later books, and when people first encounter the material, they don't focus on it as much; there is just so much else to take in. Owen explains, "Warriors call intent as a way to draw the spirit closer or to activate their connecting link with the spirit, intent, power, the abstract, or whatever you want to call it. And focusing on the calling of intent takes the focus off the internal dialogue. Chanting, or in this case, calling, traps the second attention and activates it. It's just a technique that is available."

Nate is staring at him with a strained look on his face. "So, you want me to call *intent* while I'm in the mound?"

Owen sees it as a further opportunity. The calling of *intent* isn't something he has done before in the mound, but it is something else he practices in his recapitulation crate and finds to be beneficial. Making it something to try in the mound is sound in theory. "Hey, you're going to be lying there in the dark anyway, so you might as well do something. It will keep you focused and help you stay awake." Nate crinkles up his nose and seems a bit confused. "But how am I supposed to call *intent*?"

Owen gives a quick laugh. "You just voice the word *intent* loudly and repeatedly. It would help if you had something to focus on, like the flame of a candle, but just calling should be enough."

Nate shrugs. "Sounds easy."

It is easy. Everything warriors do is simple, direct, and to the point. The challenge is commitment and persistence.

CHAPTER NINE

After eating, they agree to stretch out and rest; they have a long night ahead and think it wouldn't be a bad idea to take a nap. Each of them retreats to their own vehicle. When Owen wakes, Nate is snoring slightly from the front seat of his truck. It's getting close to seven o'clock. One of the things that concerns him about keeping vigil is mosquitoes, something he associates with the low-lying marshy area surrounding the mound site, so he puts on the long-sleeved shirt he brought and will bring his jacket and brimmed hat.

Nate soon wakes and begins preparing himself.

The two of them then put on their backpacks and walk to the mound.

"So how long am I supposed to be in here?" Nate asks when they arrive at the site.

"As long as you can." Theoretically, the whole time they are together, if he is able. "Forget about time," Owen suggests. They have agreed to be here for up to three days.

"I'd hate for you not have a turn," Nate says and smiles.

Owen doubts Nate will last that long and smiles back, saying he is sure he will get his chance.

As Nate prepares to enter the mound, Owen pulls out a roll of string from his pocket and begins uncoiling it. It's his last technique. He has saved it for effect.

"What's that?" Nate asks, seeing him stretch out a length.

"The urge to fall asleep is almost insurmountable," Owen answers. "Every effort needs to be made to fight against it. This string is for the person keeping vigil to help the person inside stay awake." Owen further explains that the string is to be looped over Nate's big toe, and that he will occasionally give a tug. The tug is to make sure Nate is fully awake, and the anticipation of the string being jerked will help him stay focused.

"What!" Nate shakes his head. "Man, that's crazy."

Owen laughs. Every effort should be made to give them the best chance for success.

"Do I have to go barefoot?" Nate asks, seemingly concerned.

Owen assures him that he doesn't have to go barefoot. The string can be looped around his big toe over his sock.

Nate doesn't have any other questions. He takes a bottle of water, an empty bottle, and a jacket he can either roll up for a pillow or put on if he gets chilled. With his items in hand, he kneels on the ground in front of the entrance, then crawls through the opening. Before he gets too settled, Owen tells him to stick out his foot, then loops the string over his toe and makes sure it is tight. Nate crawls all the way into the mound. Owen waits until Nate is comfortable, then stretches the string out. He then goes about sealing up the entrance.

"So I'm supposed to just yell '*intent*'?" Nate asks to clarify before Owen has sealed up the opening completely. Owen tells him to call clearly and steadily as if he were actually calling to someone.

After finishing the opening, Owen tells Nate to yell back to him. Nate's voice comes through moderately muffled but still easily heard. Owen says loudly that he expects to hear his calling as a steady, constant sound. He gives a tug on the string for fun, and Nate yells in protest.

Owen turns from the mound; he has his own adjustments to make. He has decided to have a fire. He'll keep it small. He didn't even bring up the issue with Nate, not wanting to deal with the whole airplanes-and-infrared thing again. Having a fire will give him something to focus on with his own calling of *intent* and help him stay awake. It will also help keep mosquitoes away.

Owen digs a fire pit. Around the edges, he clears away anything that could be ignited by a spark. There is a light breeze in the trees, but it doesn't reach ground level. He then spends some time gathering small sticks and branches.

Before moving farther from the mound to gather more firewood, he checks on Nate. He hears the call of "*intent*" but it isn't very spirited. "Louder!" he encourages.

"*Intent!*" Nate yells back at him.

Owen collects more branches. He wants a lot of branches. It will be a long night.

With everything done that needs to be completed, Owen sits on the bucket. Daylight is quickly fading. There is a feeling of heaviness in the air as twilight gathers.

Owen takes a moment to devise a strategy for his time. He feels it is important to stay with Nate and be a source of support, but he also wants to focus on his own practice. For now, he wants to focus on the growing twilight. There is such power in the transition around him.

Owen deliberately opens himself to the expanse. Here he is out in the woods again. Of all the possibilities of existence, here he is. This is his life; he is determined to make the best of it.

What catches his attention is the sound of frogs in the near distance. He hadn't noticed their croaking before, and maybe they had only started up with the coming of night. There must be water nearby, which makes sense given the surrounding low-lying area and almost guarantees mosquitoes.

Owen likes the sound of frogs. It gives dimension to the growing expanse. The frogs have their own calling ahead of them. It reminds him of Nate. He listens for a moment and doesn't hear anything, so he picks up the string at his feet and gives it a pull. "*Intent!*" is voiced immediately.

Owen returns to listening to the frogs. Their sound has increased, as if more of them are joining the chorus. It must be quite the thing being a frog, surrounded by so many others, singing for all they are worth, singing their own song of existence. It is their time on earth as well.

Owen notices the shadows of branches and trees blending.

Everything is losing definition.

But almost as a response to his awareness, the first mosquito finds him, and of course, there is another. Owen takes the lighter from his pocket and lights the small piece of crumpled newspaper he had placed at the bottom of a clump of pine needles. The flame catches easily and spreads. The smoke is a welcome sight. He adds the smallest twigs he can find.

Owen thinks of Nate and listens, and sure enough, he can hear the calling. It sounds strong and focused enough, and when he listens further, he hears it again. He goes back to feeding the fire.

Slowly, the darkness becomes complete. Owen is surrounded by the night. It is just him and the space beyond him. He is here to meet infinity and push forward in a concentrated effort. He is aware of the barrier of perception. He is on one side where he has been all his life, and on the other side is a never-ending immensity to explore. All Owen cares about is going forward.

Owen is ready. His attempt again will be to turn off the internal dialogue. He is accruing inner silence. With all his focus, he will push through the barrier of perception and make himself available to the unknown.

The fire continues to produce smoke, but it isn't overwhelming. He hasn't noticed a mosquito for a while. It is time to start his calling.

Owen has never done his calling outdoors and is a bit hesitant. His concern is that someone might hear him and come to investigate. He knows his concern is unfounded because there can't be anyone around for quite a distance, and who would come over in the night anyway? Owen doesn't want any more excuses.

He spends a moment focusing on the power of *spirit*. It is what he wants to attract. The *spirit* is everywhere as a force. He wants to bring it closer and polish his connection. The *spirit's* only intent is to express itself. He wants to be a conduit for that expression.

"*Intent!*"

The sound of his voice penetrates the space around him. He listens for the sound of frogs, but they have ceased. He hates to disturb them, but this is his destiny; as an expression of *spirit* this is his direction.

"*Intent!*"

Owen focuses on annunciating clearly and being deliberate in his effort to reach toward the unknown. But he does decide to make at least one attempt to be loud enough that Nate can hear him. His thought is that if Nate knows he is also calling, it will be support for his continuing effort.

"*Intent*!"

Owen adds a stick to the fire and stares into the flames. "*Intent*!"

His interest is to relax his awareness as a way to focus his attention on the flames and the power of *spirit*.

"*Intent*!"

The space takes over. His focus gathers. He settles in.

"*Intent!*"

It is like pushing off from shore.

CHAPTER TEN

What? Where? What?
Everything is darkness as he struggles against the darkness. It's a big yelling. The yelling is inside him, but comes from somewhere else. The realization hits him: it is Nate yelling in the mound!

In a rush, he drops to the ground and then scrambles on all fours to the mound.

Nate is yelling. The mound shakes, dirt is flying. "Nate!" he yells, but nothing changes. "Nate!"

From inside his own escalating panic, Owen realizes that Nate is struggling to get out. Owen has just enough time to realize the mound won't hold Nate when Nate bursts through the top. Owen is thrown back but scrambles forward. "Nate!" he yells, but Nate's desperation is so complete as he struggles to get out that Owen's only thought is that if Nate does get out, he could hurt himself, so he throws himself into the fury of what is Nate and wraps his arms around. Nate's body is completely tense, but the surprise is that Nate's weight yields and begins to fall backward, so as Owen holds on, his own legs are lifted by the leverage of their fall. He keeps holding on as Nate is pinned below his waist in the mound. They both are caught as Nate becomes bent over backward, but Nate's body shifts to the side against the counterbalance of weight and force, so Owen has just enough time to recognize the slow roll and decide to hold on no matter what as the combined weight of their turning and twisting gathers momentum until Nate's legs are pulled out of the mound and they both fall in a heap to the ground.

Owen instantly rolls on top of him to hold him down. For better leverage, he thrusts his knees up until he is sitting on top of him, ready for whatever. "Nate!" he yells, but nothing comes. The full tension of Nate's muscles, firing with fear, has subsided. Owen doesn't know what to think. He tries again to connect with Nate by yelling his name, but nothing registers. He looks closely through the darkness. Nate's eyes are open; it is the blank look on his face that concerns him. Nate seems dazed. But at least he isn't yelling. Owen takes the time to adjust his grip in case Nate is readying himself. But nothing happens. The struggle has gone out of him. It sends Owen into a whole new kind of panic. Has Nate passed out? Owen bends down to look closer at his face. His eyes stare wide, as if they are seeing, but Nate isn't seeing him. His mouth is open; he seems to be breathing. The clue he holds onto is the body's firm rigidity beneath him. The explanation that bursts upon him is that Nate's assemblage point has shifted. What he needs to do comes to him just as quickly. He needs to get water to splash on Nate's face; it's what don Juan always did to Carlos in similar situations. He has a bottle of water in his backpack, but doesn't want to leave, yet getting water is critical. Owen pushes himself to his feet while staying bent over and still pushing down on Nate lying beneath him. Nate doesn't react, so he decides to go for the water. He turns and rushes to find his backpack, then hurries back. Pulling out the bottle, he tries to splash Nate's face, but it isn't easy with Nate lying down, so he ends up pouring water over him.

Nate sputters against the water, but when Owen tries to speak to him, there is no response. Owen needs more water. What he really needs to do is submerge Nate as don Juan did to Carlos. That is the way to gain cohesion. He remembers the stream where they washed off. He has to get Nate to the stream; it is an absolute certainty. Immediately, he lifts Nate to his feet and tries to walk with him, but Nate's legs aren't working. He puts both arms around Nate from behind and tries to drag him by the arms, but it will take too long to get Nate back to the vehicles. Nate seems able to stand on his own. Owen puts an arm around him from the side, leans heavily, and holds Nate tight against him, beginning to walk. Nate's legs still don't work well, so Owen leans further to the side to take most of Nate's weight.

He struggles to get Nate to the trail and then toward the vehicles. Owen is relieved at how well he can see. It is even lighter out from under the trees. When he reaches the open space where the vehicles are parked, he helps Nate into the back seat of his truck and shuts the door. He starts his vehicle, turns it around, and heads toward the stream.

Owen drives as fast as he can. It is getting light out. As he drives over the bridge, he parks as soon as he can get Nate down the embankment. He gets Nate out of the back seat, holds him tight against him again, and steps him slowly down the slope. Reaching the edge of the stream, Owen continues walking directly into the water, holding Nate. There is no need to be gentle, so when he reaches the deeper water near the base of the bridge, he pushes Nate in and follows after him.

Nate reacts to going underwater as if being shot out of a cannon. He leaps to his feet, gasping for breath. Owen is surprised by the sudden intensity of his reaction and gives Nate a moment to get his wits about him. He then tells Nate he needs to continue being submerged and dunks him again.

This time, when Nate shoots out of the water, he rushes across the stream to the other side. Owen is surprised at how fast he moves and has to hurry after him. But at least Nate has become lively. Catching up to him, Owen grabs Nate by the shirt and pulls him back into deeper water. "It's OK, Nate," he says, trying to sound convincing. "You're OK." Owen throws him in again.

The only thing that seems to register with Nate is blind panic. As soon as he gets his feet under him, he is off, rushing in the other direction. Owen has to catch up to him and drag him back. "Stop! Stop!" Nate protests. Hearing him speak is a good sign, but Owen doesn't think Nate is anywhere near recovered. He remembers how long don Juan would submerge Carlos to be sure he had gained cohesion. "It's for your own good," he explains, then throws him back in without expecting Nate to understand.

Nate gets up and rushes away, and Owen rushes after him, grabs him, and drags him back to deeper water before shoving him in. This time, when Nate gets to his feet, he dashes upstream, and before Owen can reach him, he is in shallower water, his legs moving faster. It takes everything Owen has to cut him off and drag him back. Owen again explains to Nate that what he is doing is for his own good before tossing him in.

Nate gets to his feet and tries to rush away again, but Owen catches him and throws him back. When Nate gets to his feet, Owen grabs him before he can leave the deeper water.

This time, when he stands up, Nate doesn't try to run and rubs both hands over his face to get the water out of his eyes. He then coughs and coughs again. Owen is glad Nate hasn't tried to run away because he is getting exhausted.

They stand near each other in the water. Nate begins to walk, but he isn't hurrying; he walks out of the deep water to the bank and sits down. Owen waits a moment, and when nothing changes, he walks past Nate and sits on the bank a few feet away so as not to alarm him.

Owen assesses the situation. It is definitely daylight now, which means Nate was in the mound the entire night. The last thing he remembers was fighting to stay awake himself.

As for what happened to Nate and his condition, Owen believes his assemblage point must have shifted. He could dunk Nate some more, but he doesn't feel it is absolutely necessary and decides to wait. Otherwise, he thinks the best thing to do is get Nate up and moving. Owen is feeling chilled by the cool air and being wet. He imagines Nate is feeling the same, so he decides the best thing to do is get Nate out of the water. "Can you walk?"

Nate doesn't answer, but in the next moment, he is standing and walking across the stream. Owen would like a better chance to determine Nate's condition, but if Nate is walking on his own and not motivated by panic, then maybe that's the best that can happen. If he doesn't think Nate is cohesive enough, he can always bring him back to the water. For now, he is OK with just following Nate back to the vehicle. After making his way up the embankment, Nate gets into the back seat. Owen opens the front door, gets behind the wheel, and starts the drive back to the site.

He looks in the rearview mirror and sees Nate staring absently out the window. It makes him wonder whether Nate is just stunned or worse. Recovering from an assemblage point shift is not easy. He needs some kind of response from him to determine his condition. "So what's goin' on?" he asks, glancing at the road, then back at Nate. "Are you all rright?" Nate keeps looking out the window.

Owen needs some kind of response. After arriving back at the site and parking the truck, he turns around in his seat and asks Nate if he thinks he can walk around, but Nate only shrugs. The look on his face is pure annoyance. Owen has to decide what to do. He should get Nate walking so he can assess his condition, but then he thinks of another question to ask, one that is very pertinent to their situation and could be very revealing. It is a chance to figure out what happened in the mound. "So what do you remember?"

Nate only shrugs again, and Owen is insistent. "Try to

remember." If he can't remember, it would indicate that his assemblage point actually has shifted; his usual Continuity of perception would have been turned off. It suddenly becomes crucial to determine. "Try to remember, Nate."

This time, Nate does respond, in a tone of great irritation. "All I remember is some asshole trying to drown me!"

Owen laughs, surprised by the level of indignation, but is relieved that Nate has at least responded to him. "Hey, I had to come up with something," he says in an effort both to defend and explain himself.

"But I thought we weren't supposed to touch each other," Nate says in an accusatory tone.

Nate is again using the system to confront him. But Owen has little tolerance. "Hey, we weren't having a confrontation. I was saving your damn life!"

Nate hesitates only a moment.

"So how is drowning someone supposed to be helpful?" he retorts. It is obvious that Nate is only offended; a flash of vehemence has crossed his face.

"It's what don Juan used to do to Carlos, remember?" Owen says, pushing back at him. Nate needs to understand how serious this is. "Man, you were out of it."

His words and strong tone have at least thwarted the thrust of accusation. Nate returns to staring out the window. Owen is determined to get an answer to what he considers the most important issue. "So do you remember anything?" he asks. "Before you were in the water?"

Nate glances at him, then turns away again, yet in continuing to watch him in the rearview mirror, Owen can see that Nate is actually thinking, making an effort to recollect.

"I think I remember walking," he replies half-heartedly.

It's a start. "Do you remember anything before that?" Owen asks. Nate is again thinking. "Not really." There is an element of surprise in his voice. After another moment of pondering, he asks, "So what the hell happened?" The tone Owen now hears from the backseat has a strong measure of growing concern.

Owen wants to be careful and not risk alarming Nate by telling him what he thinks happened; he is not sure how Nate will respond, but he doesn't want to be dismissive and inflame his suspicions. Owen truly doesn't know what to say, yet his hesitation has exactly the effect he was hoping to avoid.

"So what happened?" Nate asks in a tone of sharp consternation and demand. He is now looking directly at him in the mirror. It is as if every bit of Owen's inability to come up with any explanation has magnified his sense of alarm.

Owen still hesitates, trying to come up with something that won't run the risk of being disturbing, but he can't think of anything and decides to be direct. "I think your assemblage point shifted."

Nate takes in what he says. "So why do you think that?"

Owen feels there isn't any use in being evasive, though he isn't sure how much sense Nate is going to make out of what he tells him. "Because you were yelling."

For a moment, Nate is only silent. "I was yelling?" he repeats, seemingly confused. "What was I yelling about?"

Owen realizes he is getting dragged further down a path he doesn't want to go, but he doesn't see how he can avoid the direction. "I think something scared you," he finally says.

"What scared me?"

It is an easy enough question to answer, and Owen says he has no idea what scared him.

"Where was I?" Nate asks.

Owen answers directly. "In the mound." "Then what happened?" Nate questions.

Owen again feels the pressure of being steered toward being forced to reveal something that can't be helpful, so he comes up with his most tempered response. "You came out."

Nate takes a moment to fully take in what was said. "I came

out?" He is both confused and concerned. "What do you mean, I came out?"

Owen feels as if a light is being shone upon him. But the bottom line is, he feels he needs to be truthful. It is the obligation of one warrior to another, though he does feel he can at least cushion the effect his words might have and does his best. "You just came out through the top."

There is another long pause in the seat behind him.

In the next instant, the door opens, and Nate is out of the truck and walking down the trail. Owen jumps out and starts after him. "Nate!" he calls, but Nate keeps walking, fast and determined.

Owen hurries after him but makes no effort to catch up. He is close enough behind, however, to see Nate react in shock when he reaches the mound. "What the hell!" he exclaims.

Owen steps to the mound after him. The scene is dramatic. The mound looks as if it exploded. Branches stick up and out in all directions from around the hole at the top. Sheets of newspaper are scattered about. Most of the mound is a bare frame.

CHAPTER ELEVEN

"What the hell!" Nate repeats, completely appalled. There is a look of utter dismay on his face. His arms are extended from his sides with his palms up, and his whole body turns from side to side as he looks over the devastation.

Owen stands next to Nate, surveying the site. He is tempted to say something to be calming, but nothing comes. He is shocked himself. What happened was extreme.

"So what the hell?" Nate exclaims again, still amazed. But now he has turned to him for an explanation. Owen's reaction is to want to be a stabilizing force and give some kind of answer, but all he has is what he has already offered. "Man, I really just think your assemblage point shifted."

Nate isn't consoled in the least. As if it were possible, his incredulity threatens to escalate. "But how can that be?" he asks, desperately struggling to make sense. Nate looks at the disaster of the mound, then back at him, then back at the disaster. His face is frozen in a look of complete disbelief.

For the moment, Owen is left chasing after Nate, appalled. After catching up and feeling his own rush of amazement, he finds himself in a new direction of incredulity, and he can't help but exclaim, "I guess it worked!" The realization becomes overwhelming. "It just worked!" He punctuates his new direction with a high laugh.

But Nate only looks at him, then back at the mound, then back at him, wearing the same strained look of confusion and dismay. Yet, still looking at the mound, Owen remains filled with amazement. "It's what we were trying to do!" he exclaims. It is all clear to him now, so as the ramifications continue to expand, he can only laugh again. "It worked! Your assemblage point shifted!"

Nate is still looking at him, struggling to make sense, and, in an effort to rescue Nate and to follow the momentum pushing out of him, Owen continues his line of thinking. "You were trying to shut off your internal dialogue, and you did."

The magnitude of what he hears himself say is overwhelming. By the look on Nate's face, the need to make sense remains paramount, so Owen tries to add to his explanation. "Everything depends on turning off your internal dialogue, and when that happens, the world collapses."

Nate doesn't stop staring at him. "So I stopped the world?"

Owen is relieved that he is getting it. "Yes, I think you absolutely did!" He laughs again in amazement. As further explanation, he then offers the image Nate used himself. "You turned the radio dial!"

He watches as pure incredulity washes over Nate's face. Owen lets his own incredulity lead him. "Everything was set up for it!" He knows Nate needs details, and as they come to him, he blurts them out. "Being in the mound shut you off from the outside world and exposed you to the earth's energy. The calling distracted your attention, and the idea of the string being pulled kept you focused."

Nate is looking at him quizzically, so Owen adds, "You said you can't remember anything; that's the indication that the assemblage point shifted."

Nate continues to look at him and seems to be adding up everything as he is being told. "But maybe I was just sleepwalking," he then suggests, having come up with an alternative explanation.

Owen laughs. It's a crazy idea. But he doesn't want to dismiss the possibility. Yet he isn't about to have his enthusiasm deterred. "Have you ever sleepwalked before?"

Nate answers that he hasn't.

Owen takes it as confirmation, then thinks of something more to add to his conclusion. "And your body was stiff. Remember, that's an indication that the assemblage point has shifted."

Nate takes in what has been said and at least seems to somewhat believe Owen. He returns to looking at the mound and shakes his head. "This is some crazy shit!"

"Hell yes, it's crazy!" But Owen wants to convince him of the magnitude of what he did. It is the critical accomplishment of a warrior: shifting the assemblage point is the line that divides being a warrior from the general realm of simply being alive. "You've crossed the line. You broke through!"

But Nate isn't able to match his enthusiasm. "But I didn't do anything."

"That's just it!" Owen only laughs. "That's how it works! We set it up and it happened! That's all it really takes!"

Nate isn't quick to agree, yet he's obviously impressed. He continues to look at the mound. "So why did I break out?"

It's the obvious question. Owen doesn't have a clear answer.

Something huge hovers between them.

They continue looking at the mound, then at the sheets of newspaper scattered about. What has happened is amazing.

Yet after a while, the immensity of the event begins to lose its sharp edges. Something remarkable has happened, but eventually it becomes mostly just the two of them standing together, looking at the mound.

They are standing in wet clothes in the cool morning air. Owen suddenly feels a chill move through him. He has to assume

Nate is feeling chilled as well. After another moment, he suggests they walk back.

By the time they reach his vehicle, they are both shaking and quickly jump into his truck. Owen starts it up and turns on the heat. But they are still in their wet clothes, so they jump out of the truck to stop shaking and strip down. They are left without anything dry to put on. The clothes they left to dry on their vehicles yesterday after rinsing off in the stream are wet with dew, and just about everything else they had to wear went into the water this morning. Owen comes up with a pair of dry socks, and Nate manages to find a T-shirt. Otherwise, they wrap themselves in the sleeping bags they find in the back of their vehicles and jump back into Owen's truck.

The two of them continue to shiver as they sit in the truck, trying to get warm. "Oh man, oh man," Nate says from the backseat. The chill has definitely settled into their bones.

But after a while, the chill subsides, and they are both just sitting there, warming themselves.

Owen feels his amazement at what happened at the mound return. It's a big deal. In all the years he has been involved with the material, he has never had such a dramatic confirmation of its validity.

And he doesn't want to keep the feeling to himself. "Wow," he says, amazed, letting the feeling push out of him. For the moment, he rocks back and forth.

Owen's impression is that things just came together. "It's like the stars lined up."

Nate stays silent for a moment. "So why do you think I was yelling?" he then asks.

Owen has to laugh. The question indicates what Nate has focused on in thinking about the event. He has no clear idea why

Nate was yelling. "I think maybe you just scared yourself," Owen says, feeling obligated to come up with some kind of explanation. "Remember, anytime you disengage from the first attention, it is like dying, because everything you perceive is turned off, or there can be some bleed-through from some other radio station, but it is more like a hallucination. You probably were just hallucinating." It's more likely the case of what happened, and after hearing himself mention it, he feels strongly that it is a probable explanation.

"Do you think I could have entered another world?" Nate then asks.

Owen laughs again. It's obvious that Nate is more focused on his imagination than on the explanation Owen just gave him. Maybe it's no surprise that Nate has chosen the outlandish. What happened does seem otherworldly.

Owen doesn't want to be dismissive and takes a moment to consider the question seriously. It's possible and surely within the realm of what can happen when someone enters the second attention, but it would mean Nate was able to assemble another world, which seems too advanced. "It would mean you were able to completely tune into another radio station. I don't think you're ready for that."

"Yeah, but something had to happen. I mean, I didn't break out of the mound for no reason."

It's true, and for the moment, Owen is forced to speculate. Nate was definitely terrified, but it's likely that having everything around him turned off, sensing the presence of something massive, the second attention, and maybe having his mind project his fear into the situation would be enough to scare him.

Yet something about the incident has come to dominate Owen's interest. What happened really shouldn't have happened in the normal progression of things; it usually takes years of effort and the relentless pushing of a teacher before the assemblage point loosens enough to shift on its own, and Nate is so young and inexperienced. Yes, Nate could be a natural talent, but there is another critical factor. "I think the most important thing is you just did it," he says, taking time to form his words to communicate his reasoning. "You didn't think about it, so you didn't know enough to get in your own way. You didn't not believe. Remember, the easiest thing is for the assemblage point to shift, but the hardest thing is to be convinced; it's why a teacher has to work so hard to get someone to believe things are possible. You didn't hinder yourself or cut yourself off from being in contact with the spirit." Owen truly believes it's the real key to what happened.

When Owen looks in the rearview mirror, he sees Nate staring out the window again. He thinks of something else to add to his explanation. "Remember, a shift of the assemblage point happens to ordinary people all the time. It happens in dreams. It can also happen due to illness, stress, or drugs and alcohol." Owen is trying to get Nate's attention. "You're not on drugs, are you?" he asks in an attempt at lightness.

Nate assures that he is not on drugs.

Owen feels he has put the final piece of the puzzle in place and looks out the window himself.

Suddenly, the vehicle becomes very hot. Owen quickly turns off the heat and shuts off the engine. He rolls down the windows. But the heat is still too much, and he throws the sleeping bag off his shoulders. Even that is not enough, so he gets out of the truck to take the sleeping bag off completely. Nate has overheated as well and gets out on the other side. They both end up walking around to cool off.

The two of them stand looking around. They are mostly naked. The day is bright. The trees around them are still and tall.

Owen steps out of the parking area to urinate, and Nate does the same. They both then go back to standing around. After a while, they decide to eat something. It has been the better part of a day since either of them has eaten anything, and they both are suddenly hungry. After washing their hands and taking out their coolers from their vehicles, they stand around eating. Being almost naked isn't comfortable. They check on their clothes. Nothing is close to being dry.

After eating, Nate gets into the front seat of his truck, and after a few more moments, he decides he wants to go to sleep. Owen isn't sure it's a good idea. He remembers don Juan being adamant at times that Carlos not fall asleep while he was recovering from events involving his assemblage point shift, yet Nate says he remembers times from the books when Carlos would sleep for long periods after something like that happened to him. Owen admits he's not sure about the right way to proceed, and Nate insists he feels fine. Owen doubts he could recover so quickly, but he doesn't care to argue. Watching Nate get comfortable, Owen feels tired as well and gets into his own vehicle.

But before falling asleep, alone for the first time since being woken by Nate yelling from the mound, Owen takes a moment for himself. He opens himself to the full scope of what has happened and lets the weight settle on him. He is a man trying to make sense of the world. He is following a path that makes the most sense to him of anything he has ever encountered. He has been working on concepts for years that he believed in but never experienced, so he has been proceeding on faith and intuition. He has now received confirmation that the most remarkable things he believes in, the things that have changed his notion of what it means to be alive, are actually real. He shouldn't be surprised, because he has believed it all along, but having it happen is such a relief.

CHAPTER TWELVE

Owen falls asleep, and when he wakes, Nate is still stretched out in the front seat of his truck. He gets out of his vehicle, steps into the brush, and urinates. Afterward, he checks his clothes. The day has warmed. The sun is drying his clothes, and the ones he wore yesterday are pretty much dry, but the ones he had on this morning are still quite damp when he turns them over. He takes the time to turn Nate's clothes over as well. Owen wonders how long Nate will sleep. He doesn't want to waste the rest of the day. Owen makes no effort to be quiet as he walks around and opens the back of his truck to get another bottle of water.

Nate finally stirs, though he isn't quick to get up. Owen decides to move things along. "Hey, eternity is waiting," he says, in an attempt at lightness, through the open window where Nate remains stretched out.

Nate sits up but seems groggy. His face looks filled with sleep.

Owen understands that Nate could still be half-asleep, but he also feels the need to be sure Nate isn't suffering any lingering effects of what happened earlier. "How ya feeling?" he asks.

Nate says he feels OK.

"So what do you think we should do?" Owen then asks, being direct in moving Nate along.

Nate acts like he doesn't want to think about it, but he does get out of the truck.

"We still have the day ahead of us," Owen states. "I need to get my chance in the mound."

It is another attempt at lightness. Yes, it makes sense that he gets a chance to be in the mound, but the mound is destroyed, and he doesn't think it can be repaired quickly. But they should decide about it, if not for tonight, then maybe later. Starting to fix it would at least give them something to do, and they should get moving around. When he mentions that they should take a look at the mound to see if it can be repaired, Nate is willing. Nate checks his own clothes and decides his shorts are at least dry enough. He puts them on. When Owen checks his shorts again, they are still damp but should dry on his body. His shirt should dry as well, so he puts it on.

They walk together to the mound. But soon after arriving, Owen realizes that returning to the mound might not have been such a good idea; it still looks terrible, and Nate is again appalled by what he sees. "That's crazy," he keeps saying, and he is thrown into another round of speculation about what could have been going on with him to cause him to break out. Owen is convinced he was hallucinating and tries to assure Nate that it isn't any big deal, that people hallucinate for all kinds of reasons. "But I don't remember a thing," Nate bemoans. Owen is sure he doesn't. It only confirms that when the assemblage point shifts past a certain point, normal perception is turned off.

Owen is thinking about finding an opportunity to take Nate away from the site while idly picking up the torn pieces of newspaper scattered about and crumpling them before tossing them into the white bucket. Nate helps for a bit and then starts talking about what it would take to put the mound back together. At first, he seems interested only in examining the broken sticks. Nate assesses that some of the frame sticks will need to be replaced, which means taking apart some of the frame. He begins pulling broken sticks out of the frame. Owen is pleased by Nate's change of focus and moves in to help. Even if the mound doesn't get completely fixed, it will be good to get started. The mound is something they will want to use again.

The work proceeds. Only a couple of sticks are actually broken, and after deciding how many sticks need to be replaced, they spend time searching for and finding new sticks that will work. While they work, Owen stays very aware of Nate. Nate is making an effort and can focus, but the bouncy enthusiasm that seems to be his trademark is missing. But Owen isn't going to make too much of it; rebuilding the frame is a drawn-out process that requires a more methodical approach. And the sustained effort can only be a good thing for Nate; it has to be helpful to have something to focus on and further solidify his cohesion.

The biggest challenge will be replacing the dirt that is scattered in all directions. There isn't enough dirt left in Nate's truck. They should be able to get dirt from somewhere if they want to complete the mound.

They finish rebuilding the frame. The decision then is what to do next. It still seems too much to run around finding dirt. So, what are they going to do with the rest of the afternoon? They decide to walk back to the vehicles.

Nate wants to take another nap. Owen very much feels it isn't a good idea. When he takes another chance to look closely at him, Nate seems listless; his eyes don't seem fully focused. Owen also doesn't want to argue about going back to sleep, so he suggests something they could do, a technique from the books, something all warriors must practice. "Hey, we're out here to work on the material."

He suggests they practice "The right way of walking." It involves walking with the fingers curled to draw attention to the body and with the eyes slightly crossed while staring at the horizon. The idea is that, by not focusing on anything in particular, the first attention is flooded with peripheral stimuli and becomes overloaded trying to interpret perception. The result is that the inner dialogue shuts off, and yes, it can lead to the worldview collapsing.

It's a fairly simple technique, but as Owen reviews it with Nate, he becomes less enthused. Flooding Nate's attention could make his assemblage point even less stable, but at least they will be walking, which should help ground him as well as keep Nate from the chance of a nap. Nate agrees to go along with the idea.

They walk down the two-track and then onto the dirt road. It takes them to the stream. That doesn't seem like a good idea either. Seeing the water reminds Nate of what he went through earlier that day when Owen dunked him. Owen can almost see Nate's jaw clench, and he becomes very quiet. Owen is quick to keep going past the stream, but with every step they take, they have to take one back. The day is moving toward evening. There is no doubt they will want to spend the night at the tent site. They probably should get moving in that direction. After walking a while longer, they turn around and head back to their vehicles.

They grab their sleeping bags and anything else they might need and head to the site. It is good timing; twilight is descending. They take time to prepare the site and break sticks for a fire.

Owen's interest is in quieting himself. He tells Nate he is going to practice gazing. Nate seems aware of the concept but doesn't ask for clarification, so Owen believes he is familiar enough with gazing to practice on his own if he chooses. Owen moves to the edge of the opening and sits facing the wall of greenery. The power of growing twilight is palpable.

Gazing is the not-doing of looking, a perceptual game of focusing on features of the world that are ordinarily overlooked. Owen practiced gazing the last time they were out at this site. By gazing, a warrior expands the world by enlarging his perception of it, and yes, the goal is to turn off the internal dialogue. He takes time to absorb every detail of the leaves in front of him, from the outline of the edges to the delicate pattern of veins. But another concept from the books has become available to him. It was mentioned that, as human beings, the eyes are relied upon too much to perceive the world, make judgments about those perceptions, interpret them, and conclude with others a shared description of the nature of reality. It was suggested that the ears and hearing be used to take some pressure off the eyes in perceiving.

Owen is aware of a seeming contradiction between the two techniques: on the one hand, focusing on using the eyes in a different way of perceiving while gazing; and on the other, not using the eyes at all and focusing on the ears and hearing to perceive the world around him. But he feels he can combine the two techniques to achieve the true goal: interrupting the continuous flow of usual perception, leading to a description of the world upheld by his constant talking to himself. He immerses himself in gazing at the details of leaves while opening himself to the sounds of birds and small animals. A rolling breeze drifts through the landscape. He follows with his ears its unfurling pattern of ebb and flow.

Darkness grows until it is complete. What he hears is Nate stirring, and evidence of a fire appears against the wall of greenery in front of him. He continues listening to Nate's movements. What catches his attention is that Nate doesn't settle back down. There is a restlessness in his actions. Owen decides to get up and sit next to him again.

Owen sits down and gets comfortable. He is looking forward

to staring into the fire. But what catches his attention is Nate's breathing. The fact that he hears it at all is a surprise. It seems uneven and labored, and when he looks over at him, he becomes concerned.

"What's going on?"

Owen, noticing his discomfort, gives him permission to not hold back. He breathes deep and then more rapidly.

"Something's not right."

Owen's concern escalates, though his understanding of what is happening is clear. It is what has worried him for a while.

"I think your assemblage point is shifting again. It never stabilized after your time in the mound. It's understandable. That was quite a jolt you took."

Owen's words do nothing to soothe him. Nate gets up and begins walking around, shaking his hands and arms.

"It's like I can't get control of myself."

His words only confirm what Owen is thinking.

The big question is what to do about it. Nate's condition cannot be willed away. Maybe it will pass. Owen thinks of something to say to him, but nothing clear comes to mind.

"Just keep breathing. Keep walking around."

Nate does just that. Both his breathing and his shaking become exaggerated. It is obvious he is not improving.

"It's like something is trying to come out of me."

Owen notices the panic in his voice.

"What should I do?"

Owen is starting to feel panicked himself. He still believes Nate's assemblage point will settle down, but he can't be sure when. Nate is in a tough spot.

Owen remembers something from the books and immediately gets to his feet.

"We should jog in place. Remember, it's what don Juan had Carlos do."

To offer assurance, Owen is willing to jog himself; they are in this together.

The two of them begin jogging. It feels like the right thing to do.

They continue jogging. Their effort surely captures their attention. Owen can only hope it is enough to restore Nate's continuity.

They jog until nearly exhausted. Owen stops first, then Nate. They both bend over, breathing heavily. Owen waits another moment before asking.

"Feeling any better?"

Nate makes a serious effort to assess himself.

"Not really."

Now Owen is really concerned. The fact that they are isolated out in the middle of the night is daunting. What he realizes is that they have to get to water, to the stream. It's the only thing that makes any sense. If Nate can't get himself under control, Owen will have to dunk him again.

But he doesn't want to say that to Nate, not knowing how he will react. The bottom line is they can't stay here.

"We need to walk."

"In the dark?"

Owen knows it is a desperate move that reflects his assessment of their situation, but there is no way to hide it.

"You have to keep moving, Nate."

They decide to leave everything behind. Nate knows the way. There is a faint trail. Nate has a flashlight, but the beam is weak and won't be much help.

Making their way through the brush at night is much worse than in daylight. But finally, they make it. Nate wants to get in his truck and just leave, but Owen doesn't let him. Nate is in no condition to drive. So they keep walking in the same direction as that afternoon. When they reach the river, Nate doesn't seem to have gotten worse, so Owen doesn't feel the need to dunk him. It is a relief to know the water is near if he needs it. They keep walking. The night is pitch black. A wind rustles through the trees that line the road. Their eyes have adjusted enough to see the road in front of them, but nothing else.

They keep walking.

Nate finally asks, "So how long we going to do this?"

Owen hadn't thought about it. Though he is aware that for every step they take, it is another step they will have to take to get back. The key is for Nate to become stabilized again. How long that takes, he can't be sure.

"Do you think there are bears out here?"

The question stops Owen dead in his tracks. Bears! He hadn't even thought about it. But the idea quickly escalates into a volume that presses down on him like a heavy weight.

"You know the area. Are there bears out here?"

Nate stands next to him. The night suddenly becomes oppressive.

"There could be."

The thought of bears becomes a force, colliding inside him from all directions. Owen suddenly finds himself standing in the middle of nowhere, in complete darkness, with trees rustling all around.

Nate turns on the flashlight he has been carrying and flashes it against a solid expanse of foliage. The weak beam only accentuates their vulnerability. If bears wanted to get them, they wouldn't have a chance.

Owen tries to get control of himself, but it isn't possible. Such fear overtakes him that the only thing he is aware of is that his ears are burning. He is at the night's mercy. He is the one breathing heavily. It is a long way back to their vehicles. The more pressing issue, of course, is that a bear could be right in front of them. He has to think of something. He remembers that in bear country, you need to make noise, so hopefully a bear is more afraid of you than you are of him.

"Hey!"

Nate takes the cue.

"Hey!"

There is no doubt now that they are turning around and heading back. Owen struggles for any shred of composure.

"Hey bear!"

But their verbal outbursts are sporadic and barely penetrate the darkness, and their footsteps seem to outdistance the sound. Owen is desperate to come up with something. Their only chance is to let a bear know they are coming, with the understanding that bears might be more afraid of them. An idea comes to him.

"We need to sing something."

"Like what?"

"It doesn't matter. Anything."

Something bursts into mind. The song is universal, the epitome of sophomoric inanity. He is sure Nate knows it.

"Let's sing the beer song, ninety-nine bottles."

Nate does know it.

They immediately start singing loudly.

"Ninety-nine bottles of beer on the wall, ninety-nine bottles of beer...you take one down and pass it around, ninety-eight bottles of beer on the wall. Ninety-eight bottles of beer on the wall, ninety-eight bottles of beer...."

They walk as fast as they can in complete darkness, singing loud and off-key, like two drunks coming home from the bar.

"Seventy-eight bottles of beer on the wall, seventy-eight bottles of beer...."

When they finally reach their vehicles, Nate strides directly to his truck, opens the door, and gets in. Owen is right behind, not letting him close the door.

"I'm out of here."

"You can't drive, Nate."

Owen doesn't hesitate to grab the keys from the ignition.

"Give me my damn keys!"

"Be smart about it!"

"Fuck off!"

Nate slams the door.

"Nate!"

But Nate doesn't even look at him. Through the window, he sits with his arms crossed, staring straight ahead.

CHAPTER THIRTEEN

What transpires is a hellish night. As much as Owen tries, Nate won't talk to him, and he is forced to retreat to his own vehicle. Knowing he won't be able to find the tent site by himself in the dark, he tries to get some sleep, but he grows cold and has to start the SUV and turn on the heater. When it gets too hot, he turns the vehicle off. The back-and-forth continues throughout the night, and he sleeps maybe an hour or two. When daylight arrives, he makes his way to the tent and crashes. What wakes him is the sweltering heat inside the tent from the direct sunlight. When he hears Nate moving around outside, he waits a while, then feels forced to get up. Nate is extremely apologetic about what happened. Owen isn't quick to respond, but after another moment, he asks how Nate is feeling. Nate says he is feeling all right. Things eventually return to normal between them. They can then laugh about what happened. They both admit to being on the verge of losing it. The idea of bears blasts them. They both expect one to jump out any second. All Nate keeps saying is how much he hates bears. Owen says that if they ever needed a demonstration of the frailty of human beings and how little really holds them together, they sure got it. Eventually, their attention turns to the rest of the day. They talk about getting more dirt and covering the mound, but neither of them is interested in scrounging for dirt. When Owen suggests they could practice the "right way of walking" again, Nate is quick to say that after last night, he has had enough of walking. After thinking about what else to do, nothing immediately comes to mind, and it is Nate who suggests maybe they have done enough for now. It is pretty much the same conclusion they came to after their first meeting. But their time together has been eventful and intense. They both admit feeling like they have been out there for closer to a week.

On the drive home, Owen opens himself to everything that went on with him and Nate. What a crazy experience! Another one! What most impresses him is that something actually happened again. For whatever reason, the combination of him and Nate is causing action. There is no doubt *spirit* is at work. It is what they are focused on. *Spirit* is Always ready to be involved as the force that guides men's lives; they just have to open to it, be ready to be directed, and, most importantly, believe with unbending intent.

Back home, Owen moves about doing some things. He goes to bed early and sleeps like the dead. In the morning, he does a light tai chi workout and spends time in his recapitulation crate. His aim is to consolidate his gains. Again, there is the sense that he may notice a difference in his session after his time with Nate, but nothing is obvious. The rest of the day, he focuses on the details of his life.

Everything changes, however, when that evening he checks his email and finds a message from their downline contact in the system, which Nate has also forwarded to him after receiving the same email. The email is an appeal for help. The downline pair is being hassled by at least two other downline teams. One member of the pair is being stalked so persistently in her personal life that she is close to quitting. It is the other member who is giving the call for help, knowing that, according to the system's guidelines, if her partner quits, she will be forced from the round as well and will have to wait out the rest of the six months. She is desperate for that not to happen and very strongly communicates how important it is for her to stay in the round and continue working with the material. She ends the email by saying they will meet anytime, anyplace.

Ah geez! Owen's reaction is pure annoyance. A new round has hardly begun, and already people are asking for help, while others have nothing better to do than bother someone else. It is another indication of the kind of people who get involved with the system. Their only attraction to the material is its otherworldly nature, so they bring all kinds of weird notions and indulgence to the system. Owen has experienced it enough before. And the timing is terrible. He and Nate don't need any distractions.

But Owen is obligated to respond. It's another demand of the system. At the start of each round, each pair is also given the email address of another pair, who is given the address of another pair, and so on. It is a safety-net component of the system. Because working with the material is so challenging, it can be easy to get bogged down in opinion and interpretation, and people, by nature, are petty and easily sidetracked into defending their ideas. If a team of warriors reaches an absolute impasse that threatens their ability to continue working together, they can reach out to their downline pair for input. The third party is usually used to mediate disputes and offer suggestions and clarification. Owen has always found the role of the third party essential to the system's continued operation. There have been times when he has done more work on the material as a third-party mediator than with his own partner.

But this situation is unlike anything he has ever encountered:

people using their downline pair's contact information to locate and harass them. And two pairs of partners have joined together to gang up on an upline team? It is an absolute aberration! Owen needs to make sure he understands the email correctly and read it again. And what are he and Nate supposed to do about it? His reaction is to email the woman and copy Nate, asking how they can help.

Her reply is that they need help developing a strategy. The woman's name is Gail. Owen asks what kind of strategy she has in mind, and Gail replies that hashing out a strategy will require a lot of discussion and that they don't have much time, so it would be better to meet in person. She apologizes profusely for any inconvenience and assures them that she wouldn't ask if she weren't so desperate. Gail again states how much working with the material means to her. She promises not to take up much of their time and repeats that she and her partner will agree to meet anytime, anywhere.

Owen isn't interested in getting together. But what can they do? The idea that meeting with the women shouldn't take up much of their time is encouraging, but Owen also has to look at the big picture. He and Nate have something happening that needs to be protected, but who is he to know the designs of power? Because he believes the system is a vehicle of spirit, he feels obligated to at least take the next step. But he isn't about to get caught up in someone else's gyrations. He and Nate's obligation is to hear the women out and offer suggestions. That's as far as they need to take it. Owen emails his thoughts and gets Nate's full agreement. Owen expresses his concern that meeting with Gail and her partner might interfere with him and Nate getting together next, but Nate replies that he won't be able to get away for more than a short period over the next few days. So, in that sense, meeting with the two women will at least give them the chance to get together in some capacity. And it will be in a different kind of setting. The opportunity for them is to turn the encounter into a challenge. There is no reason not to use the meeting as a chance to work with the material.

They need to come up with their own strategy. The challenge is cultivating conscious awareness and impeccability, not just reacting. It will give them a chance to practice sobriety, control, and discipline in an engaging situation. It is very important in the life of a warrior to take everything they do as deadly serious, yet against the backdrop of infinity, nothing can be taken seriously at all. With that in mind, they decide to play a little good cop, bad cop. They can treat the situation as a not-doing, a chance to practice controlled folly. Owen will be the good cop because being sweet and understanding isn't his natural inclination, and the not-doing of acting out a role will force him to be strategic in how he responds. Beyond that, they decide to just let the encounter unfold.

It is then a matter of when to get together. Because of his limited availability, the decision is left up to Nate. Nate says he could be available in the afternoon the day after tomorrow. The time is specific enough, so it will be a good test to see if the women are serious about meeting whenever. Gail emails her response, saying she only needs to know where to meet. Owen again leaves it up to Nate. Owen even offers to drive farther toward him if Nate is time-constrained. Nate says it isn't necessary and picks a location halfway between them, a strip mall off the highway with a casual restaurant. Owen forwards the information to Gail, and she says they will be there; the time decided is three o'clock.

When the time comes to make the hour-plus drive, Owen starts early. He intends to allow plenty of time and to arrive first. His aim is to control the battlefield, the first precept of stalking for a warrior, because he remembers how poorly he followed that principle when first meeting Nate and the trouble it caused him. Owen finds the restaurant easily enough. It isn't the family-style restaurant he was expecting, but it seems more like a trendy eatery. The name "Jonesy's" is stretched across the front in bold, bright letters. His final focus is a warrior's directive to be open and light, to have a sense of play but be absolutely serious: "A man goes to knowledge as he goes to war, wide-awake, with fear, with respect, and with absolute assurance."

Walking into the place, there is hardly anyone there, though he does notice a young woman sitting alone at a far table, and by the searching look she gives him, he has to think it could be one of the women he is to meet. He is surprised because he is a good fifteen minutes early, but when the woman sheepishly smiles at him, he feels forced to walk over. She asks if he is Nate or Owen. Owen introduces himself, and the woman says her name is Ronnie.

He sits down, disappointed at having lost his chance to control the battlefield of their first encounter and equally disappointed by his first impression of the woman. She seems disheveled and timid. Her longish light-brown hair hangs about her face and shoulders, and she seems nervous, almost skittish. She could be pretty if she weren't so withdrawn, but what most catches his attention is her small head. Sitting hunched forward, she seems wrapped up in a gray jacket.

Owen exchanges pleasantries with the woman, then dives right into the situation between them. Being alone with her at least gives him the opportunity to gather information. "So you're having a little trouble?" he asks, trying to be light and jovial.

"Oh, terrible," the woman says without hesitating. She shakes her head. "Really bad." It's as if the mere mention of her situation causes her dismay. "The guys keep coming after me," she bemoans. "I don't know what their deal is."

Owen is momentarily taken aback by the woman's unabashed response. And if another team has done a number on her, he doubts it was difficult. Owen actually feels somewhat repelled by the woman; she has such weak, retreating energy. It's going to be a challenge for him to be encouraging. He can't help but wonder why people like her even get involved with the system. It's not a game.

Without further preliminaries, the woman dives into telling her story, as if she needs only an audience. She says the guys are everywhere. They show up at work and at stores when she goes out. She says she even took all kinds of different roads to get here when she left home. "I could lose my job!" she complains. "People at work keep questioning me. It's embarrassing."

Owen's immediate thought is that embarrassment isn't a big deal. In fact, embarrassment is something warriors can use as a way to attack their self-importance, as a strategy to shrink their notion of themselves. From that perspective, the guys are actually offering her an opportunity, though he is sure it would be difficult for her to see it that way.

The woman begins telling him about her latest encounter with the guys. "I was at my boyfriend's last night, and we were just watching TV." Her eyes grow wide, and her hands begin gesturing. "And all of a sudden, there's this thumping on the wall. I'm all pins and needles anyway, so I almost go through the roof, and the thumping just keeps getting louder and louder until there's like a thousand different things...." The woman suddenly stares at him as if he were her source of energy. "It's like the walls were coming down; there was thumping everywhere. So my boyfriend runs to the window and sees tennis balls flying at the house. He can't see anything beyond the lights, but all these tennis balls are flying out of the darkness." Her hands fly about her face, mimicking the tennis balls, as she speaks in rapid-fire. "Of course, I'm freaking out, and he knows I know something, but I can't even imagine what to tell him. Then everything goes really quiet. And suddenly the doorbell rings. We hurry up and turn out all the lights, and there's this guy standing at the door. My boyfriend is pissed now and gets his gun, and when the doorbell rings again, he opens it and points it at the guy. But it's just a pizza guy. My boyfriend is sure the guy is part of what's going on because we didn't order any pizza, so he drags the guy inside and scares the hell out of him, and the guy pees his pants! When my boyfriend lets him go, the guy calls the cops, and now my boyfriend is in jail!"

What! Owen can hardly believe what he is hearing. With Ronnie staring at him, he feels forced to keep his composure, yet it takes everything he has to keep a straight face. "And now my boyfriend is breaking up with me!" she exclaims. She turns and sits back in her seat, thrusting her arms down across her chest and lowering her head in a gesture of complete despair.

Owen is relieved that her attention is no longer focused on him, but what is he supposed to do? It's the craziest thing he has ever heard! Part of him just wants to laugh. "Wow!" is all he manages to say, and he shakes his head. If it weren't for Ronnie's obvious devastation after reliving her story, he'd have a hard time believing her.

Otherwise, Owen is at a complete loss. The thought he clings to is that he has decided to be positive and encouraging. He struggles to gather himself. What comes to mind is that this woman had better start acting like a warrior, or she doesn't have a chance. The words of don Juan almost scream in his ear: "To the average person, everything is either a blessing or a curse, but to a warrior, there are only challenges."

"They won't leave me alone," Ronnie whines. "I just can't take it anymore. They're ruining my life!"

Owen has to come up with a way to approach this. He attempts to be rational, feeling the need to give the woman something to hold on to that will at least stabilize her, so as soon as an idea comes to him, he goes with it. "You know the guys can't touch you, right?" His idea is to at least help her feel secure in her personal safety, so he points out that there can be no physical contact between participants, or they are disqualified.

But before he says anything else, Ronnie's whole face suddenly brightens as if a light has burst from within her. She immediately leaps from her chair and rushes forward. Recovering from his surprise, Owen turns toward the direction she runs and sees another woman come through the door. The two meet in the center of the floor and rush into each other's arms. The woman immediately consoles Ronnie as best she can. "There, there," she says, as if comforting a child. "You poor thing." The safety of the woman's arms gives Ronnie full permission to abandon herself, and she sobs and stammers all at once.

Owen is appalled. The situation has deteriorated to the obscene. While staying fully engaged with Ronnie, the woman suddenly looks over at him, catches his eye, and gives him a wink. It is a gesture of acknowledgment, but it also signals that she isn't fully absorbed in the situation. Owen is greatly relieved; at least this woman might somewhat have her wits about her. She is slightly taller than Ronnie, but even at first glance, she is much more substantial. She is older, in her mid to late thirties, thick but not heavy. She is dressed professionally in a navy pantsuit and looks as if she might have come from an office.

As soon as Ronnie's initial hysteria subsides, the woman gently turns her and, with an arm still around her, guides her back to the table. She continues to make a great effort to comfort and console, yet when they near the table, the woman breaks from Ronnie for a moment to give him her full attention. "Are you Owen or Nate?" she says, looking at him and smiling politely. Owen stands and introduces himself, and the woman extends her hand, introducing herself as Gail. "Thanks for coming," she says as they shake hands. She is nice-looking in a modest way, with clear eyes, full cheeks and lips, nicely done dark hair framing her face, and tasteful makeup. Gail then returns her attention to Ronnie. "There, there," she says, pulling her close in an effort to reconnect with Ronnie and her trauma. She even pats Ronnie on the head and then presses her head to her shoulder to soothe her. "Those nasty guys aren't going to bother you. Everything is going to be fine. We'll get through this." The tone of her voice is as if consoling a ten-year-old!

Owen struggles against being sickened by such a blatant display of histrionics and unabashed appeasement. Gail then helps Ronnie into her chair. With her back to him and from the throes of her involvement, she suddenly turns slightly and, with great speed, reaches into her purse and shoves at him a twenty-dollar bill and asks him to go get them some drinks. She even manages to say he can get something for himself. Owen is shocked; he has suddenly been reduced to being an errand boy! But on the other hand, he is more than glad to get away from the crazy situation and let the two women have their time together.

CHAPTER FOURTEEN

Owen walks to the food counters. He remains unsettled by the crazy situation he has found himself in. What is it with people? Yet getting away from the women at the table has offered him some relief, and he focuses on getting something to drink. He notices the place is set up cafeteria-style. A long line of display cases and counters stretches in front of him, and on the wall behind hang huge, glossy close-up photos of food and drink, pictured against bright-colored backgrounds and framed in neon light. Owen is only interested in something to drink, but looking up at the menu, he sees all kinds of choices. Looking more closely, it seems the place's goal is to offer customers as many choices as possible: there are slurpies, smoothies, coffee, iced coffee, juices, and flavored waters. He has no idea what the women might want.

Owen takes a moment, then decides to have fun with his selection; it is his acknowledgment of the crazy situation he is involved in. And if the women cared what they got, they would have said something. When a bored-looking, pudgy girl in a purple blouse with dark makeup circling her eyes asks if she can help, he decides to choose the wildest thing that catches his attention and orders mango- kiwi smoothies, three of them.

As the drinks are being made, Owen glances back at the two women huddled together. The last thing he wants to do is have to return to some kind of mania, but it's the situation before him. "Controlled folly," he admonishes to himself. A warrior acts as if he doesn't have a care in the world. He centers himself to be ready for whatever.

When the drinks are ready, Owen pays the girl and picks up the tray to carry it to the table, but as he turns, he sees Nate has walked through the door. Nate is looking around, and Owen catches his attention. Nate walks over, and they greet. Owen is quick to fill him in on what is going on. "Man, we got a weird one." Nate wants to know more, but Owen doesn't want to be too conspicuous, so he nods toward the two women. "Just be ready," he says. "Get yourself a drink and I'll meet you." Owen starts back to the table.

Gail seems to have calmed Ronnie down, and both women are sitting up as he arrives. "Thanks much," Gail says, smiling at him, taking two of the drinks and handing one to Ronnie. Owen hands her the change before sitting down next to her. "We really appreciate you coming," she says, with a note of formality. "We know it's not the usual request, but as you can tell, we have ourselves a challenge." Yes, Owen would sure say she does, and he likes that Gail has at least used the word "challenge." He hopes she has shifted Ronnie's attitude toward how a warrior deals with the world.

Owen lets them know that Nate has arrived, and they wait for him to join them. Taking a sip of his drink, he finds it just as sickly sweet as he imagined.

When Nate arrives at the table, Owen makes the introductions. Gail stands and extends her hand, while Ronnie remains seated. Nate takes one of the remaining seats on the opposite side of the table next to Ronnie. As a group, they are now seated in a roughly half-moon shape, with Owen and Nate at the ends. "So, what's going on?" Nate asks.

"We have a real challenge on our hands," Gail answers. "And we're looking for some ideas."

"What have you come up with?" Nate asks. He leans forward, ready to get down to business.

"Well, our whole goal so far has been to keep Ronnie away from the guys," Gail answers. "But it isn't working."

"She knows they can't touch her, right?" Nate asks, referring to the rule Owen brought up earlier about no physical contact between participants, and says he has already mentioned it to Ronnie. "So what's the big deal then?" Nate says bluntly. He sits back in his seat. "She should just ignore them." "It's not so easy," Gail explains quickly. "The guys are relentless, and they show up everywhere."

Nate's reaction is to laugh. "A couple of guys bothering her is the least of her problems. We're facing infinity here."

Gail understands but is quick to come to Ronnie's defense. "She's just getting started. It's a lot to handle for a beginner."

"Well, maybe she's in the wrong game," Nate surmises, continuing his hard stand. Owen understands what Nate is doing; he's coming with both barrels blazing in his role as the bad cop.

Gail seems taken aback by Nate's directness, but quickly regains her composure and returns to defending Ronnie. "It doesn't matter so much where she starts but how far she can travel the path."

"But she has to get out of the starting gate," Nate counters. "She'll be fine," Gail answers. "We just have to get through this."

Owen thinks that maybe Nate is being too adamant in his role as bad cop, and to counteract his approach, Owen realizes it is time for him to get involved, time for his good cop to appear. "Let's take a look at this," he says, preparing himself for an attempt to find common ground.

But Nate jumps in again. "Hey, we have a lot going on. This is a big effort for us to come all the way out here. If she wants us to help her find a solution, that's fine, but she needs to step up."

"She'll step up," Gail says. "And believe me, we're only grateful for you to give us your time, and we understand how serious this is." Tensions escalate. Owen is surprised by how vehemently Gail pushes back against Nate. She seems almost desperate in her determination to defend Ronnie. And Ronnie might not deserve it; Owen has to believe Gail can see that she's a mess.

A realization then hits him, whole and complete: Gail isn't so much defending Ronnie as protecting her own involvement with the material. She is fighting to stay in the round. If Ronnie quits, she is out of the round as well. She is accepting her warrior's challenge to take advantage of every situation, even if it means being involved with a miserable person like Ronnie. And in dealing with her, Gail will have to practice discipline, resolve, and ingenuity, maybe like never before in her life. Coming across a person like Ronnie on her path should be treated as a find, a true chance to practice these attributes and temper her warrior's spirit.

If his interpretation is true, Owen is only impressed. He recognizes his own challenge. If he has decided to play good cop, he needs to jump in. "Now wait a minute," he says, sensing the need to be a peacemaker. "There are different ways to look at this. Let's step back a minute." He has forced everyone to give him their attention. For the moment, he isn't sure what to say. "Let's look at the big picture," he continues, feeling for a thread. "These guys have presented themselves, and obviously there is the chance to create a challenge."

Gail is immediately relieved. "Absolutely," she says and smiles.

Based on what Gail has already said, Owen believes he has found a place to start. "These guys are fixated on Ronnie because, from their perspective, they are getting a positive response. But if that fixation is broken, they could easily go away."

Gail almost beams in agreement. It's as if he has thrown her a lifeline. Owen is starting to feel solid in his position.

But before their conversation can go any further, Ronnie suddenly stiffens. It's as if her whole body spasms. "They're here!" Her eyes widen with terror.

In unison, they all look toward the front, where Ronnie is staring, but no one has come through the door. They turn back to Ronnie. She reacts again in terror, letting out a guttural moan. This time, when he looks, Owen sees the last of a guy leaping across the bank of windows that stretches across the front of the eatery. It is just a quick glimpse, yet as he continues looking, he sees another guy leap out from the right edge of the windows and begin leaping across. His leaps are big and extended, and he is wearing a black, billowy cape or coat. For a moment, the guy is blocked by the doorway. Then he appears on the other side, and with a couple more leaps, he is across the bank of windows and disappears.

Ronnie is beside herself with fear. Gail presses against her with an arm around her shoulder. "It's OK, it's OK." Owen looks at Nate, who shrugs in a gesture of not knowing what to think.

Looking back at the windows, another guy is starting across, this time from the left. He is a different guy, shorter and without the cape. He jumps with his feet together, arms at his sides, as if he were on a pogo stick. Dressed in black, he is wearing a bowler hat.

As soon as the guy reaches the other side, another guy starts from that end, but he must be crouched or crawling because only his head is visible as he moves across the solid section that extends a couple of feet below the windows. The effect is of a seemingly detached head floating through open space. At one point, the guy turns and smiles at them. His face is painted white, as if he were a mime. He then opens his eyes wide and blinks, forming his mouth into a surprised "O" before turning and continuing his journey. It is a surprise when he reaches the door area that blocks him from view. After not seeing him for a moment, he emerges on the other side looking ten feet tall. He has to be on someone's shoulders.

Owen finds himself smiling; these guys are at least creative. If it weren't for Ronnie's reaction, he could be greatly amused. When Owen looks again, one of the guys has started from the left and is dragging his leg. He seems to be in great pain and shakes his fist at the sky as if cursing his fate.

Ronnie moans uncontrollably. Gail urges her not to look, but she seems unable to break her gaze.

Then nothing further happens. After waiting several moments, their only conclusion is that the guys have stopped.

He and Nate look at each other and suddenly laugh in amazement. "Well, that was sure something," Owen says in a deadpan tone. Gail works hard to calm Ronnie. Owen is both appalled by how abandoned Ronnie is in her dismay and impressed by how completely Gail gives herself over to bolstering Ronnie and bringing her under control. There is little doubt about the ferocity of Gail's struggle to keep herself involved in the round.

And Gail does get Ronnie under control. She remains upset, but her distress seems limited to feeling sorry for herself.

Gail gathers herself and sits upright. "Well, as you can see, the guys don't plan on stopping anytime soon." A flash of fierceness in her eyes communicates determination.

Owen's focus remains on Gail. He thinks she might have extensive experience with the material and could be advanced, maybe more than anyone he has ever met. But he also recognizes the seriousness of her predicament. If the guys are that determined to harass Ronnie, there will be other opportunities when she won't be protected, and if Ronnie continues to be so affected, she probably doesn't have a chance. According to the system, all

Ronnie has to do is say, "Quit," and the guys will be forced to leave her alone, but both she and, consequently, Gail will be out of the round.

Because of his interest in Gail, Owen feels motivated to take the lead in his role as good cop. The place to start seems to be where they left off. After meeting the guys and seeing their demonstration, though, he feels he has a deeper understanding of the situation. "These guys are obviously off on a nut. They probably think they are practicing stalking or controlled folly or something, but I don't think what they are doing is well rooted in the material." Owen is following the only line of thinking that has presented itself. "I doubt they have any real staying power. If their fixation is broken, they will easily lose interest and get bored."

"But they said they have already tried keeping Ronnie away from them," Nate replies.

"But how much?" Owen asks.

Gail says they have been able to have Ronnie stay at friends' houses where the guys don't bother her, but the real problem is at work, where the guys wait for her in the parking lot and even come into her workplace.

Her time at work seems to be the core issue. Owen suggests that Ronnie take some time off, maybe even a vacation, but Ronnie says she doesn't have any vacation time; she just started the job. Owen then suggests she call in sick, but Ronnie says that if she does, she is afraid she will lose her job. Owen asks what kind of job she has, and Ronnie says she is a receptionist. Owen is sure there must be other receptionist jobs, but Ronnie says jobs are hard to come by; it took her weeks to find this one.

Owen is only feeling resistance, and if Ronnie is unwilling to put in any effort, it will be hard to help her.

"So how did the guys know you'd be here?" Nate suddenly asks. It's a good point. The guys must have followed her. Ronnie says she was constantly checking her rearview mirror. "But the guys were all ready for a show," Nate says. There is little doubt he feels he is onto something. "They must have known ahead of time we were going to meet."

It's true; the guys were prepared, and they wouldn't have gone through all the effort of props and dressing up if they didn't think they'd have an audience. The realization changes the dynamic of what happened.

"We believe they're intercepting Ronnie's email," Gail admits. Her tone is almost a confession. "Which means they're probably intercepting mine."

The information highlights a new angle. But as Owen thinks about it, the fact that the guys have access to Gail's email might even bolster his idea. "But the guys aren't bothering you."

Gail says they haven't, at least so far.

"Yet the guys could probably know where you live and where you work."

Gail agrees. But when Owen looks at the three of them, he can tell they aren't getting his point. Owen delivers it as if he were delivering a punch line. "The guys don't bother you because they don't think they're going to get the same kind of reaction."

What he has said makes immediate sense to everyone. Ronnie is set to start complaining again, "But what can I do?"

Yet in the next instant, Gail cuts her off. "Hey, you're going to have to do something," she says. "You know you're not going to get a free pass." Gail's tone has shifted. There is a definite edge to her voice. "You have a decision to make. You're at a crossroads. Either you let these guys stop you or you find a way."

Gail's change of approach is a surprise to everyone. Owen is relieved that Gail is taking a stand. He realizes she is also risking her involvement in the round, but she must believe the time is right to take that chance.

Gail drives home her point to Ronnie. "Otherwise, you have to quit. This just might not be for you."

Gail has applied the full force of her leverage. Faced with the withdrawal of her support, Ronnie would be absolutely lost. The realization seems to hit Ronnie hard. She is suddenly isolated and looks down, her arms crossed over her chest, in response to what can only be seen as a reprimand.

But in the next instant, Ronnie seems to rally herself. She lifts her head and wonders if she can get another position with the company. Right now, as the receptionist, the guys appear at the front window and even come in to bother her, so maybe she could get a job in the back of the business doing filing or data processing. She thinks a position might be coming available. Gail is immediately encouraging and even offers to meet her somewhere, drive her to work, and pick her up afterward to avoid the guys bothering her in the parking lot.

So, there it is. They have at least settled on a direction. Everyone is relieved, and it seems like a natural conclusion. The solution was staring them in the face. All Ronnie had to do was make an effort. But in the next instant, Owen feels it came too easily. There is something about the timing of Gail's change in approach to Ronnie. Owen laid out the issues of their situation, issues Gail was aware of and had presented before her, but she let him be the one to state the obvious, as if coming from someone else, the solution would carry more weight, or at least add weight to her argument. Owen can't help but wonder if that was her intention all along, and after gaining Owen and Nate as cohorts, Gail felt comfortable enough with their support to apply pressure on Ronnie without it seeming like it was coming just from her. Ronnie couldn't so easily dismiss her or think Gail was being personal in her attack. Gail knew Ronnie would hate to lose contact with her, and he believes she played that angle perfectly.

Owen is surprised. Gail could have used them to carry out

her plan. If that was her intent, it was an impressive strategy. But there is no way to know, because once they reach a solution, there is no reason for them to continue talking. Gail is profuse in expressing her gratitude to the two of them. She stands, shakes their hands, and says they couldn't have done it without them. She doesn't want to hold them up any longer. They all wish each other well. Even Ronnie is smiling. All Owen can think about is how adroitly Gail handled the situation. And he can't blame Gail for using them; a warrior uses everything available, with the understanding that a warrior is to be used by the world as well.

CHAPTER FIFTEEN

The four of them walk out of the restaurant together. They take a moment to look around in all directions to make sure the guys are nowhere in sight. Owen and Nate even walk the women to their vehicles. Quick goodbyes are exchanged, and the women thank them again.

"Well, that was sure something," Nate says, shaking his head as they watch the two women drive away.

Owen gives a low laugh. "Geez."

"That girl doesn't have a snowball's chance in hell," Nate states. Owen only smiles. He knows Nate is talking about Ronnie, but it's Gail who has his attention. He is still impressed with how effectively she set up and took advantage of the situation. He doubts Nate even has a clue about what really went on.

Owen and Nate spend a few moments talking about their next time together. Nate says he has the dirt lined up and should be ready to meet at the site the day after tomorrow. He will confirm by email. They share one last laugh about their crazy meeting with the women, then turn and walk in opposite directions to their vehicles. On the drive back to his place, Owen idly thinks about what happened at the meeting with the women, but what he thinks about most is Gail. Her handling of Ronnie, him, and Nate, and the entire situation was a fine display of warrior-ship. It makes him wonder what else she has accomplished. It would be great to meet someone of real quality. And he likes that Gail is an attractive enough woman, though his foremost interest is in her as another warrior. Maybe she is an opportunity. It could be a direction of spirit. He has her email address and could ask her to meet. He won't contact her for a while, but decides at some point it will be interesting to know what happens with her and Ronnie.

Arriving home, Owen moves about the house. It isn't long before the doorbell rings. Reaching the door, he doesn't see anyone beyond the frosted glass, so he opens the door to look further. He notices a black rose on the porch, with a note beneath it. Picking it up, the note reads, "Pleased to meet ya!"

Damn! Owen is appalled. Now the guys have found him! He is quick to step out onto the porch and look around, but only sees a silver car moving down at the end of the street.

Owen is quick to email Nate about the rose and note, and it isn't long before Nate emails back that he got them as well.

It means the guys know where they live! Now they are involved! It's shocking to believe that the guys would go to such lengths as to follow them home. And having roses with them can only mean they planned to follow them all along! But how did they follow them? Owen didn't notice anyone behind him as he drove. But if they got into Ronnie's and Gail's email, they would have gotten their email addresses as well, and maybe traced them back to their home addresses. Owen isn't much of a computer guy, so he's not sure how all that works, but the bottom line is the guys know where they live.

But what can be the point? All Owen can think is that the guys are really having a time amusing themselves. Don't they have better things to do? Are they now going to try to harass the two of them and follow them around? For one thing, the guys aren't going to get the same kind of reaction from him and Nate as they got from Ronnie. But the idea of waiting around for the guys to make the next move is only annoying.

The first thing he decides to do is email Gail and let her know of the developments. Gail emails back, profusely apologizing for getting them involved. Owen is sure their emails are being intercepted and decides to send a message to the guys when he replies to Gail, saying the guys must be clueless wannabes who are more interested in indulgences than in being warriors.

The question then is what to do. Owen still feels the guys are just a bother, but he also has to take what has happened in the context of power. In that sense, he has to look at the guys as at least a challenge. But what most gets his attention is that the guys showing up on his doorstep have given him a reason to get back in contact with Gail much sooner than expected, and that's a good thing. When Nate emails his suggestion that they just wait for the guys to make a move, Owen doesn't care to be so passive. It's the idea of making contact with Gail that has taken over his focus; she is someone he would like to know more about, someone with whom he could become involved.

But what should be his next step? He can't say too much in emails if the guys are intercepting them. If they are going to work together, they will have to meet in person. It would cause another encounter with Gail, and that is really what he wants.

When Owen emails his suggestion that they get together again and meet at the same place, and everyone agrees, he realizes that he is taking the lead, and that's fine with him. What he wants to be sure about is that their meeting won't interfere with him, Nate, and their trip to the woods. After some emailing back and forth, it was decided that the four of them would meet at four o'clock the day after tomorrow, and he and Nate would get back out to the mound site the following morning. Everything seems to have fallen into place. Owen is pleased. He is curious to see what will happen. When the time comes, Owen arrives early again, and this time he is first to show. There are a few people in the place, and the table they sat at before is open, so he decides to sit there again. To avoid drawing attention to himself, he orders a drink, this time something he might enjoy, an iced coffee.

Nate is next to walk through the door, and the two of them spend a few moments joking about the fine mess they've gotten themselves into. Soon, Gail and Ronnie arrive together. Everyone is in a good mood, except for Ronnie, who still seems shell-shocked. She says two of the guys showed up at her work again yesterday and that someone buzzed her apartment in the middle of the night. Owen repeats his belief that the guys will keep doing things like that as long as they get a positive response. He then asks about any progress they're making with Ronnie's strategy to find a different place to stay and get a new position at work. Ronnie says a place to stay won't be a problem, but the new position at work could take some time. She says she is looking into the possibility of a different job altogether.

Before they go further with their talking, the rest of them decide to get drinks. When everyone returns, they quickly get settled.

Owen announces that he fully expects the guys to show up again. His statement causes Ronnie to recoil, but Gail quickly brings her under control. Owen believes he is only stating the obvious and is sure the others have thought of it as well. If the guys are intercepting their emails, they know their group will be meeting, and if they're serious about their little game, they won't be able to pass up the chance to make contact. Owen then suggests a strategy: when the guys show up, they need to remain unaffected and even laugh at them. Owen believes that just going against their expectations might be enough to break their fixation. "I just don't think these guys are going to have much staying power," he adds, repeating the point he made before. "There just isn't that much to motivate them."

"And we have to control the battlefield," Nate adds. Yes, it's what Owen believes.

But what Nate says next makes it evident that he is thinking in a whole different direction. "So maybe we can turn the tables on them," he suggests. "I have a buddy who's a cop. Maybe we can follow them back to their cars, get their license plate numbers and find out where they live. Then we can bother them. It will be like stalking the stalkers."

Nate is excited about his proposal, but Owen isn't as positive about it. The last thing he wants to get involved in is a bunch of gyration. Chasing people around and staking out where they live seems a bit ridiculous.

"It would definitely change their focus," Nate offers.

Owen agrees that it would, but it seems juvenile, and the strategy lacks any real foundation in the material. They would simply be reducing themselves to the inane level of the guys.

"I think the thing that is most important," Gail then states. "Is that we treat the guys as worthy opponents. They can be an opportunity for us if we approach them as a challenge in the context of the books."

That's something Owen can agree with.

"Maybe we could use them as petty tyrants," Nate then offers.

Now that's extreme. The use of petty tyrants in the books is an advanced technique that centers around finding people in positions of power that warriors put themselves under the control of, so that they are forced to practice the attributes of warriorship and polish their link with *intent* under difficult and trying circumstances. The degree to which that was done by don Juan in the books was absolutely profound. Owen thinks that even thinking in that direction is definitely too much for them, so he is surprised when Gail picks up on the idea.

"Nothing can temper the spirit of a warrior as much as the challenge of dealing with impossible people in positions of power," she says, seeming to quote from the material. "We could somehow find a way to put ourselves at the mercy of these guys."

"We could use ourselves as bait!" Nate interjects.

Owen finds the idea outlandish but is willing to find out what they are thinking.

But he doesn't get the chance. The guys suddenly show up. Ronnie sees them first, and all her composure instantly crumbles. Gail is immediately against her. What pleases Owen most is the accuracy of his prediction that the guys would make an appearance.

Two heads stick out, peering from the far-left side of the bank of windows, one atop the other. They both wear hats and have their faces painted white. They look up and down at each other, then back at the group several times in a mock consultation, before their heads retreat from view.

Owen attempts to pull the four of them together. "OK, let's have fun with this."

Nate doesn't need any encouragement. "It's show time!"

For a moment, they sit waiting for what will happen next. Three heads pop out, one on top of the other, from the right edge of the windows, causing the impression that with the other two heads on the opposite side of the windows, there are now more than four guys. All the composure Gail has been struggling to instill in Ronnie is lost as she involuntarily gasps with dread. It is as if the guys have tapped into her innermost fears.

The three heads look up and down at each other as if fervently plotting their next move. For support, Owen moves his chair closer to Gail. Taking the effort as his cue, Nate moves closer to Ronnie. Nate suggests they wave at the guys. "They're a bunch of clowns," Nate offers to Ronnie for support.

The show begins in earnest. The guys start walking back and

forth in front of the windows in various postures and poses, and with different props. At one point, one of the guys even displays a fake animal head impaled on a spear. It is all very clever and dramatic, but soon feels like it has been done before. Even Ronnie doesn't seem so affected.

All that changes, however, when two guys from each opposite edge walk toward each other and meet in the middle. The door suddenly opens! The guys are coming in! They fill the doorway in a gathering mass and then start forward. There is a rush of surprise among the group seated at the table. "Here we go!" Owen manages to say. "Hold together!"

The guys rush straight at Ronnie, flailing their arms and hands like maniac demons. Ronnie falls apart and would collapse under the table if it weren't for Gail and Nate pressing against her. Owen's best reaction is to sit stoically and smile. The guys dance in front of them, making ludicrous gestures at Ronnie.

The onslaught continues. Gail is desperate to bolster a cowering Ronnie. Owen struggles to stay nonchalant, but it is difficult to see what the women are going through. It takes every bit of his control not to change tactics and start yelling at the guys. Suddenly, he hears a voice directed toward them from the middle of the room. As soon as he hears what is being said, he knows it must be an employee. "What is going on here? What are you doing?"

The guys in front of him move apart enough for Owen to see what looks like the manager coming toward them, in uniform and wearing a hat. He is a portly, middle-aged Middle Eastern man, shaking his finger. "You must stop this right now! This can't be happening!" The guys offer no resistance and split into two groups that move around the man. The manager keeps coming forward until he is in front of the table in the middle of them, turning around and trying to focus on everyone at once. "This can't be happening! You must stop!" The manager has not attempted to discern who is the cause of the disturbance, and

Owen sees a chance to gain an ally. "Sir, we have been sitting here—." But the manager isn't interested in determining the source of the problem; he just wants the situation to end. "Get out!" he admonishes. "You must get out!" At least his focus is on the guys who have moved around him to the other side of the table and are making another attempt to get close to Ronnie. "Stop this right now!" The guys then break from Ronnie and gather like a cloud before rushing out of the restaurant, cackling and flapping their arms.

Nate is suddenly up from the table and running after them! Owen is stunned! What is Nate doing?

But Owen is forced to confront the angry manager standing directly in front of him. "You must go," the manager says, waving both arms as if dispersing a plague. "You have to leave."

Owen hardly cares about reasoning with the man. His attention is on the fact that Nate has run after the guys. What is he thinking? Then it hits him: Nate could get into a confrontation! The realization expands until he is overwhelmed. If Nate gets physical with the guys, he is automatically out of the round. And Owen is out too! Everything that has been happening between them would be over!

Owen's shock catapults into absolute panic. His life suddenly depends on Nate not getting knocked out of the round!

In the next instant, he turns to Gail, huddled with Ronnie, and tells her he has to go, then, in one motion, he is up from his chair, pushing past the manager.

Owen rushes out of the restaurant and stands in the street, scanning the parking lot in all directions but seeing no one. It's incomprehensible that they could have disappeared so fast! To his right is an alleyway a few doors down, at the corner of the line of stores that divides the two sections of buildings. It's the only place they could have disappeared so quickly.

Suddenly, Gail and Ronnie are by his side. "What's going on?" Gail asks, alarmed.

"I have to find Nate," he says, heading toward the alleyway. Reaching the corner, he is dismayed not to see anyone, yet it isn't likely they could have gone anywhere else. It means they are moving fast. He is tempted to run but resists further panic. The two women suddenly appear beside him again. "You don't need to be here," he says. "We're in this together," Gail answers. He doesn't care what they do; his obligation is to Nate.

The alley is maybe forty yards long and surely leads to a service area at the back of the buildings. It has to be where they have gone. "Nate!" he yells as he starts down the alley, his voice rebounding off the walls. "Nate!"

Suddenly, he sees one of the guys poke his head around the corner at the far end! Owen is heading in the right direction. "Nate!"

"What are you going to do?" Gail asks.

He has no idea what he is going to do; he only knows he is going forward.

Suddenly, another of the guys steps out from the corner of the building across the alley, and then the first guy steps out across from him. They stand as bookends against the open space, taking an exaggerated stance with their legs spread and their arms crossed over their chests. Owen can't believe they're serious about any confrontation. He isn't interested in playing games. "Nate!"

But as he walks closer, the guys step toward each other, clearly intent on blocking his passage. Owen is surprised but not deterred. Everything he has been working for with the material has come to this. He still can't believe the guys are trying to stop him, but he slows his pace. The two women, however, take the guys seriously and suddenly appear on either side, pressing against him. He doesn't have time to be distracted.

As he continues forward, he is expecting the guys to turn and flee at any moment, but they seem determined to hold their ground. For him, the real seriousness lies in what could be happening with Nate. If Nate gets carried away and does something, then Owen loses everything. Working with Nate is the best chance of his life! "Nate!"

Suddenly, he feels the two women nearly huddle under his arms in fright. He attempts to shake them while staying focused on the guys. But to stay against him, each woman clutches one of his arms. Now they are a huge hindrance.

The final straw comes when the two women intertwine their hands with his. He imagines them paralyzed with fear and vehemently tries to shake himself free, but they hang on tight. They are only twenty or so feet from the guys. Owen needs to be ready.

Owen struggles with the women as he tries to decide what the guys are willing to do. It is impossible to believe, but he feels the two women actually pulling down on him; in unison, he feels their dead weight and only thinks they are collapsing. He is becoming desperate. Forced to use his strength, he struggles to hold the women up as he readies for the encounter with the guys.

What he experiences next shatters his comprehension. It is a maddening sensation. Forced to look down, he sees a bizarre sight. Both women are desperately gnawing at his wrists. His mind somersaults, and at once he is overcome by a monstrous sensation of physical revulsion and pain. In the next instant, he looks up to see both guys rushing at him.

Owen's mind explodes. His body reacts; he has fallen into a trap! The guys and the women are together! He only has time to brace himself before the guys leap upon him. He is suddenly in a fight for his life. It is all he can do to stay upright. Then, from around a corner, he sees another of the guys running at him. Owen struggles to keep his feet.

In the next instant, he sees Nate running toward him from around the corner. Owen's reaction is a spasm of hope, believing Nate is coming to help, until he sees the steely determination on his face and realizes Nate is part of the plot. He recoils in shock.

His mind has no precedent for what is happening. All hope is lost. As the other guy jumps on him, Owen knows he is done for. He is going down. There is no telling what will happen. Suddenly, lights appear before his eyes, and the light around him grows darker as his vision blurs; he feels at the edge of an abyss. In the last instant he can stand, he directs all his attention to his training. In some sense, he has been preparing for this moment all his life. His command to himself is to let go, yield, relinquish, and trust. As his last effort, he focuses on the words of don Juan: "Abandon the self and fear nothing."

CHAPTER SIXTEEN

The expanse is everything, and he is of the expanse. There is nothing not of him, but he is not anything at all. There is the expanse, and there is him floating. It is only the awareness of him floating that is of any difference.

The difference continues until the expanse becomes something beyond him, like a shading or a density. The separateness continues until it is mostly him aware of the expanse retreating.

Where is he? The thought comes to him as part of his separateness until the thought itself is big enough to have meaning. He is somewhere, but where? That too grows into a meaning he tries to understand.

Suddenly, he feels something. Feeling is of him and something he has to decide about because it is not something beyond, so when he feels it again, he has to concentrate before he is sure what is happening. He feels wetness. But where is wetness? There is light beyond him, and there are things that have shape.

When the wetness comes again, there is direction, and he focuses his attention, but tries too much, and there is a weight that becomes his head. He stops trying. Then there is wetness, and he again tries. Toward the wetness is movement that becomes something else, until that something fills up the light and becomes someone looking at him. There is a flood of familiarity he struggles to piece together, but the person is gone before he can understand. Then it hits him; the woman is Ronnie, and Ronnie is a part of everything that happened to him! He struggles to gather understanding, but only the realization that something happened persists. He remembers Ronnie being frightened and her chewing on his arm.

Suddenly, there is great movement as someone returns to everything around him. There is a kind of darkness as the person becomes mostly everything. She is looking down at him with a very smiling face, and he knows her, until he realizes it is Gail. She looks very pleased to be looking at him.

"Hello traveler," she says. Her voice is like bubbles. "Good to have you back."

The words are shapes that have entered him, and he struggles to bring them into focus. Gail's face lowers until it is close to him. It is her face that has meaning. Just by looking at her face, the space changes as if it were changing colors.

There are other images around her face as if they are coming out of her face; people were jumping on him, and Gail was biting his hand. Through the images, he hears Gail say that everything is all right.

But everything is not all right. They were jumping on him. "You're going to be fine, Owen."

It's the sound of her voice he focuses on. It sounds nice. He only wants it to be nice, but they tricked him. It is that thought he wants to make big because it is what really matters.

"Try to remember," Gail says, her face very close to him.

All he can remember is people jumping on him, and it was such a shock because she was a part of it. "You jumped on me." The words come out of him as if expanding from his thinking.

Gail's reaction is to smile. Her eyes are very kind; she is showing him kindness. "Try to think past that, Owen."

But he doesn't want to think beyond that because it is most important.

Gail remains smiling at him. She is only kindness, but what he remembers wasn't kindness at all. "We didn't do anything to hurt you, Owen, I promise, and I promise I'll tell you everything, but for right now, it's very important that you try to remember. Try to remember what happened after we jumped on you."

He doesn't want to remember because Gail is trying to get him to remember. The thought that suddenly bursts on him is that he is in a strange place. "Where am I?"

"You're with friends."

But he is not with friends. They tricked him and jumped on him, and now he is in a strange place.

"Listen, Owen. We think your assemblage point shifted," Gail continues. "It's very important that you try to remember. Try to remember what happened after you went to the ground."

He looks at her face as the center of what is happening, but when he looks closer, the weight of trying to understand becomes too much, and everything starts to expand. His vision begins to blur. There is the feeling of falling backward.

When he is aware again, it is from the feeling of wetness. He looks down and sees Ronnie running a wet towel over his feet. He feels wetness on his forehead and reaches up to feel a wet towel. When he looks back at Ronnie, she is looking at him, then immediately gets up and leaves the room.

Owen looks around. It is very important to decide where he is, but nothing looks familiar. He sees a dresser off to the side and part of a chair. He must be in a bedroom.

Soon, Gail is coming through the door. She walks straight to him and sits down. Her face is very open and smiling, the way it was before. "How are you feeling?" she asks, bringing her face closer.

He is feeling all right. Then he is not interested in how he is feeling. A sudden rush of questions rises up.

"Where am I?"

"You're in a house with friends," she answers. "No one is going to harm you."

He wants to believe her, but the images of what happened to him gather again. "You were biting my arm."

Gail laughs, though it is more like a giggle. "That was just to distract you," she says in a tone of amusement. "We knew getting you to the ground wouldn't be easy."

What she said is new, and he needs to understand it. "Why were you getting me on the ground?"

Gail laughs again. She seems to be enjoying herself very much. "We were just having fun. We were trying to get your attention. We wanted to meet you."

Meet him? What she has said doesn't make any sense. He is focusing on what she has said as something very basic. "You could just meet me?"

Gail laughs with genuine delight. "Well, that wouldn't have been very interesting, and it wouldn't have been much of a challenge. You presented yourself, and we wanted to make an impression. You were someone we wanted to meet, and we wanted you to want to meet us."

What she says is very confusing. His head begins to swirl. Another thought bursts upon him. They jumped on him, and Nate jumped on him as well. They had a confrontation! They had physical contact! It means he and Nate are kicked out of the system! "The round is over," he bemoans, feeling the full weight of the realization settle on him. He stops looking at Gail and stares up at the ceiling in dismay.

Gail laughs again, this time with a gleeful cackle, as if what he has said is very funny. "You weren't going to see Nate anymore anyway," she says. "At least not for a while. Your first encounters scared the hell out of him. He needed a break."

What? Owen looks at her, but she only smiles at him. His head suddenly reels. It's as if what she has just said is the most amazing thing he has heard so far. Nate wasn't going to continue? He thought he and Nate had a connection; they were making real progress with the material. Following the path is all that matters. What Gail has told him about Nate is the final straw; any hope he had of understanding what has gone on completely collapses.

"It's why we had to move so fast," Gail adds, with genuine delight. "We didn't have much time. So we came up with our little plan."

Owen hardly pays attention to what she says anymore; it is too much to decide whether what she tells him is true. All he knows is that he has been thoroughly tricked by people he doesn't know. The ramifications press upon him as something very disturbing.

"Listen, Owen," Gail then says. "The thing to focus on is your assemblage point shifted. It's a big deal. As you know, it's the key to the warrior's world."

What gets his attention is the change in her voice. The tone of her voice has become earnest, almost pleading. "Try to remember, Owen. It's very important."

He knows it is important, and for a moment, he can focus on what she is saying as a way to explain what has happened to him. He tries to remember, but nothing comes to mind. He is surprised. He should remember something.

"Try harder," Gail implores when he tells her nothing is coming. He does try. And there is an awareness like shadows of images and people and activity around him, but just beyond him, like on the other side of a veil or a barrier, he expects to get beyond at any moment, but can't. And it doesn't make sense that he can't remember, but as hard as he tries, nothing more comes.

The effort is exhausting, and he lets his head fall back and stares at the ceiling again.

Gail consoles him. "It's all right." She is then encouraging.

"It's a good thing. Not being able to remember is a sign that your assemblage point did shift."

He would like to believe her, but all he can focus on is being in a strange place with strange people; he has no idea how he got here. What Gail says next surprises him, though he isn't able to muster much interest. She says someone would like to meet him if he is up to it. He doesn't know what he is up for, and what she is asking is just another thing beyond him. Before he thinks of answering, Gail seems to have decided for him by standing and leaving the room.

CHAPTER SEVENTEEN

He is alone in a strange room in some house; he has no idea where he is. Owen can't believe what he has gotten himself into. It is beyond anything he could have imagined. He has been attacked by a group of warriors, and his assemblage point has shifted. His mind can go in so many directions, trying to explain what happened, but he has no hope of being sure of anything. He has to come up with something. Whatever he is involved in isn't going to stop anytime soon. The thought that comes to him is that he could get up and leave, but where would he go? He doesn't know where his vehicle is.

Owen's speculation is suddenly cut short by the sound of something in the hallway. The low, mechanical squeaking is advancing toward him, and he has just enough time to ready himself before the squeaking slows and an old man appears in the doorway. The old man has longish white hair and a trimmed white beard, beams at him with pleasant eyes, and has tubes in his nose. He is pushing an oxygen cart.

Owen's body reacts strongly. He believes another onslaught is upon him. Owen tries to center himself and prepare for whatever happens.

The old man maneuvers his cart into the room and continues smiling, obviously trying to make him feel at ease. Owen only stares back at the man; he could be anything at all in the universe.

"So how is our warrior-traveler?" the old man asks as he shuffles in.

Owen isn't familiar with the term, but he understands the man's interest is to be polite. Owen returns a measure of politeness by saying he is feeling all right.

"Good, good," the man says and seems genuinely pleased. "And I believe congratulations are in order."

Owen isn't sure to what the old man is referring.

"As you know, a shifting of the assemblage point is a great achievement," the old man states.

Yes, shifting the assemblage point is a great accomplishment, though he hardly feels he had much to do with it; if his assemblage point did shifted, it did so on its own as a result of the bunch of them jumping on him and taking him down.

When he gets closer, the old man takes a moment to move the chair toward him. He then parks his oxygen tank off to the side and sits. The old man is directly in front of him, still beaming with delight.

Owen's full focus is on steadying himself. He realizes he is at the man's mercy.

"I am Les Henry," the old man says, giving a slight bow of his head, "and I am at your service."

Owen's body reacts with a jolt. He recognizes the introduction as a warrior's from the books. Don Juan explained the introduction as a warrior's, stating his individuality in the presence of the spirit that guides all things. It is further evidence to Owen that he is not dealing with an ordinary person. Yet knowing what he does about what happened to him has already determined that. What further convinces him that he is at least dealing with a warrior is that the man's eyes are very bright and his forearms and hands are lean and muscular. The old man looks plenty healthy, and Owen can only conclude that the oxygen tank has to be some kind of prop to put him at ease. He continues to brace himself for another round of deception.

"This is my home, and you are welcome." The man continues to smile at him.

Owen appreciates the gesture, but it doesn't offer much.

His next thought is that he has to take some initiative; he can't keep being passive; he needs to take some control. The only thing that comes to him is to be direct. This guy is surely the group's leader. "Are you a nagual?"

The old man reacts as if Owen has just said the funniest thing. He laughs, tilts his head back, then looks to see if Owen is serious. "A nagual, huh?" the old man repeats, then laughs again in another short burst. "Oh, that is rich." He looks at Owen and smiles with genuine mirth. "Nope, just an interested old man."

Owen is not buying what the guy says because he is not buying anything about what is going on; he is in the middle of a bizarre situation and is not taking anything at face value. And the way Les acts is a perfect example of what a nagual would do. When dealing with the ordinary world, a nagual, as the leader of a party of practitioners, would never reveal himself and would operate behind a front of warriors as a strategy to deflect attention away from himself. Owen is anxious to know whether the man is really a nagual; if so, it would mean the group of warriors who attacked him is advanced. It would be remarkable. He comes up with another question intended to elicit a revealing answer. "Are you a member of a party?" he asks, using the term "party" intentionally, as it refers to a group of practitioners connected to a nagual.

But the old man only shakes his head and chuckles, seemingly amused. "Sorry to disappoint you, but there's no party here." The old man then stares at him with widened eyes. "And what about you? Are you a member of a party?"

It's Owen's turn to be surprised. When the old man continues to stare at him as if genuinely trying to discern what he is looking at, Owen realizes that the guy is serious and trying to figure him out as well.

"You have to admit," the old guy continues. "Some remarkable things have been happening with you."

Owen suddenly feels scrambled again. The guy's question has shifted the focus back to him. And the guy thinks he could be a party member, which would mean he is connected to a nagual himself. It's too much to think about, and from his confusion, Owen only shakes his head.

"Well, we're glad to make your acquaintance," the old guy says. Owen notices a warmth in his statement. "I imagine you might be hungry."

Just the mention of food elicits a strong reaction from him. Owen hasn't thought about food at all, but as soon as it is mentioned, he suddenly becomes ravenous. It is a shock to realize how easily he can be affected by something the old man has said. He has no idea how long it has been since he last ate. "What time is it?"

Les shrugs. "Somewhere past nine o'clock."

Nine o'clock! They met at the café at four! Owen is appalled. That was five hours ago! Could he have been out of it for so long?

Les laughs at his dismay. "The world is a very strange place."

Owen feels he is on the verge of falling to another level of uncertainty and devastation.

Les then invites him to join them when he is ready. "Turn left out the door, then turn left again." Les makes an effort to stand, turns around, and shuffles out of the room. Owen listens as the squeaky sound of the cart fades away.

CHAPTER EIGHTEEN

After the old man has left, Owen closes his eyes and falls back against the bed. A wave of being overwhelmed washes over him.

He then experiences a tantrum, a flash of complete annoyance and utter dismay, born of feeling at a loss, of being vulnerable, because of what was done to him, the situation he has found himself in, and the realization that he has been so dominated, so completely played. How could he have been so gullible? Next, Owen experiences a strange reaction that comes from the very depths of him, something he has never felt before, as if from a different part of himself, from a place he never knew existed. It starts as a shiver that goes through him, then a shake. His whole body is involved. It starts in his feet and then moves to the top of his head. He is shocked. It is something he would never suspect his body to be capable of. He is breathing heavily.

His reaction is to speculate. What was that! Though he is quickly convinced, he cannot come up with any true answer. The world is a mysterious place. There are facets of himself he can't even imagine. He believed that before, but now he has true confirmation.

The whole experience passes as quickly as it came. He is left with the awareness of being in a strange bed, in a strange house, with people he doesn't know who have done something remarkable to him.

He has to do something. His life is in the balance.

Owen takes a moment to look around. What catches his attention is the door across the room from him, which he hopes leads to a bathroom. He needs to use one. Finally, he gets out of bed. The first thing he notices is that he is fully clothed. Stepping to the door, he opens it and finds a small, bright bathroom. After urinating, he washes his hands and splashes water on his face. Returning to the bedroom, he glances around for his socks and shoes. Finding them, he puts them on and instantly feels better.

He still has to decide what to do. There is again the temptation to flee, and he has to believe he would eventually figure out where he is and find his way home, but the idea doesn't feel like it offers much. The fact that he has encountered a group of practitioners is intriguing if he allows it to be; in all his years of working with the material, he has never even heard of an operating group of practitioners. Both Les and Gail have tried to make it clear that he is with friends, but he doesn't believe it. The only thing he becomes convinced of is that he needs to act like a warrior, but no clear direction comes to mind. He has to do something. The key for Owen seems to be that he can't take himself too seriously. He is a person on his way to dying, and against that magnitude, he has nothing to defend. He has to be ready for whatever. His trust has to be in the spirit.

Owen straightens himself and takes a deep breath. After another moment, he walks out of the room. He turns left and follows a short hallway. When he reaches the open space at the end, he turns left again.

Across the open space of the house, he sees Les and Gail sitting with a younger guy at an island counter in the kitchen. "Ah, there he is," Les announces, raising a hand in greeting. The other two turn to face him. Les is the picture of joviality. Gail and the guy also smile broadly as he approaches, and Owen can't help but smile in greeting. As he reaches the table where they are sitting, the young guy is introduced as Daniel. He has dark eyes and hair, an open face, and gentle features. He is surely one of the guys involved in the prank. Owen shakes hands with him and, in an attempt to be engaging, remarks that he believes they have met before. Everyone laughs, acknowledging the unusual situation.

"You look to be in good shape," Les says, sounding pleased. "No worse for wear."

Owen isn't sure what shape he's in, but admits to feeling all right.

He senses that the three of them are relieved.

There are a couple of open stools around the counter, and Owen takes a seat at an end, which puts him across from Les. Daniel is the closest to him, and Gail sits in the middle of the three.

"Your vehicle is out front," Les says. "The keys are under the floor mat. You can leave at any time."

Owen appreciates the effort to be assured.

Gail asks if he would like something to eat. He was hungry earlier, but eating isn't an issue at the moment. Yet Gail has offered, and it has been a while since he last ate, so he accepts. Gail steps to the refrigerator, pulls out a bowl, and sets it in front of him, along with a small bowl from the cupboard and a serving spoon and fork from a drawer. She asks if he would like something to drink, and he says water will be fine. As she pours him a glass from a pitcher in the refrigerator, he spoons some of the pasta salad into the bowl. He can see chunks of chicken, halves of grapes, and slices of almond in a cream sauce with pasta. It looks good. He takes a bite, and it is good.

But he is mostly interested in continuing to talk with the others. He realizes they are being polite in their silence, giving him time to eat. The others watching him eat make him self-conscious and even less hungry, so he decides to start the conversation himself. "So I'm assuming I didn't just drive here," he says, trying to restore the joviality they initially shared.

The three of them chuckle in unison.

"No, you definitely weren't in any condition to drive," Gail answers. The three of them smile at him, and Owen smiles back.

Yet in that small exchange, Owen feels the strangeness of his situation highlighted. He has no idea what has gone on.

"And one of the guys drove your vehicle," Les offers. "And if you're wondering how you got into a strange bed, it's not every day that an unconscious person gets carried through the front door."

The three of them laugh together, admitting their amazement, but instead of laughing with them, Owen looks closely at Les. He still can't believe what happened and needs any information he can get. "So I was passed out?" he asks.

"Sort of, or at least dazed, and stiff as a board," Les answers.

It is Gail who then speaks. "You scared the hell out of us," she says, smiling at him from across the counter. "We initially thought you had a stroke or something."

That's new. Owen wants her to continue.

"Everyone was running around," Gail adds. "A couple of the guys who were borrowed from an acting class just ran off."

Owen is suddenly struggling to piece together what happened.

"The worst was when these two women came up and started yelling to call 911," Gail says, amazed. The incident has obviously made a strong impression on her, and she continues to recall it. "By then, we figured out that your assemblage point must have shifted, so we loaded you into a vehicle and told the ladies we could beat the ambulance to the hospital."

All of them laugh at her recounting. Owen can only smile. He greatly appreciates Gail's willingness to share details and wants to keep her talking. "And all you wanted to do was introduce yourself?" he asks, recalling what she told him earlier.

The three of them laugh in unison. "Like I told you," Gail answers, "we only wanted to get your attention. Getting you to the ground was supposed to be the end of our prank. It was like an exclamation point. We expected everyone to get up and have a good laugh."

Owen thinks he might understand; he remembers Gail saying they viewed him as a challenge. But what suddenly grabs his attention is how fooled he was; he didn't have a clue, and it seems unfathomable. "I can't believe I never suspected a thing," he says, shaking his head, unable to contain his disbelief.

The three of them laugh uproariously. They are the picture of delight.

"We didn't have much time," Gails says, continuing her explanation. There is a sense that she is fulfilling her earlier promise to tell him what happened. "As I told you before, Nate wasn't going to meet with you anymore, so we had to act fast and thought of the situation with Ronnie and me to make contact. But then you were leading us along. Remember, it was you who called for the second meeting."

Yes, he did call for the second meeting; he remembers being interested in reconnecting with Gail, so he wasn't just being led along. Suddenly, all the details of what went on are becoming too much to keep track of. He thinks of the guys in their costumes, Gail and Ronnie putting on their charade, and Nate being part of it. That's what truly has his attention; he remembers the sight of Nate running at him from around the corner and how determined he looked. He thinks of the coordination between the women as they grabbed his arms and started gnawing at his wrists. Owen is staggered. "Wow," is all he manages to say, and he shakes his head, admitting he feels overwhelmed.

The others are getting a kick out of his dilemma, and the ramifications keep coming. He thinks of the story they told him about Ronnie and her boyfriend and the guys coming to her work. He remembers Gail and Nate coming close to arguing. It was all made up! It's like there were scripts they had practiced!

Owen is desperate to understand. It just doesn't make sense. They had only a couple of days to pull it off! "So much happened," he manages to say, feeling compelled to say something to keep his equilibrium.

The others agree, amazed.

"It definitely took on a life of its own," Gail says, herself hugely impressed. "We put the whole thing in the hands of power, and spirit led us along."

Owen still isn't fully getting it, but what grows to dominate him again is the realization that he didn't have a clue. They played him perfectly! It's appalling that he could be so completely fooled! He never would have believed he could be so gullible!

He isn't hungry anymore, but he takes a bite of food just to settle himself. He then shakes his head again. The ramifications have continued to mount, becoming dizzying. He feels he has to say something, if only to steady himself. "I just can't believe I so completely fell for it," he says, to stay focused on what has become the focal point of his intrigue.

The others again laugh.

"Actually, you didn't have a chance," Les says.

Owen looks at him to make sure he heard correctly, and Les only smiles. But Les says nothing more, and Owen needs to know what he means. He can't believe it could have been that easy. "So how'd you know I'd fall for it?" he asks, feeling forced to admit his interest. It's the part he can't understand; he never would have believed he could be so predictable. They were able to lead him out of the restaurant into a back alley!

"We discovered your hinge of weakness," Les offers, smiling as if he knows something of great importance. "It sealed your fate."

Owen has no idea what he is getting at.

Les is beaming at him. "Remember in the books, a warrior finds the weakness of any situation and applies pressure."

Owen does remember, though he doesn't see how it relates to him. Les hesitates another moment. "Well, as soon as we discovered your hinge of weakness, the outcome was all but guaranteed; it was just a matter of us being able to pull it off."

He still doesn't understand, and Les doesn't add anything else.

As Les continues smiling at him, he is sure Les is holding back, deliberately building suspense and having some fun with him. He can't help but feel a little annoyed at being toyed with. He feels he has no choice but to play along because he is hooked; it means too much to him not to know what Les is thinking.

"So what was my weakness?" he finally feels forced to ask.

Les looks at the others, then back at him. He is grinning as if beyond himself with delight. "Well, it's also your greatest strength."

Owen is completely at his mercy. Any attempt to disguise his interest has completely failed. "So what is it?" His voice even cracks.

Les throws up his hands, announcing with grand revelation. "Because you want it so bad!"

What? Owen isn't sure. He's not getting it. The moment feels anticlimactic, as if whatever Les is trying to communicate to him has slipped through his fingers. The others laugh with abandon, a clear indication that there's something he's missing.

"Wanting it so badly is also your greatest strength," Les reiterates, his arms still raised above his head. "Your determination to stay involved with the system meant you'd do anything. So when Nate chased after the guys, we knew you'd be afraid of being knocked out of the round and would chase after him."

Suddenly, the magnitude strikes him full force. It's true!

There is no way he wouldn't have followed after Nate! He remembers the moment when it hit him that he might be forced out of the round! It was like a bomb going off inside him. His whole life was in jeopardy!

"From there, it was like rolling downhill," Gail says. "The pieces just kept coming together. The only thing left for us was the challenge of seeing it through." The three of them laugh and smile as if they are having the time of their lives.

Owen feels staggered by the immensity of what he has discovered. He was never in control; he never had a chance to be. He has no choice but to suddenly think of himself differently.

Owen tries to remain steady amid the magnitude of his awareness, but the volume is too much; he feels himself begin to waver under the onslaught. He places both hands on the table to steady himself.

"Are you all right?" he hears Les ask.

He's not all right. The room begins to spin; his vision blurs. The others grow concerned. He hears Les say he should lie down. Yes, he should lie down, but when he tries to stand, his legs don't work well, and the others suddenly crowd around him for support. They lead him to the couch, and he falls into it. But he doesn't want to lie down; instead, he stretches out. Gail brings him a glass of water, and he drinks it, but it doesn't help. He feels he is in a space that is somewhere but really nowhere at all.

"His assemblage point must be shifting again," Les determines to the others.

Owen believes him, but the awareness doesn't help with what he is going through. The space inside him is vast and keeps shifting back and forth. When asked if he would like to go to the room and lie down, he agrees.

CHAPTER NINETEEN

The space around him is completely dark. He remembers asking that the light be left on. After he fell asleep, someone must have turned it off.

He is quick to remember what happened when he needs to assess his situation. After meeting with the group in the kitchen, he became overwhelmed when he heard how they had tricked him. It took everything he had to remain stable. What he remembers is being uncomfortable with them staring at him on the couch.

But that only explains how he woke in darkness. The other elements of what happened hover around him. When he lines up the events of yesterday in a kind of sequence, the magnitude is overwhelming. He was attacked or tricked by a group of warriors, and his assemblage point probably shifted; he must have blacked out and been carried to someone's house. But he has been through all that before. Going over the events again doesn't offer much. The issue is that he has to decide how to proceed, and for the moment, he is at a loss.

He wonders what time it is. At least the question gives him something solid to focus on. As a rule, he prefers not to be aware of time when working with the material, focusing instead on a more organic unfolding of experience not defined by reference to any linear construct. But at the moment, it would be a big help to know whether it was getting toward morning or still in the middle of the night. If it really mattered, he should be able to find his way to his vehicle and his dashboard clock, but that doesn't make any sense.

Owen sits up on the edge of the bed. His first effort is to assess his condition, and after a moment he decides he feels decent, nothing too different. He then stands, steps to the window, and separates two slats in the blind. Looking out, he can see through a lesser darkness a line of trees across a small lawn. He determines that the light he sees is residual from lighting elsewhere, not the coming of dawn.

Owen sits back on the bed but doesn't feel like lying down. Agitation builds. He half expects to feel the shiver and shake that went through him before he got up last evening to meet the others, but nothing happens. The details of his situation rise again, crystallizing around him. He has been attacked by a group of warriors, and he is in a strange house. But he is intent on not letting his agitation escalate. What most has his attention is feeling stuck and having to wait for something to happen next. It could take hours.

When he wakes again, it is light out. His initial surprise is that he actually fell back asleep. But what time is it? The question now is, how late is it in the morning? He gets up and uses the bathroom. He then washes his face vigorously and runs wet fingers through his hair. He feels fine; he can't detect any aftereffects of what he experienced yesterday.

He then takes time to center himself, to be ready to deal with what is in front of him. He is reminded that a warrior does his best then lets go. As always, he intends to have his actions be guided by *power*, the force of *infinity*.

Finally, he just leaves the room and makes his way into the

great-room area. No one is there. Owen takes a moment to look around, but isn't interested much in the details.

On the island counter in the kitchen, there are a pitcher of water and a pitcher of orange juice, along with a couple of glasses and a note that reads, "Out back." Owen is thirsty and drinks half a glass of water before heading down the hall to the back of the house. The hallway passes a few closed doors, which he assumes are bedrooms. At the end, he walks into a curious space. It is clearly a built-on addition and a sunroom, set at an angle at the back of the house. The room feels like its own contained space, with a perimeter of full windows. There are only throw cushions for furniture, along with two upright chairs. Owen is sure the room's off-angle is designed to take advantage of the streaming sunlight that fills it.

Opening the door to the outside, Owen finds a short balcony with a small metal-mesh-top table and two matching chairs; it must be a perfect place for private enjoyment. Looking out from the balcony, he stares over the tops of several roofs. They all end at a level just below his feet, giving the impression of looking out over an expanse. The impression he gets is one of quietude and tranquility. But he doesn't care to linger. Owen continues his exploration by walking downstairs to face the building that a moment ago was the first roof in front of him. It seems to be a garage, and from the bottom of the stairs, a narrow walkway extends in both directions along the garage exterior. To the right, he glimpses a couple of cars parked in what he assumes to be the driveway at the front of the house, so he turns left. The walkway follows the garage wall on one side and the house's tall wall on the other, forming a narrow passage.

Reaching the corner of the house, the walkway turns left into open space. Across a small area of lawn, the walkway leads through a row of tall, dense shrubs. Owen follows the path. As he approaches the opening, he can see another wall of shrubs on the opposite side of a yard or courtyard.

Owen passes through the shrubs and sees four members of the group to his left, sitting cross-legged with their backs against upright posts near the exterior wall of the house. Beside Les sits a guy he hasn't met, whom he assumes is another member of the group involved in the prank. On the other side of Les sit Gail and Daniel. The people sitting give no sign of recognizing him and stare straight ahead, their eyes half-closed. Owen suspects what they are doing and watches closely. Sure enough, he notices their heads shift slowly from side to side. They are gazing.

Two kinds of gazing are described in the books, and the one they appear to be practicing involves harnessing the sun's energy. The understanding is that people, as sentient beings, are born with a finite amount of energy and have no way to gain more except by tapping into an external source. Any source of light will do, but the sun is strong and readily available. The practice is to take in the sun's light through the left eye while sweeping one's gaze across the sun with half-closed eyes. While sweeping the gaze from left to right, the practitioner slowly exhales, then slowly inhales as the gaze sweeps back to the left. Owen has practiced this before and found it very relaxing and invigorating. It seems like the perfect thing for him to do right now, so when he sees an open post next to Daniel, he walks past the group and sits down. He begins with his head on his left shoulder, slowly inhales, and lets the filling of his breath coordinate with the sweep of his half-closed eyes across the sun. He is very aware of letting the sunlight enter through his left eye as prescribed. When his head reaches the end of the sweep, it is in time with the completion of his full inhale. He pauses a moment, then slowly begins exhaling while sweeping his gaze in the other direction.

It is a fine practice; he can feel his whole being open to it. The sun is a little high in the sky, so he has to tilt his head slightly toward it, but it's still very accessible. He is taking in the sun's energy. It feels radiant and good.

The practice can go on for hours, and Owen is prepared to stay as long as the others. It is not easy for him to sit cross-legged for extended periods, but he is determined to ignore any discomfort and focus on relaxing and opening. As with anything of this nature, the main challenge is to quiet the mind. He is aware of the group around him and lets their collective focus guide him.

It isn't long, however, before he notices movement to his side. When he glances over, he sees that the others are getting up. Owen stops gazing and waits to see what will happen. When the others are on their feet, he decides to join them.

After standing, Owen meets the others' eyes. They all smile and are quick to greet him. He is introduced to Jessie, a young guy he hasn't met before. Jessie is smaller than Nate, with the same build, but a much quieter demeanor. Jessie is bearded, with retreating eyes behind glasses and a thin smile; he is indeed one of the guys involved in the prank. Owen shakes hands with him, and they exchange a quick nod of acknowledgment.

Everyone stretches their bodies and comments on the beautiful morning.

Owen stretches his body fully, reminded of don Juan's advice to stretch the body often, especially after any long period of inactivity. Owen waits for someone to take the lead in what comes next.

The others soon turn and walk back toward the opening in the shrubs, where the walkway leads to the house. Owen is prepared to follow, but he notices Les staying behind. When Les walks over to a round table surrounded by patio chairs, Owen takes it as an invitation.

They are going to have a conversation. Owen reminds himself to be on his guard around these people. What most instills that reaction in him is the fact that Les doesn't have his oxygen tank; it is an indication that the tank was really a prop, surely meant to disarm him into thinking Les was just a doddering old man.

"So you slept well, I take it?" Les asks before sitting down.

"As well as can be expected," Owen answers. To be engaging, he adds, "Although I'm not sure anyone ever gets used to waking up in a strange bed."

Les smiles openly. "Well, I hope it was comfortable?" Owen assures that it was.

"And no aftereffects?" Les asks.

Owen understands the question as Les referring to what might have happened to him as a result of the shifting of his assemblage point and everything else that went on with him. He takes the opportunity to reassess himself and tells Les he feels fine.

"Good, good to hear," Les offers, and he seems genuinely pleased. "Having your assemblage point shift is quite an event." He then adds, "And quite an accomplishment, so again, congratulations."

Owen thanks him and appreciates the sentiment, though he is again very aware that the shifting of his assemblage point had little to do with him and was the result of what the group did to him. It reminds him of what he is dealing with and his decision not to be led along. "So you folks gaze a lot?" Owen then asks, in an innocuous attempt to direct the conversation.

"We often do," Les answers, seemingly comfortable with the change of direction. "It's a good way to start the day."

"And you're not a party?" Owen asks, smiling, trying to turn the conversation in a more serious direction while making it clear he knows it's the same question he asked yesterday. He still isn't sure, given the scope of what they did to him, the skill required to carry out their prank, the fact that a group was involved, and how much their actions had to be dictated by the spirit, which means they must have a strong connecting link. The bottom line is that he still thinks Les could be a nagual, and that information is extremely important.

Les's response is to immediately smile back at him, making it obvious he is aware of what Owen is getting at. "Just a group of practitioners," he answers.

Owen doesn't feel the need to pursue the issue further, but he is intent on getting more information. "So how many are there in your group?"

Les looks at him, assessing the full meaning of the question. "You've pretty much met everyone."

Pretty much? It means there could be more. Owen looks at him to see if there's anything he hasn't been told, and Les seems to recognize what he is thinking and attempts to clarify. "I mean, there are always people on the periphery. We're just a group of people attracted to working with the books. And some people are more attracted than others."

The answer seems reasonable enough. "So how did you all get together?" What has piqued his curiosity is that he has never known of a group of practitioners.

Les sits back in his chair, reacting as if the question has made him think about something he hasn't considered much. "People know each other. Some of us have known each other for years. Some people have met through the system."

Owen takes the answer in. It doesn't offer much. He then thinks of a question that might lead somewhere and will at least let Les know he is paying attention to the details around him. "I see you don't have your oxygen tank with you," he says, waiting to see how Les will react.

Les continues to look at him directly, then smiles before answering. "I need the oxygen less in the mornings. It's the humidity that gets me."

Again, it's an honest enough answer, though it isn't enough to convince Owen that the oxygen tank wasn't a prop.

Les suddenly leans forward and clasps his hands on the table in front of him. "Listen," he says, continuing to look at Owen directly and smiling. "I understand you're a bit suspicious because of what happened to you, and I'm not interested in convincing you of anything otherwise. What happened was also amazing to us. You offered us a challenge, and we accepted it. We believe power gave us a demonstration. There isn't much more to it than that."

Les's directness catches Owen off guard, and he feels forced to smile, realizing he has been caught being too blatant in his attempt to understand.

"It's obvious you've done some work," Les continues. "We're glad to meet you."

Owen appreciates the sentiment and can't fault Les for being assertive.

"Let me ask you something." Les then says, leaning back in his chair. He clasps his hands behind his head. "Does the term *warrior- traveler* mean anything to you?"

Owen isn't sure what he's talking about. The question comes out of the blue, and when he looks at Les and sees him watching closely, he wonders whether Les's intent is to disarm him. He isn't familiar with the term, though he does remember Les using it to address him when they first met. "No," he answers.

"How about the term d*ark sea of awareness*?"

It is another great-sounding term, but again, nothing he is familiar with.

"What about m*ud shadows*?"

Now that is something Owen would definitely have remembered if he had encountered it, and he has to wonder what Les is getting at. There is a sense that Les is building another drama. Owen can't help but be curious, but he doesn't want to get caught up in any suspense Les might be trying to create.

Les doesn't stretch the tension further and suddenly beams with delight. "Owen, it's been nice meeting you, and I don't know if our paths will cross again, but I think it's important that I let you know there's another book out there."

What? Owen is again caught off guard by the quick turn in their conversation. Another book? What is he talking about?

Les leans forward. "By some of the things you have said, we don't think you are aware that another book came out."

What could he have said? He is tempted to replay his conversations with the group in his mind, yet he recognizes that the availability of another book is the larger issue.

"What kind of book?"

"A book by Carlos." "When?"

"It's been over a year."

That doesn't make sense. "But Carlos is dead."

Les says the book was released posthumously.

Owen thinks he knows what Les is talking about. Other books have come out, some about Carlos and some by Carlos, but mostly books that comment on the material or describe techniques and procedures. Owen has never been interested. He has to think Les is referring to them. But there is a factor that will differentiate what Les is talking about. "Is don Juan in it?"

Les nods his head, obviously pleased with what he has offered.

But Owen still isn't sure it is anything new. "Is it another in the series?"

"Eh, it's a little different," Les answers. "What's the name of it?"

"*The Active Side of Infinity.*"

The title is definitely something he hasn't heard before.

Owen wonders why he hasn't heard about a new book, but in the next instant he knows the answer. He has been out of the system for a while and hasn't paid attention to what is happening online. He hasn't been in contact with anyone working with the material. "Is it good?" he finally asks.

Les answers unequivocally. "Unbelievable."

Owen's interest is piqued, and his mind is starting to race. Another don Juan book would be remarkable. He has based his life on those books. A new book would mean a lot. He hears himself asking Les if the book is available.

"All the usual places."

Owen is suddenly beside himself. His reaction is from a deeply personal space.

Les breaks out laughing. "Hard to imagine, isn't it? There's a whole chunk of new material out there."

Is Les fueling his intrigue? It hardly matters, and he suddenly finds himself caught between wanting to learn more about Les and the others and the force of having new material available. "Another book," he hears himself say. "Wow, that's crazy." He struggles to keep his composure. Another book would mean everything; if there is new material, it could expand his awareness and understanding. It would advance his life!

His interest in how he deals with Les and the others has completely evaporated. He surely won't be much for any more conversation.

Owen sits there until, in the next instant, it is as if an inner force propels him. As soon as he tries to explain that he should be going, Les dismisses him with a wave of his hand. "There will be plenty of time."

Owen is out of his chair. But he realizes he has no idea where he is.

Les is quick to give him directions. A couple of turns, and he will hit the main road, turn right, and he'll be a mile from the highway. Owen is off. He hears Les laughing and is almost through the line of shrubs when Les calls after him. "Be sure to come back and tell us what you think!"

CHAPTER TWENTY

Owen can't get over it! Another Carlos book! It will mean everything to have more access to don Juan's world!

But by the time he gets to the highway, he is beginning to have his doubts. What most catches his attention is how quickly things change with Les. One moment, he is starting to press Les, trying to learn more about him and figure out what is going on with him and the group; the next, he is hurrying out of the house. How did that happen? Did Les play him again? If Les wanted to deflect attention from himself, then coming up with the idea of another don Juan book would definitely capture his attention. It's almost the same kind of thing done to him when they knew he would chase after Nate. Les had to know he would be forced to react if he truly believed another book was available. Owen can't help but be appalled. How could he so easily be manipulated?

Of course, there really could be another don Juan book. But there hasn't been one in years, and Carlos is dead. Owen feels he has no choice but to find out; it is testimony to how deeply Les has hooked into his greatest hopes. Les is either an accomplished warrior or a devious madman. The problem is that Owen has no idea whether he can tell the difference. If he finds out there isn't a book, maybe he should just be done with those people. But he can't dismiss the feeling that they could be serious practitioners, and it would be astounding to have met up with such a group. What he is left to think about is where he was in his life yesterday and where he is now; how much his world has changed.

For now, he needs to figure out whether there really is a new book. When he stops at his favorite bookstore and asks about The Active Side of Infinity, he is shocked to find that such a title exists! The bookstore is out of stock at the moment, but they could order the book and have it in a few days. That's not good enough. He leaves the bookstore and makes the half-hour drive to the big-chain bookstore in the bigger city.

And there it is! *The Active Side of Infinity*. It isn't a big book, and Owen only takes time to make sure it is about Carlos's involvement with don Juan before buying it. He can hardly believe his good fortune and drives straight home. After a quick check of his emails and phone messages and after taking care of a few immediate matters, he is set to block off a chunk of time and start reading. It is a nice day out, and he moves the lounge chair to his favorite reading place on the small deck off the back of his house. A breeze is blowing, sunlight blinks through the leaves of the maple tree above him.

Reading the don Juan books is one of his absolute favorite things to do, and he now has a completely new book to delve into! He truly is in a remarkable space. Before opening the book, he looks up into the trees, then out to the sky. It is a big world. The majesty and mystery of existence extend around him.

The book is immediately different from the others in that it isn't a chronological continuation of Carlos's involvement with don Juan; the book is more episodic, "a warrior's collection of memorable events," as Carlos calls it. Still, there is immediately plenty of interaction between Carlos and don Juan. And there is don Juan in all his glory, with his far-reaching insight into the depths of human experience and the nature of existence, and his magnificent and cutting humor.

It is so good to be back in don Juan's world again! As with all his books, Owen allows his first reading to be an absolute romp. His only interest is to be completely absorbed, fully open to being moved as far and as fast as possible in any direction the material takes him. There will be plenty of other readings for him to take notes, try to understand, and catalog the concepts.

The situations Carlos gets himself into are outrageous and amazingly hilarious. Owen can only imagine being challenged by situations that would shake him to his very core. Carlos is the perfect bumbling and doubtful buffoon as well as the tenacious and hungry student.

Owen does come across the term *warrior-traveler* that Les referred to. Curiously, it was not used in the other books, but is a perfect description of don Juan's legacy of practitioners who traveled a journey of awareness into the unknown and were at war with misconception and ignorance, while exploring the possibility of human consciousness.

The *dark sea of awareness* is another term he encounters for the first time, another one of the terms mentioned by Les. The *dark sea of awareness* is the vast dimension of consciousness extending beyond the known, connected to every sentient being by the assemblage point

Owen takes time to eat and do a few other things around the house, but only as a break before getting back to his reading. It is a bit disappointing that he is going to read the entire book in one day, but he can hardly stop. It is just so much fun. He loves having his head spun around; he loves being appalled and amazed.

Toward the end of the book, Owen comes to a chapter titled

"Mud Shadows." He remembers the term from his conversation with Les. Throughout the book, don Juan makes cryptic statements to Carlos about man "not being in control of his own mind," or that the mind we use daily for everything is a "foreign installation," but don Juan always refuses to elaborate, saying Carlos isn't ready for a full explanation. Carlos dismisses don Juan's remarks as another didactic device and a drama-building maneuver to capture his attention. One evening, as darkness settles and they sit quietly, don Juan directs Carlos to pay close attention without focusing his eyes, telling him he will see a fleeting shadow cross his field of vision. It takes Carlos a moment to engage the necessary awareness, but he sees a strange, fleeting black shadow projected onto the tree foliage. Carlos's awareness expands until he can see black shadows flying in the air around him. But nothing prepares him for don Juan's explanation, that the creatures are something warriors have been aware of for generations as the "topic of topics," that man has a companion for life, that man's existence is dominated by a predator from the universe at large that feeds off man's energy, keeping man barely alive, and that the relationship between the predator and man is the same as that between man and chickens. Man is raised and kept for food.

Carlos is so affronted by what don Juan is saying that he is unable to give the idea any real credence. Don Juan goes on to say that the mud shadows, also called "flyers" because of the way they leap around, actually feed on an energetic shell, or "glowing coat of awareness," that naturally grows around a human being. By keeping the shell cropped close to the ground, the flyers render a person weak and docile yet still able to actively focus on perpetuating their self-reflection as the source of their awareness, thereby causing energetic growth that replenishes the shell, serving as a constant source of food for the predator. Carlos protests vehemently. That man is raised for food is such an odious proposition. Don Juan is nonplussed and delivers a coup de grâce to Carlos's reason by saying that, to keep humankind obedient and meek, the flyers have incorporated a stupendous maneuver, from the point of view of a fighting strategist, and a horrendous one from the point of view of those who suffer it. The predators have given humankind their own flyer's mind, which is morose and contradictory, filled with fear of being discovered at any minute, thus keeping humankind endlessly fretting and active over concerns of the self, which is the perfect condition for growing the flyer's food.

Carlos is beside himself with rebellion. What don Juan is proposing is monstrous! It has all the makings of a cheap sci-fi horror film. Don Juan laughs and says he couldn't agree more, then simply gives Carlos another demonstration of the mud shadow's existence. He takes Carlos to a deserted area and, after having him enter inner silence by turning off his internal dialogue, Carlos sees a gigantic shadow, perhaps fifteen feet across, making heavy, plodding leaps across the bottom of a desert valley. When a mud shadow nearly lands on him, Carlos reacts with utter terror, trying to shake off whatever might have come to eat him.

As much as Carlos wants to protest against the nature of what he has seen and don Juan's explanations of the creature's existence and their odious relationship with humankind, he cannot dismiss don Juan's reasoning. Don Juan appeals to Carlos's analytical mind, asking him to explain the contradiction between the intelligence of man, the technician, and the stupidity of his systems of belief and behavior. Warriors believe the predators have given us our systems of beliefs, our ideas of good and evil, and our social mores. They are the ones who set up our hopes and expectations, dreams of success or fear of failure. They have given us covetousness, greed, and cowardice. It is the predators who make us complacent, routine, and egomaniacal.

Carlos's analytical mind swings back and forth like a yo-yo, but after a while and given further time to think about the flyers, he is unable to deny that what don Juan is proposing does make sense as an energetic fact. It explains every kind of human contradiction he can think of. As he looks closer at the world around him, there seems to be evidence everywhere, and the more he talked to and observed his fellow men and himself, the more intense the conviction that something was rendering us incapable of any activity, any interaction, or any thought that didn't have the self as its focal point. His concern, as well as that of everyone he knew, was self-reflection. And that universality of focus leads to a stultifying homogeneity. He couldn't help but agree with don Juan that "every human being on this earth seems to have exactly the same reactions, the same thoughts, the same feelings. They seem to respond in more or less the same way to the same stimuli. Those reactions seem to be sort of fogged up by the language they speak, but if we scrape that off, they are exactly the same reactions that besiege every human being." Carlos is thrown into a spiral of anguish for humankind and ends up weeping for his father, the most considerate being he ever knew, so tender, so gentle, so helpless, who never had a chance.

After finishing the chapter, Owen is left with the same reaction as Carlos, absolutely staggered. The idea of a predator is too ghastly, revolting, and assaulting to even consider the possibility that it could exist. He is unable to continue reading and has to get up and move around. He goes into the house and busies himself, then takes up some mindless work in the yard. Yet, as someone committed to remaining open to all possibilities about the nature of existence, he has to consider what don Juan is saying about the flyers. And if it were true, there is no denying it would explain a lot. It has always amazed him how great the gap is between people's hopes and intentions, their understanding of what they need to do to live a good and conscious life, and what is actually done. People are undeniably their own worst enemies. If people put half as much energy and focus into living their true beliefs as they do into perpetuating their madness, the world would be a much different place. Why is humankind so easily thwarted? Over the years of reading and working to understand the don Juan material, Owen thought that ignorance and slavery to self-importance explained the human condition, but the concept of the flyers takes that understanding to a whole new level. And when he looks out over the landscape of humanity, he is amazed by the dazzling accomplishments of technology, while man the social creature hasn't advanced at all and continues in an endless spiral of conflict and war, perpetuated by self-interest, suspicion, and self-righteous indignation. Evidence of human delusion and indulgence is everywhere, yet people have such a hard time relating it to their own choices and seem condemned to endlessly repeat their mistakes and blame others. How can it happen over and over, and yet everyone continues to think they are on the verge of advancing and getting their understanding right? No one seems to recognize that there must be an inherent flaw or fault in being human, or at least there has been no widespread recognition of it. People seem so anxious to stumble toward hopes and dreams without ever truly considering that they are simply involved in a repeating pattern of empty expectation that has been going on for thousands of years. Now, to think that humankind really is just a trapped creature, and that the predictability of endless self-serving projection and mania that keep him spinning around in place is the result of a predator that makes him easy prey and an easy source of food! The flyer's mind becomes a logical explanation. "Man, the magical being that he is destined to be, is no longer magical. There are no more dreams for man but the dreams of an animal who is being raised to become a piece of meat: trite, conventional, imbecilic."

Owen is left reeling. He just can't get over what don Juan says about man the technician, and the marvelous things created, contrasted against man the social creature, who ends up condemned to live such small and petty lives, especially against the backdrop of the possibilities available. He thinks of all the people he knows and can find no true exception, and he has to include himself in that scrutiny. For all his effort and gyration, he really hasn't gotten anywhere beyond his usual patterns, especially considering how much he believes to be available and how much he believes he knows how to proceed. Still, he gets in his own way and is quick to sabotage himself. His life seems to be an endless cycle of stops and starts, two steps forward and two steps back.

Yet what he focuses on is that don Juan said there was an escape, a way to defeat the flyers and their debilitating action. Don Juan said that there is an inherent weakness in the flyer's mind. The flyer's mind "has no concentration whatsoever." And the way to defeat the flyer's mind is to burden it with discipline. But by discipline, he didn't mean harsh routines. "Warriors understand discipline as the capacity to face with serenity odds that are not included in our expectations. For them, discipline is an art: the art of facing infinity without flinching, not because they are strong and tough but because they are filled with awe." Don Juan goes on to explain how discipline becomes a deterrent. "Warriors say that discipline makes the glowing coat of awareness unpalatable to the flyer. The result is that the predators become bewildered. An inedible glowing coat of awareness is not part of their cognition. After being bewildered, they don't have any recourse other than refraining from continuing their nefarious task."

Don Juan continued, "And if the predators don't eat our coat of awareness for a while, it'll keep on growing, beyond the level of the toes. Once it extends beyond the toes, it regrows to its natural size. As awareness reaches levels higher than the toes, tremendous maneuvers of perception become a matter of course." Warriors burden the flyer's mind with discipline by taxing it with inner silence, having found that it will eventually flee. "The flyers are an essential part of the universe...they are the means by which the universe tests us."

After finishing the book, and for the next couple of days, Owen is dominated by the concept of the flyers. Nothing else matters. The concept of the flyers completely overshadows the rest of the material. If he is dominated by mud shadows and used for food, what else is there to think about? He feels he is being forced to face the great truth of humankind's existence. But in reality, he has to wonder whether the idea of being dominated by mud shadows changes anything all that much. The other books brought to light the madness of human beings, the power of ignorance, and enslavement to self-image. Self-importance has been called the three-thousand-headed monster. Isn't that obstacle enough? Does the revelation of mud shadows as an energetic predator expand humankind's predicament that much more? Being enslaved is being enslaved. The contrast between man the engineer and man the social creature is definitely revealing, but after all is said and done, has anything really changed? The degree to which humankind is dominated and disconnected from its true nature seems the same. And the solution to both the flyers and the notion of the three-headed monster is also the same: discipline is still the answer; impeccability and the redeployment of energy are still the approach.

The thought that keeps returning to him is that Les, Gail, and the others have also had to deal with the concept of the flyers. He wonders what kind of response they have come up with. They seem to be serious enough people. He is especially looking forward to talking with Les. Owen appreciates Les telling him about the book.

Owen is sure Les would like to hear from him after reading the book. After another day, his interest in seeing Les grows strong enough that he decides to visit. He could just drive out to see Les, but he doesn't want to risk missing him. He also thinks it best to let Les know he is coming, as it might allow Les to set aside some time and focus on what could be a long, in-depth conversation. He doesn't have a direct way to contact Les, so he decides to go through Nate. Nate is his point of contact with the group anyway. He emails Nate to let him know he would like to go to the house and that tomorrow, around noon, would be good. It isn't long before Nate emails back saying that six o'clock would be better. Owen is fine with that, so six o'clock it is.

CHAPTER TWENTY-ONE

When the time comes, Owen makes the drive to the house and reaches the area with time to spare. Not wanting to arrive too early, he fills up with gas at a station and then spends several minutes sitting in the parking lot before making the final drive. Pulling up to the house, he is a little disappointed to see several cars out front; he was hoping to be able to talk with Les alone but is not deterred. Walking up to the front door, he rings the doorbell.

Nate answers! It is the first time they have seen each other since Owen was jumped on, and it feels like a reunion! They both laugh, shake hands, and give a quick embrace. As Owen steps through the door, Ronnie comes forward to greet him! Except for the moment of waking up and seeing her at the foot of the bed, he hasn't seen her since the encounter, and they are both happy to see each other. Ronnie looks so different. She is open and bright, a completely different woman from the one he originally met. Of course she is, because she was putting on such an act for him, and seeing her now is testimony to how well she disguised herself. They both did a great job of fooling him completely. Owen has no trouble admitting their accomplishment and shakes his head, still amazed. "You really got me." The three of them laugh together.

Ronnie and Nate turn and lead him into the house, and the rest of the group is waiting for him by the kitchen and living area. Owen is surprised to see everyone he has met so far. They are all glad to see him. Owen takes a moment to look over at Les, who is standing by the couch next to his oxygen tank. They nod a greeting and share a smile.

"So how does the world look today?" Gail asks as she steps forward to meet him, smiling broadly.

They are all aware that he has just read the book and must be very curious about his reaction. Owen can't help but shake his head again. He makes no effort to hide the effect the book has had on him and groans in awe and dismay. "Unbelievable," he says. The others laugh in unison.

"Like a big punch in the stomach?" Gail continues. Owen readily agrees.

"Like a swift kick in the teeth," Nate laughs. Owen agrees to that as well.

"Like your head wants to explode," Jessie chimes in.

Yes, yes. Owen catches on; they are having fun with him. He smiles and nods acknowledgment.

"Like you're upside down," Ronnie throws in. They all share a laugh.

But their shouting out continues.

"We are trapped in madness," Daniel announces. "There is a predator among us," Nate adds.

Jessie has more to offer. "The world is not what it seems."

Owen becomes unsure about what is going on and realizes that their shouting is deliberate, but they all continue to look at him and smile. He is suddenly uncomfortable being the center of attention.

Music suddenly starts. The group then separates. Owen is left to wonder what is happening. The music rises to a volume and rolls funky and wild.

Gail and Nate then face each other and begin doing some kind of strange dance. They sort of squat with their hands on their thighs, then lift one leg at a time before dropping it down. Soon, the others join in, first Ronnie and then the two guys. They are all smiling and having a good time. Owen glances over at Les, who is only looking on, delighted in watching the performance.

Owen can't help but think whatever they are doing is for his benefit, yet they seem aware of only each other. They continue their dance, raising one leg while squatting, then letting it fall. There is a sense of great weight, as if each is trying to exaggerate being as huge as possible. They look like giant frogs or sumo wrestlers posturing for each other. Owen realizes what they are doing: they are imitating the great bulk and heaviness of the mud shadows as described in the book! It makes him laugh. It's the craziest thing! Their imitation is quite good; there is a feeling of great plodding mass. Suddenly, words to the music kick in, and they all sing along. "Would you like to dance with me? We're doing the cosmic slop." They dance for each other and sing unabashedly. "Would you like to dance with me? We're doing the cosmic slop." They are having great fun. It's a real hoot. By the level of their abandonment, it is obvious they've done this before. Owen understands their dancing as making fun of their predicament of being held captive by entities of the universe—a perfect warrior response. Laughter bubbles out of him.

Gail turns to him and takes his hand. His initial response is hesitation at being dragged into something he didn't choose, but they are just having fun, and he is all for it. The concept of the mud shadows has reduced everything to madness anyway, so he allows himself to be led forward. Letting go of his hand, Gail turns to him and picks up the rhythm of the others. For a moment, he is overcome by self-conscious awkwardness as he searches for the rhythm, but he focuses on Gail and tries to follow. He raises his leg and lets it fall. He intends to feel as huge as possible. It's like opening to a direction. The volume of the dancing carries him.

The rhythm does come to him; he dances with Gail and the others. The dancing is perfect folly. When the words come around again, Owen sings with the group. "Would you like to dance with me? We're doing the cosmic slop?" Everyone is smiling and having a great time. "Would you like to dance with me? We're doing the cosmic slop."

But there is also a seriousness to their imitation. They are all aware of the monstrosity of their situation, with the mud shadows, and are making fun of their plight as a form of release; they are mocking their oppressor. In that sense, he is grateful for the chance and only wants to give himself over, because the concept of the mud shadows has put great pressure on him. He is glad for the chance to not care and have fun with it; he dances for release as well.

Owen raises his thigh and leg until his massiveness is as big as possible. He lets go, dropping his weight to the ground and stomping his foot.

It's almost like a contest, but they are all in it together. How huge and massive can they all be?

As he continues to be big and huge and to connect with the bigness and hugeness of the others around him, it becomes less and less of an effort to keep dancing. It is as if the volume of dancing itself and the volume of the others around him are pulling him along. It's a curious sensation that he gives himself over to, as everyone around him dances with the same level of abandon.

Yet at one point, he feels himself becoming separate from his dancing. There is a flash of concern, but he is having too much fun and believes too much in the direction. As the separateness continues, he has to wonder whether he could stop dancing even if he wanted to, and it is a shock to realize he probably can't. The dancing has taken over him; it has moved beyond his own volition. At the same time, the room begins to waver as it too loses certainty.

Owen has no doubt his assemblage point is shifting again. He knows it is a good thing; it is what he has been working toward. It's a great accomplishment, the threshold every warrior strives to cross, and he knows it is just a matter of letting himself go and following the movement, but he also feels a rising reluctance. Entering the second attention is entering the unknown. It is dangerous. There is no knowing where the movement will take him. Part of him believes he should just trust and grab his cubicle of chance, while another part believes he is not ready. What he senses strongly is that the shifting of his assemblage point needs to be his choice, on his terms, and this isn't the right situation. It's a bodily sensation that has the direct result of him instinctively pulling back instead of letting go. He needs to stop. But how? There is no connection at all to him dancing anymore.

Without a doubt, he knows his awareness is on the verge of being whisked away. Everything around him is separating and moving away; he feels himself becoming lighter and lighter. What truly throws him into a panic is when he tries to anchor his focus by grasping onto something solid and looks over to see Les staring fixedly at him. Owen is shocked by the certainty that Les is aware of what is happening and has probably set him up again; he has fallen into another trap. Owen's reaction is to resist with every fiber of his being; he wants the dancing to stop! He knows he has to break the fixation with his dancing and forces himself to look around. He remembers the technique from the books for breaking fixation and rolls his eyes counterclockwise, instantly experiencing a small measure of relief.

Owen feels dizzy. He is not so much afraid of falling as he is relieved to think he isn't getting any worse.

Gail and Nate are suddenly at his side, leading him to the couch.

He falls into it. He hears Les direct someone to get water.

The room is still wavering, but the sensation doesn't seem to be escalating. He is aware of perspiring. He is offered a glass of water, which he shakes his head to refuse. Les instructs everyone to step back.

Owen sits back against the couch with his eyes closed. He seems stabilized and stays very focused on what is happening to him. The second attention is the direction of his life and where he wants to go. He feels a space and awareness, a huge potential.

"Is he all right?" he hears someone ask. It is one of the guys. Les says they will have to wait to see.

Owen feels a sense of separateness within himself. It is as if the elements of him are only loosely tethered together. His mind seems separate from his body. His chest cavity feels a great distance from his legs.

"What's going on?" Ronnie asks, genuinely concerned.

Les says he is sure Owen's assemblage point is shifting again, and a flutter of surprise passes through the group. When Daniel wonders how it could have moved, Les replies that Owen's assemblage point probably hasn't fully stabilized since its last shift, when they jumped on him, and that it was probably kept loose by the shock of learning about the flyers. Les also thinks the newness of the dancing might have had something to do with it.

Owen takes in what Les has said and agrees with him. Otherwise, he is aware of his breathing and focuses on keeping it steady.

"So is he in the second attention?" Nate asks.

"There's no way of telling," Les answers.

"Is he stiff?" Daniel asks.

"Don't bother him," Les instructs.

Owen senses their concern and amazement; he is amazed and

concerned himself. His assemblage point has shifted again. But his focus remains on maintaining his sense of control. He knows he is in a precarious situation and remains motionless, eyes closed.

Les again says there is no way to be sure, but if Owen's assemblage point has shifted, he is in the realm of *intent*.

"He is on the verge of infinity," he explains, in an attempt to satisfy their curiosity. "The wings of his perception are unfolding."

A ripple of amazement moves through the group. Hearing the profundity of Les's statement, Owen feels a wave of nervousness. He is on the verge of something, though he mostly feels past the most intense moment.

"Remember, we are nothing but energy imbued with perception," Les continues.

There is a flutter of intrigue among the group

It is Nate who asks. "Could he be in another dimension?"

"That's up to him and his connection with *power*," Les answers.

Owen continues to agree with Les and is very interested in hearing what else Les has to say. The direction of his life depends on how he handles his new development.

But when nothing more is said, Owen finds himself in a strange position. Being at the center of attention, with them all standing around, looking down, it is as if he were a patient surrounded by consulting physicians. Even with his eyes closed, he can feel the pressure of their focus.

"Is it possible he could disappear?" Nate wants to know.

Owen hears Les's low laugh. "That's a bit extreme," he says. "Although there are examples in the books of people disappearing into the unknown, remember that all we truly are is organic matter focused by our assemblage point. But to disappear would mean he has crossed the barrier of perception; it would mean his assemblage point has stabilized at another position, and there's no way of knowing whether he is capable of that. It would be far-fetched. That's a very advanced maneuver."

"So what is he doing?" Ronnie asks.

"Could he be hallucinating?" Jessie suggests.

Les again says there is no way of knowing. "Maybe he's just resting," he offers, before injecting a note of mirth. "Though that would be pretty hard to do with all of you staring at him."

Owen can appreciate Les's intent to make light of his situation, and again, he is aware that their attention is focused on him.

The truth is, he has now passed the point of crisis, and remaining motionless with his eyes closed is mostly an extension of his attempt to keep the others talking about him and, most importantly, to hear what Les has to say to gain more understanding.

But the seriousness of their interest seems to have passed. Owen suddenly finds himself in a difficult situation. Les might realize he is only sitting there, listening to them. Keeping his eyes closed only prolongs the situation. Opening his eyes and admitting he is fine will only confirm their suspicions.

"Maybe we should check if he is stiff," Nate suggests.

"Or maybe we should just tickle his ears," Les answers.

A low laugh sputters through the group.

There is no doubt Les is having fun with him. Owen is again the focus of Les's folly. It annoys him, but he is mostly annoyed with himself. He is aware of them watching every move on his face. The longer he lies motionless with his eyes closed, the longer he prolongs the inevitable; he will have to open his eyes at some point.

CHAPTER TWENTY-TWO

Owen remains lying on the couch with his eyes closed as the center of attention until he feels he has no choice but to end the moment.

He smiles, then opens his eyes to see them all looking down at him. A burst of laughter from the group makes Owen sit up and shake his head. Everyone seems relieved.

Les tells everyone to step back and give him some room. When the glass of water is offered again, he accepts it and drinks. He takes a moment to assess his condition. His head feels a bit fuzzy, but otherwise, he feels mostly cohesive; he definitely doesn't feel he is going anywhere, and the episode of his assemblage point shifting has passed for the most part.

When Les asks everyone to move farther away, they turn and walk to the kitchen area. Soon, it is just he and Les. Les sits in the chair next to him.

"You all right?" Les asks, expressing genuine concern.

Owen believes he is.

"Looks like you got a tiger by the tail," Les adds.

Owen can only agree. But as he continues to sit and grows more confident in his recovery, he becomes increasingly aware of his annoyance that Les chose to have some fun with him when he was so vulnerable. The shifting of his assemblage point is nothing to be taken lightly. Yet Owen is also aware that a warrior can never take himself too seriously, and that, in warrior terms, what Les did was acceptable. He feels caught in the middle of deciding how to think about Les. To resolve his dilemma, he focuses on a question that will be very telling. It comes from wondering whether Les staged the whole situation with the dancing. Owen still feels desperate to know what he is dealing with in these people. "So how much did you know about what was going to happen?" Owen remembers looking over and seeing Les watching him intently, aware that something was going on.

The question catches Les by surprise. "You mean while you were dancing?"

"Beforehand," Owen answers. "Did you know my assemblage point would shift?"

Les gives a surprised laugh. "Oh, you give me way too much credit. I'm the one following along here. I mean, it's obvious your assemblage point has been loosened. But the dancing is something we often do when we get together. It's kind of like a team ritual, for team spirit." He gives another short laugh. "The idea of the flyers is quite the challenge for us too, you know. And then to have someone new to the concept—it seemed a good reason to celebrate."

Owen can't argue against the explanation, but he isn't willing to believe the incident occurred fully by chance. What he continues to realize is that if Les did set him up, it was another remarkable maneuver that took a keen understanding of awareness.

Les asks if he is up for eating something.

The others are in the kitchen area and seem to be getting ready for a meal. Owen isn't particularly hungry, but he doesn't want to separate himself or keep Les from joining the group, so he accepts the invitation. When Les gets up from the chair and reaches for his oxygen tank, Owen gets up as well.

As Les and Owen step into the kitchen, the others quickly make room for them. A big bowl of salad has been placed on the counter, along with a rice pilaf and a dish of broiled summer vegetables that have been pulled from the oven. Owen wonders whether they eat together a lot, then realizes the dinner might be because of his visit. It's kind of weird to think about. He was just on the verge of being whisked away into the unknown, and now he is eating with the others as if nothing happened. As a tribute to a warrior's sense of detachment, he remembers don Juan saying that a warrior, one minute, can have untold mysteries before him and in the next instant be laughing and telling jokes with friends.

After filling their plates and taking silverware from a basket, the others spread out to seats throughout the kitchen and living area. Owen sits on a stool at the island counter. The food is good.

He notices that everyone eats in silence, just as don Juan and his cohorts always did in the books. Owen can't help but be impressed to find himself in a group of practitioners. After eating, as the dishes are cleared, Owen notices Les sitting alone on the couch and walks over. He sits next to Les in the chair and lets Les know he appreciates being invited to dinner. Les says they were looking forward to having him over. Nothing else is said, and for the moment, they both seem content to relax. Owen doesn't expect the silence to last long. Too much has gone on.

The others have noticed them sitting together and begin to gravitate over. Daniel steps in behind the chair on the other side of Les, near the inset shelving in the wall that holds the stereo unit. He puts on some upbeat but unobtrusive instrumental music. Nate sits in the other chair. Ronnie and Gail sit on the couch next to Les. Owen expects a conversation to develop about the books, what happened to him, what they think might have happened to him, and what they have experienced.

A conversation does start when Ronnie asks if he thinks his assemblage point actually shifted. Owen answers assuredly that it was about to.

Gail asks if it was because of the dancing. He answers that he is sure that was part of it.

Owen is willing to be as open and available as possible. He is ready to get on a roll with their conversation. He is imagining one of those late-night sessions when all manner of questions and intrigue can be raised.

It is Les who picks up the conversation. "Obviously, Owen has worked hard to dislodge his awareness from its fixation on the first attention. It is a monumental task. You have before you someone who has endured the hardships of learning and steadfastly followed the path. Until now, he faces the unknown, the second attention. The binding force of everyday existence is releasing him from its prison, and he is becoming free to reach out and grasp the second ring of power, the gateway to untold mysteries. He is on his way to claiming his rightful human heritage as a magical being. We must wish him well."

Owen is surprised to hear himself being talked about in such terms; it feels like a tribute. He is suddenly back in the uncomfortable position of having everyone focus on him. He tries to make light of the situation by feigning surprise at what Les has said, but he feels his effort comes off as deflective and overly humble. What Les is saying isn't necessarily untrue, though Owen thinks Les is overstating his situation. He doesn't feel the need to correct or add to what Les has said. Owen waits to see what will be said next.

But Les says no more, and his words hover in the space among the group. Owen feels as if he has been left stranded on a pedestal, separated from the others. Everyone is forced to bask in the magnitude of what has been offered.

A strange thing happens. The group begins to separate. It feels as if they are giving him space, but it's not what he wants.

Gail returns to the kitchen and finishes cleaning up after dinner, with help from Jessie and Ronnie. Daniel and Nate move to the stereo and start discussing music.

Not long afterward, people begin to leave altogether. Gail is first to go, saying she has to work in the morning. Both Nate and Ronnie have to work as well and leave shortly after. Jessie soon follows.

Everyone says goodbye to everyone and is sure to include him. Owen says good night to each.

Just Les and Daniel remain. Owen expects Les to start talking to him. Maybe the others left because of some kind of signal from Les that he wanted to be alone with him. But Les soon says he is tired, stands, and rolls his oxygen tank out from the side of the couch. Before he retires, he invites Owen to stay the night in the room where he stayed previously. But before Owen makes a decision, Les and Daniel both say good night and walk to the back bedrooms.

Owen is shocked. He can't believe it! Les just left. Without talking about the book! It's what he came for, what he thought they wanted!

Les doesn't come back.

An irritation escalates. What the hell! Are they messin' with him again? He can't help but think that being left alone was intentional. He feels controlled, manipulated, imposed upon. Even leaving the stereo on feels like a mockery of his situation.

His annoyance continues. The hardest part is being forced to just sit there. There's nothing he can do about it. He becomes annoyed with himself; he was so susceptible. They knew how invested he would be in talking about the book and the flyers.

He should just leave. It's his only option. But where would that get him? The bottom line is that he wants to know more about these people; it would mean a lot to encounter others. If they did play him, it was deliberate, strategic, and almost masterful—an extension of the kind of thing they did to him with their first prank. But what could be the point? Are they simply amusing themselves?

Owen speculates on the ramifications of his situation until he is nearly exhausted. He has no choice but to accept the situation. When he gets up to retire, he is actually tired. After turning off the stereo, he walks to the bedroom.

CHAPTER TWENTY-THREE

When Owen wakes, it is daylight. He has no idea what time it is. Remnants of what happened to him last night threaten to crowd in on him, but he pushes them away. His focus is on moving forward. A warrior has to be ready for whatever. He reminds himself that everything he does is a bid for power. In the life of a warrior, there are only challenges. But he also feels a sense of resolve. He is almost desperate to understand these people and to get a sense of what he is dealing with. He gets up, uses the bathroom, and then leaves the room.

As soon as Owen enters the great room of the house, he sees Les sitting on the couch. They exchange a friendly greeting as Owen walks over and sits in the chair across from him. Les quickly asks how he is feeling, and Owen answers that he is feeling fine.

"Well, my man, it looks like *infinity* is nipping at your heels." Les grins, his comment surely referring to what happened to him last night.

Owen smiles back but hesitates to answer. He's interested in learning more about Les and the group, but it doesn't seem appropriate to dive in right away. If Les wants to take the lead initially, that's fine with him.

"So what's next?" Les then asks.

Les isn't hesitating in getting serious. Owen isn't clear on what he is thinking, so, to deflect scrutiny from himself and stay neutral in the conversation, he says the first thing that comes to mind, something glib. "In the world of *Intent* there is only intending."

Les laughs, once, as an exclamation, interpreting the statement for himself. "To intend is to wish without wishing, to do without doing."

Owen can only agree.

"And the whole goal is to be sensitive to the solicitations of *spirit*, to polish our connecting link," Les says.

Owen doesn't respond. Is Les wanting to start a serious conversation? The time for that would have been last night. Owen still feels a little sore about being abandoned.

But Les doesn't continue. In the next instant, he changes the subject. "I hope you don't mind, but could we move outdoors? Being outside is always better for me, especially in the morning."

Owen is relieved. But the fact that he is relieved is also unsettling. He has only started talking with Les, and he already feels like he is chasing after him.

Owen agrees to move outdoors, and the two of them stand. Les offers him something to drink, and he pours himself a glass of orange juice from the counter and takes it with him. They walk together down the hall and out the back door.

Walking behind, Owen notices that Les appears capable as he walks without his oxygen tank, though it has already been established that he doesn't need his oxygen as much in the morning. Given his apparent good health, Owen doesn't want to dismiss the possibility that his oxygen tank might still have been a prop to disarm him, but he is also tired of being suspicious. There is a situation ahead of him. His determination is to let their conversation unfold.

Reaching the courtyard, there isn't anyone else around. Les walks to the round patio table, and the two of them take chairs and sit across from each other.

"So I imagine our flyer friends threw you for quite a loop?" Les says, smiling as they get settled.

Les has again taken the lead in asking questions. But it is only the start of their next encounter, and the subject is an obvious one between them. Owen smiles back and gives a low laugh as he thinks about the flyers and their initial effect on him. "That's some wild stuff."

Les laughs in a genuine outburst, as if Owen's response has given him permission to express the full extent of his amazement. "Ol' Carlos has really dropped a bomb on us," he says, grinning broadly and continuing his mirth. "As if showing us unimaginable worlds wasn't enough. As if making the otherworldly nature of existence so damn rational that we feel forced to believe and pursue it. Then, to top it off, there are predators from the universe at large who treat us as enslaved prey they raise for food!"

It's almost too much. They shake their heads in unison, having reached the point of being hugely impressed. The full scope of the flyers, combined with the magnitude of the material, is staggering for anyone interested in exploring the condition of being human. In that sense, Owen recognizes an opportunity to involve Les; he has a natural curiosity.

"So what was your reaction when you first encountered the flyers?"

Les takes a moment to think before answering. "Oh, I'm sure pretty much the same as yours. I think I spent a week wandering around in circles."

They both laugh again.

"So you read the book when it first came out?" Owen asks.

He recognizes he has taken the lead in the conversation and is quick to keep going.

"Oh yes, everyone did. It was all over the internet. The whole warrior world was abuzz. It was like the proverbial wailing of despair, as if the devil himself had suddenly appeared, and of course, he sort of did." Les gives a high chuckle, amused by the image. "People were leaving the warrior's world in droves. It was too much blasphemy, too much heresy."

Owen hadn't considered the overall effect of the flyers on the broader community of practitioners. It must have been quite a shock. He can only imagine the sense of upheaval. "But it explains so much," he then says, offering a point that most impressed him.

"Oh sure, it absolutely does," Les agrees. "I mean, how else can you explain humankind's perpetual mania? What lessons are ever really learned? Sometimes humankind's only accomplishment seems to be its ability to create infinite variations on a debilitating theme."

Owen couldn't agree more, but Les was referring to humankind, the social creature. To round out the full scope of the paradox, which, to him, seems to truly point to some outside source for the degree of human contradiction, he brings up the other side of the coin. "And man the engineer is capable of such technical marvels. I mean, there hardly seems to be a problem that can't be solved. There's been such progress. Yet as a social creature, humankind hasn't gotten past square one."

"Exactly!" Les agrees. They both are awash in incredulity.

But for as much as he is enjoying getting on a roll with Les, he remains aware that he has taken the lead in their conversation, and his overriding goal is still to gather information about the group. "So how 'bout the others?" he asks, recognizing his chance. "How did they react?"

His question elicits an odd response. Les laughs as if something has struck him as uniquely funny. "Most of the others weren't involved with the material then," he answers, then looks at him. "Can you imagine your first encounter with the material being the concept of the flyers?"

Owen is taken aback. He never thought of that.

"Most of these young people had never even heard of don Juan until they heard about the flyers," Les continues. "It was what brought them to the books."

Owen lets the words sink into him until he is shocked. Wow! If his first exposure to the don Juan material had been the notion of the flyers it would have changed everything; it would have been a completely different experience. "So how'd they respond?" he asks, greatly intrigued.

Les laughs again, in true amazement. "It's the damnedest thing. While some people were running from the material, others were running toward it, and it was mostly young people."

Owen does not understand.

"It's as if it made all the sense in the world to them," Les expounds. "It's as if they were hardly surprised."

Owen is again left struggling to comprehend.

"The only thing that makes sense to me," Les continues, "is that young people have been so exposed to so many notions of alternate realities and dimensions of consciousness, it was like the notion of the flyers is simply confirmation of what they suspected all along."

Owen still isn't getting it.

"It's like the concept of the flyers spoke their language. Think about it," Les says, leaning forward to explain. "All these video games and movies these kids watch, and the books they read, are about otherworldly creatures, aliens, and other dimensions of reality. I mean, when I was growing up, there were zombies and space aliens and stuff, but these kids are absolutely inundated with this stuff. Remember, don Juan said that we are subconsciously aware we aren't alone in this world, and I just think that subconscious awareness has moved closer to the surface."

Owen follows Les, and what he has said is very interesting, but he seems to be getting off on a tangent of speculation. Owen feels the need to return to something more specific. A question comes to mind that gives him a chance to focus on the group. "So is Gail that way?"

"Oh no, not Gail," Les quickly qualifies, sitting back in his chair. "She's been with the material almost as long as I have. She's a true warrior. Gail is stupendous."

Owen is both glad and relieved to hear it. He's always thought there was a balanced quality about her.

Owen then brings the conversation back to the others. "So how do the rest of them deal with the whole flyer thing?"

Les laughs. "I don't think they really do. I mean, sometimes I think they're more interested in scaring the piss out of themselves. It's like going to a scary movie. I don't know, maybe it's not fair, but they're so dominated by the notion of the flyers that they don't have room for anything else in the material. The effort they make is mostly a reaction to the flyers."

Owen is quickly back to being incredulous. What Les has said very much brings to focus a different picture of the group.

"It's why I made such an example of you last night," Les then adds. "I hope you don't mind. I mean, I'm assuming most of what I said was true."

Les has jumped to another line of thinking, and Owen struggles to follow him, but is aware of what he is talking about and is reminded of last night when Les seemed to suddenly be extolling his virtues.

"It's just that I saw an opportunity to drive home a point," Les continues. "I wanted to highlight the contrast. Because whatever you have been able to accomplish, you haven't been motivated by the flyers."

Owen doesn't fully understand what Les is saying but is willing to go along.

"That's why the group is so fascinated by you," Les suddenly laughs. "You're like some strange cousin. It's as if they're experiencing someone who has stepped out of a different time and space. You've been working on the material for years, motivated only by the material itself, and most of the group couldn't imagine doing something like that without the flyers' escape as their driving force."

Owen lets what Les is saying gather inside until he is dumbfounded. "But the material is so powerful."

"Of course! But these young people can't see it! If you ask me, being so dominated by the flyers is a clear indication of the flyers' mind itself and proof of their existence!"

Owen is left reeling. What he is hearing is very strange. But what has his attention is how worked up Les has become. He seems very attached to what is going on with the others in the group. Owen attempts to grab onto something solid. "So what does their reaction have to do with you?"

Les's initial reaction is to be surprised at the question, but he manages to smile. "I don't know, I guess I'm just amazed. I mean, I'm involved with these people. They have my interest."

But how involved is Les with the others? Owen feels there is a possible contradiction to the attitude of a warrior, because a warrior can only be for himself, not in a selfish way. For a warrior, everything begins and ends with the self and one's personal connection to spirit. Contact with the spirit causes someone to overcome the feeling of self-importance, and the self becomes something abstract and impersonal. The only exception is if Les were the nagual. Then he would be required by power to guide his apprentices to realize the larger dimension of themselves. Owen still isn't completely sure Les isn't a nagual and recognizes the opportunity to push the issue. "But you're not the nagual, right?"

"Oh no, no," Les adamantly confirms, shaking his head.

Owen believes him. He is willing to give up on the idea, but it highlights the need to understand Les's connection to these people. "So why are you so interested?"

Les sits back in his chair, taking in Owen's words. "I don't know. Maybe it's just part of my folly. These young people are looking for direction. They sense the greater reality. They know there is so much more to the world than meets the eye."

But is it his place to try to lead them? Owen is reminded of don Juan saying that the hardest thing to do is to leave people alone. Every warrior has to find their own way; it's only their connection to *spirit* that can direct them. So, can Les afford that kind of involvement for his own practice? Owen senses an opportunity and pushes in that direction. "But how can you be so involved? This is tough stuff. A warrior needs to stay focused. That's why a warrior can only be for oneself."

"Yes, yes," Les answers, and seems to be agreeing with what Owen is saying. He then counters, "But you have to be involved with the world around you."

Owen's response immediately comes forth. "But only as a way to further your practice."

"And I believe that it is," Les replies. "I mean, there are plenty of examples in the books where practitioners were of great service to humankind." Les goes on to explain. "Both the nagual Julian and the nagual Elias were great healers who cured hundreds of people." Les is referring to two of don Juan's teachers in the books, and Owen admits that what he says is true, but Owen is also immediately aware of a key difference. "Yes, but they were naguals. Their connection to power was assured. What they were doing was the result of expressing that connection. It seems that if your connection to spirit isn't strong enough, you can't be sure you're serving the spirit or caught up in your own indulgence." Owen realizes he is being adamant in pursuing his point, but believes he might be onto something.

What he has said needs to be considered by anyone pursuing the material and indicates that he is getting close to what Les is truly about. He feels he might have penetrated his façade.

Les stays open to the full force of the argument and again sits back in his chair. "You have to admit, we're in a new era," Les then says. "The cat has been let out of the bag. What Carlos has done has the potential to redirect the course of humankind."

Owen is not sure what he is getting at and wonders whether Les has changed the subject to deflect scrutiny from himself.

"I mean, I'm sure you've thought about it," Les continues, gaining a stronger focus. "Here's Carlos…this bumbling, completely self-absorbed anthropology student with a pathology for writing down every minute detail of every incident he experiences, who thinks he is trying to learn about peyote and medicinal plants. He stumbles upon this thousands-year-old tradition of warriors dedicated to nothing but exploring the nature of existence, and he is directed by power itself to become involved and carry on the tradition. Remember how baffled don Juan and his cohorts were that Carlos was a non-Indian, yet there was no doubt that Carlos was directed to don Juan by power, the spirit itself? Remember, don Juan even directed Carlos to write books as a not-doing, as part of his warrior practice, when writing books was the furthest thing from Carlos's interest. But he was committed to don Juan and the path, so he did, and the rest is history. Look what has been unleashed on the world! Can there be any doubt it is a design of spirit?"

Yes, Owen has thought about all that himself, and it is amazing, but he still isn't sure what it has to do with Les.

"And we as the new members," Les continues. "As maybe the start of a new phase of the lineage, are forced to make sense of it and, yes, maybe get it out to the world." Having become animated by the power of his conviction, Les leans forward and looks directly at Owen in great seriousness. "Do you remember that section in the books, where don Juan talks about what modern man most needs right now is to understand the world in energetic terms? And to move away from social terms? It's the only way for humankind to save itself!"

Owen does remember. It is a part of the books that had a great effect on him.

"That's what the material has done," Les says. He again becomes emphatic. "It has given humankind insight into the only direction that can truly free him from his madness."

Owen continues to agree but is still not sure how it relates to Les, and the more Les talks, the further he gets away from that issue as the cornerstone of his own life and practice, which is how Owen sees it. He feels he has no choice but to return to the subject. "But what does that have to do with you and your involvement with the others?"

Les sits back and tilts his head. He takes a deep breath. He is making the effort to reach for something personal. "I'm an old man," he says, gazing up toward the sky. "I've had my time, and believe me, I still have plenty ahead of me." Les then lowers his gaze and looks at him with pointed conviction. "But I need to be honest with myself and look at the big picture. I know what I am up against, and I can see a future, and I want to be a part of it. The issue is still how I can best serve the spirit?"

There it is! Les's focus is on other people! As a way to perpetuate his own notions! And all a warrior can truly focus on is his connection to *spirit*, as a personalized expression of *spirit* itself; the books are very clear on that. And they are warriors, so there is no reason to hold back from each other. "So, what are you, like the pied piper of warriors?" Owen lets out a laugh for emphasis, to further drive home his point.

Les takes the full impact of the accusation and seems to be thwarted by the blow, but manages to smile. "I'm only interested in living my deepest connection."

But he's not living his deepest connection; that's the point, at least not for him personally, because his living can only be as his direct relationship with infinity. But Owen isn't going to argue the issue any further; he doesn't have any great need for Les to see it his way. For his own sake, he feels satisfied that he has at least flushed Les out into the open and has a clear view of him. Les might only be a crusader, an activist, a paper warrior.

"Maybe it's just the teacher in me," Les offers. "Maybe it's just my indulgence." His words seem like a weak effort to explain himself.

Owen doesn't know what to say. His intention wasn't to make Les uncomfortable, but he isn't willing to ignore his observations, either. "It's not easy stuff," he says, bringing their conversation to a neutral place. He realizes he is letting Les off the hook, but he doesn't need to push further.

The end of their conversation has left them on opposite sides of a fence, and Owen can't help but feel a wave of disappointment wash over him; he had such high hopes for Les, as a practitioner, as someone who might be truly accomplished, as someone better than he is.

A silence develops. There just doesn't seem to be a way to bridge the gap between them. And neither of them seems willing to duck into small talk.

They are suddenly just a couple of guys sitting together. Owen finds himself looking to the side at the line of shrubs. There just isn't much else to say. They are individual beings in relationship with *infinity*.

After another moment, Owen feels the only thing to do is end their time together. It might seem sudden and rude, but there doesn't seem to be anything left to discuss. He tells Les he should be going, and Les makes no effort to stop him. Owen stands. It is a bit awkward, but he turns and walks away.

CHAPTER TWENTY-FOUR

As Owen leaves Les's house, he believes he might be done with those people. His suspicions have been confirmed. As practitioners, they are remedial, and his biggest disappointment is with Les. Owen thought he might have found someone better than himself, someone who could show him some things and lead him. He admits that his ultimate hope was that he had come across a party, and that Les was the nagual. Don Juan said in the books that if a warrior is impeccable enough in his struggle, power has set it up so he will find a teacher on his own, and Owen thought Les might be the one. It would have made such a difference. It would have changed everything.

They are good people, but without the direction of a nagual, they are just struggling along, and the last thing he needs is to get caught up in someone else's gyration. So, it's better to know the truth and be done with it. Maybe he's destined to be on his own; it's a warrior's destiny to be solitary in his pursuit of *spirit*. And his world is very different now. His assemblage point has shifted. He has received confirmation that it is possible. It's a huge relief, and in that sense, he is grateful to the group. He can't deny some remarkable things did happen—the way they played him, the way they worked together, the force of their effort. He can't deny that *spirit* was involved.

He doesn't want to be too hasty in dismissing the group because they are the best he has ever known, so he might make contact with them again, but it will be very different. He won't have any high hopes for them, and his involvement will be on his terms, as the chance for challenge. He knows his feelings toward Les and the group stem from his disappointment, and he doesn't want that to be the reason for closing the door. Or maybe he won't feel the need to take it any further and maybe the involvement has run its course. The toughest thing for a warrior is to know when to stop. A warrior touches the world lightly and moves on.

Otherwise, Owen has to stay focused on polishing his own connection to spirit. All a warrior ever truly has is his struggle, and he has to accept that. He is quick to read the new book again. It is just so amazing, and the ramifications are profound. Being told about it by Les is something to be grateful for. This time, when he reads the book, he reads it in more detail. Like all the other books in the series, he identifies important passages and highlights concepts. He has created an extensive reference guide for the material. The challenge is to gain a deeper understanding and to integrate the vast landscape of pieces into a full picture. The scope of the material is huge.

But he also faces the challenge of living the material as a guideline to be followed. So, he's back working with the recapitulation crate. There's just so much junk that a person picks up living in this world that needs to be cleared out, and there's so much energy to reclaim. He continues to focus on his tai chi practice, the integration of body and mind, the expression of energy as the truth of every moment. It feels good to go to class and interact with classmates.

But living the material is difficult. It's so easy to be distracted by the everyday world, and in truth, there is an undeniable comfort in being absorbed by the doing of daily living. Owen is reminded of don Juan saying that, secretly no one wants the benefits of knowledge because it is so demanding, and a warrior needs to be pushed relentlessly to continue making progress. Owen has no one to push him, and he realizes that is a big obstacle for his practice; doing it on his own produces such lesser results. His own struggle seems to confirm the flyer's mind. How can he hope to defeat it? He is reminded again that a warrior spends years in a kind of limbo, where he is neither a warrior nor an ordinary man, and he believes that is where he is. He has to trust, but that doesn't make it any easier.

So, when Owen gets an email from Nate saying that Les has called a meeting for two days from now at ten o'clock in the morning, and the request is for everyone to make every effort to be there, he is surprised. He surely hadn't expected to hear from the others so soon, and after their last conversation, he thought Les might be done with him as well. So, what could they want? His first thought is they could be making another play for him, after feeling him withdraw from the group, but a meeting would be too obvious on their part, and he would never be as unsuspecting again.

For Les to call a meeting, it would have to be important. Something interesting could be happening. But how to respond? He could just dismiss the request, but he also recognizes the opportunity to be engaging. There is nothing they should be able to do to him, and he doesn't want to be a paper warrior himself, caught up in his own notions. The need is to interact. The group can be seen as his worthy opponent, depending on how things develop. All he knows is that he needs to stay engaged with the world around him; the world is his hunting ground, where he challenges himself and finds his power.

So, he decides to attend the meeting, though he doesn't feel the need to email back and feels it is only necessary to show up. On Saturday morning, he heads out just after daylight. He arrives at the house early as usual. There are already a couple of cars in the driveway, but he imagines some of the group had stayed the night. Walking up to the front door, Owen finds a note attached: "Come in. Out back." Owen opens the door and enters. Walking through the living area, he doesn't see anyone. On the kitchen counter are the usual pitchers of water and orange juice, but he doesn't stop and continues out the back of the house.

Reaching the courtyard, he finds Gail and Daniel standing together. The three of them exchange greetings. Owen casually asks what is going on, but neither of them has any idea, and he feels forced to take their response as matter-of-fact.

Soon, Jessie joins them, and then Ronnie and Nate walk through the shrub opening. Everyone is glad to see one another. It seems whenever the group gets together, there is good feeling of camaraderie and reunion. Owen allows himself to enjoy the situation but remains very aware of any signs of what might come.

The group dynamic changes, however, when Les is seen coming down the walkway. Everyone turns. What is immediately striking is that Les is wearing a huge, oversized, multi-colored top hat that is as large and audacious as his wide, beaming grin. There is no doubt Les is up to something. He marches forward, swinging his arm, leading his oxygen tank, but without the tubes connected, as if he were in a parade. For the moment, Owen focuses on the hat. Where could he have gotten such a thing? It is furry and horizontally striped, yellow, green, and red. Otherwise, Les is wearing a billowy white shirt and tan linen pants with sandals.

Stepping through the opening in the shrubs, Les quickly parks his oxygen tank and begins walking around, shaking hands and thanking everyone for coming. When he reaches him, Les seems sincerely glad to see him. His handshake is energetic and engaging but somewhat impersonal. Owen's impression is that

Les is on a mission, and his feeling is that he has just met a glad-handing politician at a county fair.

After greeting them all, Les turns to one of the patio chairs and steps up on it, then onto the table. There is a reaction of surprise among the group, and everyone steps forward to ensure his safety. But Les steadies himself and then turns to everyone. "I want to thank you all for coming." His demeanor remains light and jovial, though his manner is that of being before a group. His voice is loud and clear as if wanting to include a back row. "It's nice to know I can still draw a crowd. I know it was short notice, and I know it's early, and you all have plenty to do, so I appreciate the effort. I won't keep you long, but I ask that you indulge me a little, because as most of you know, I am a king-size indulger."

A low chuckle moves through the group. Everyone is aware of Les's penchant for drama and folly. It is obvious Les is putting on a show, and everyone seems willing to be part of an audience.

Les makes an effort to stand tall and face everyone directly. "My name is Les Henry," he starts. "And I have roamed this earth for seventy-one years." Les is asserting his individuality before the infinite and is consciously putting what happens in the realm of *spirit*. "And in that time, I have seen the world go round and round." He continues with strong projection. "And I have been a part of it. I have been a banker and a poet, a beekeeper, and a car salesman." Les is being revealing. Owen finds it interesting to learn some things about him. "I have dug ditches, literally, and for much of my time, I was a college professor, trying to distinguish the patterns of society from trends of the past.

"But through it all," he says, taking time to look at each of them, "the guiding force of my life has been the desire to make sense of this world, to stare into mystery, to exercise my intrigue and gain some understanding, and to satisfy the feeling of there being so much that is beyond me. And to that end, I have loved and I have lost, I have strived and I have tried...." Owen is surprised. Les is really going for it, throwing open his arms and reaching for what is inside. "As a person, I have stuttered around inside this skin. I have lived a life of stimulation, not to mention a life of woe and wrangling, a life of hope and best intention. I have lived my life believing my greatest moments were before me. I have pranced and danced and gazed longingly at the moon. I have battled, and I have buffooned, and I have thrown caution to the wind and heart and soul in all directions. I've chased my tail, banged my head, busted my butt, and lost my mind. There have been times when I thought I was climbing great mountains of understanding and others when my greatest hope was to be lost in space...."

Owen has to smile. As with everyone else, he is getting a kick out of Les. But there is also a nervous quality to the group, as if no one knows exactly what is happening.

Les continues. "I have been in love with nothingness and everything all at once. I have been a soldier for the forces of peace and politics and saving the world, I have been a champion of personal indulgence and the dazzling esotericism of exotic spirituality. I might also add that I was married twice and divorced both times, and I have been in love on two other occasions.

"And somewhere in the middle of all this, I came across this crazy Carlos stuff, and it quickly became the profoundest vision of anything I had ever encountered. The books whisked me to the far edges of my imagination, then exploded my mind until I was left to stagger around and laugh myself silly. Yet the books were never anything more than rational; they just made so much sense, from a place inside of me that had never been so deeply touched. The material didn't require leaps of faith or lining up other ideas and shooting them down. It only confirmed my deepest intuition and inspired my greatest rational ability. And I couldn't get enough. All I ever wanted was a direction I could believe in, a vision big enough to encompass my deepest inclinations, to include everything I could imagine possible to being alive and human."

Owen is impressed. Les has adopted the role of orator. He is reaching for the crowd, reaching for something inside himself, reaching for a connection to something beyond.

"So I have pursued the material with all the power I had available. I dove into the world of don Juan with gusto, swam in its glory, bathed in its expanse, submerged myself in its sublime, and my only goal has been to continue its path, to be consumed by its magnitude." At this point, Les pauses to hook up his oxygen. Nate and Daniel help him. Les directs that the tank be placed up on one of the chairs so the tubes reach where he is standing.

"But the books are a call to action!" he starts again in earnest, raising a finger to the crowd. "To anyone who has respect for his living, life has to be lived. What else is there? So I have kept moving toward the light, as the only light in the sky. I have thrown myself against the barrier of perception. I have tried to slip through on the wings of folly. And I have had my moments. But the further I have gone, the more aware I have become of the obstacles before me. And now I am faced with the twilight of my years. I have learned to laugh at the bitter taste of defeat, and in my humility, I admit to having stepped back and bowed my head. I can feel death's prowl. But the path is still open, and my only challenge is to traverse its length, and there I look breathlessly, breathlessly upon its wonders. All I have is my struggle. And as I look out over the landscape of my life, my greatest hindrance to my progress is having never fully accepted my fate, of never having accepted my true ticket to impeccability, the acceptance of my own warrior's death that promises to both separate and liberate me from the world around. So before *infinity* as my witness, and before you as my friends, I announce as my conclusion that I am not dead enough…dead to hope… dead to desire…dead to definition…dead to self…dead to doing...and yes, my dear friends and acquaintances, dead to you!"

Owen is shocked. He realizes what Les is doing. He is claiming his practice for himself. It is what Owen was pushing toward when they last talked. Les must have taken his words to heart. Les admits that he is not fully serving his connection with spirit and rededicates himself in front of those closest to him. It is a warrior's maneuver. His effort is bombastic and gutsy, surely in response to the awareness that the spirit only responds to gestures of largesse. Les looks up at the sky as if appealing to infinity itself, then looks down and addresses the group. "My only interest is to abandon all bastions of refuge and take my place in the indefinable mystery. My only concern is my relationship with infinity. I am the one who will face my death. You cannot help me, and I cannot help you. My intention is to become a dead man, deader than I have ever been, as dead as humanly possible. And from my warrior's spirit, I can wish you well, but on the other hand, I must confess that from my warrior's spirit, you all can just go to hell!"

Les has reached his crescendo and punctuated it by dismissing everyone around him. A huge weight has descended on the group. Yet in the next instant, a burst of laughter erupts next to him.

It is Gail, and she suddenly yells at Les. "Oh, you're a long way from being dead, old man! You're not even close!"

There is palpable shock among the rest of them. Everyone looks at Gail, then at Les, then back at Gail.

"There's plenty of indulgence left in you," Gail accuses. "You're right; you are the king of indulgers. The three-thousand-headed monster is alive and well in you. You are perfect flyer food." After his initial surprise, Les grins down at her. "Ah yes, confirmation from the person who knows me best. I am nothing without my folly!"

But Gail is not deterred. "You love to talk a good game. You always have an answer. You love being the wise old man."

Gail is attacking him! What surprises Owen is the vehemence with which she shouts at Les, as if something held back is being released.

"You know my madness," Les answers. "Now you'll know my determination!"

"How much longer are you going to fool yourself?" Gail shouts at him.

Owen can hardly believe what he is witnessing. Two warriors he thought were close are yelling at each other. For the moment, the incongruity is so great that he recoils into his own space. From there, he wonders if this is staged. He can't help himself. Could they be doing this for his benefit, to catch him off guard, knowing he has stepped back from them? He quickly looks at the others for any sign of collusion, but their looks of shock and dismay seem genuine.

The confrontation continues. Les seems driven toward complete abandonment. "I admit it all. I am nothing, but I am not nothing enough!"

"It's not enough to play the clown," Gail shouts at him, not buying any of his high-minded notions.

But her words only spur Les on. "I am the king of half-ass," he responds, looking up at the sky and raising his arms again.

"Ah, you're as bloated as a toad...."

"No, dead I tell you!" Les shouts above her. "Only dead. I'll be the damnedest dead you've ever seen..."

Then, as if on cue, and at the height of pitch between them, Les suddenly collapses into coughing and gasping for breath. Owen is stunned. He expects something to change, some indication that they have reached the end of their performance, but the others rush to help Les down from the table, except for Gail, who remains separate and defiant. "Be dead, old man! Just be dead!"

CHAPTER TWENTY-FIVE

Everyone is deeply concerned about Les, who seems to be in genuine distress, except for Gail, who hasn't moved. After helping him down from the table, the others guide him into a chair, and he collapses backward. His eyes are closed. He might have passed out. "Get him some water," Ronnie urges, and Daniel rushes toward the house.

The rest of the group gathers around Les. His hat has fallen off, and his hair is mussed. Ronnie unbuttons the top of his shirt. They help him sit up to make sure he doesn't fall out of the chair. Daniel returns from the house with a glass of water.

Gail steps forward to take the glass from him. She splashes Les's face and tells him to drink. Les follows her instructions and, after drinking, leans forward. He looks exhausted. There is no doubt he has exerted himself to the limit.

"Keep breathing," Gail instructs. She helps Les sit up so he can breathe more easily. His eyes are open, but he looks dazed. Gail adjusts his oxygen tank.

But the more drastic change is in Gail's tone. "There, there,' she says with great concern, "you're going to be all right." It is as if she is comforting a child. And just a moment before, it seemed she wanted to rip Les apart. Owen doesn't know what to think, but in the next instant he recognizes that Gail has given a demonstration of her fluidity as a warrior, her ability to give herself over to the situation immediately at hand. A moment ago, Les had been the worthy opponent she attacked mercilessly, and now he is the person in great need of her care.

Gail continues to dote on Les as if he were the most important person. "You're just a crazy old goat. You know I love you."

After a few more moments of attending to Les, Gail asks if he would like to go back to the house, and he says he would. When he tries to stand, Daniel and Nate are immediately at his side, helping him up. Les steadies himself, then begins to walk. The rest of the group huddles around him. Ronnie takes control of the oxygen cart, and Jessie collects the big hat and the glass of water. Gail stays close behind Les, and Owen brings up the rear.

They all proceed slowly to the house. Les climbs the stairs one at a time, then enters the door and walks down the hallway to the living area. When he reaches the couch, he is helped into it. Jessie hands him the glass of water, and he drinks. Ronnie gets some pillows from one of the bedrooms and helps him get comfortable. Les at least seems stable. With nothing else to do, the group steps back as they continue to watch him.

Les continues to recover. Finally, he says he wants to go to his room. He stands. Jessie and Nate walk with him. Afterward, they return to sit with the group. A silence has settled.

The moment shifts, however, when Gail suddenly speaks, surprising everyone. "Les is right," she says. She hesitates, letting her words gather everyone's attention. "He is not dead enough to himself, but then none of us are. And it's the thing that matters most." Gail addresses the group. As Owen looks at her, he notices the same fierceness in her eyes as when she was yelling at Les. "We all have to die to the world and the self we know. Otherwise, we are only playing at being warriors. Each of us has to face infinity on our own."

The others have all adjusted themselves to face her.

"We have to consider the fact that, as a group, we are only hindering ourselves. We have become a crutch for each other to avoid facing our greatest challenges." Gail has picked up on Les's line of thinking about his connection with the group. "I think we have to consider breaking up our involvement."

It is Ronnie who immediately reacts to what Gail is saying. "But I couldn't survive on my own!"

Nate backs her up. "None of us could."

Gail doesn't hesitate to respond. "You've never tried. And there are no guarantees. Each of us only has a chance to live our connection."

"But there's been progress," Ronnie says in defense of her position. She is pushing back against Gail. "We're trying. This is hard. You're the one who always says the way to proceed is to not hurry, but not to stop."

Gail takes in what Ronnie has said. "I realize I should speak for myself," she says. "I only want to move forward. My connection with spirit can be the only thing I care about. Like Les, I've been at this for years, and I'm shocked by how much is available and appalled by the power that holds us back. Indolence and laziness are elements of our world, and it is easy to fool yourself. All our effort has to be to disengage from what is bleeding our energy."

"And you think working with the group bleeds your energy?" Daniel asks.

"I have to be open to the possibility," Gail replies. "It can definitely take up my focus."

"But you're the one who said we have to use the group to challenge and motivate us," Nate says, taking up the group's defense.

Gail stands up to the accusation. "I think we have to consider that, for all our effort, we may only be trapped in another doing.

Maybe the group has outlived its usefulness. A warrior has to be ruthless, first and foremost with themselves."

"I agree we have to be better," Daniel interjects into the argument. "We can always do better. But I don't think there is any need to end our involvement."

There is immediate agreement among the others.

Gail is forced to bolster herself. "Like I said, I can only speak for myself. Les has at least broken the pattern. I need to examine my position."

"I don't see why you can't use the group as a challenge," Ronnie says. Her eyes are wide and adamant.

"I can only follow a path with heart," Gail answers. "And right now, I 'm not feeling it."

It is a devastating blow to the group, but after recoiling, Ronnie pushes forward again. "We know we have to be better. We can always be better. And we know each of us is on our own. But the group can be there for support. You're the one always talking about the power of group energy."

Ronnie's tone is defensive. The group is obviously feeling abandoned. Gail takes on the force of their displeasure but remains steadfast, staring into empty space in front of her. A silence develops. Each of the group has retreated to a position.

Daniel is the one to offer something. He speaks as if the words have gathered inside him. "We know things have to change. What if we approached the group differently?"

Gail doesn't respond. It is as if something in her has deflated, already escaped. She doesn't seem willing to replace it. But Daniel has asked a direct question. He deserves an answer. "I don't even know where all of you are at with the material," she says.

Ronnie jumps in. "It means everything to us. It is the world. There's no going back."

Her words have struck a chord. Everyone agrees.

"The books are a call to action," Gail says, picking up on

Ronnie's direction of thinking. "The only way to *power* is in what we do."

Everyone agrees with that as well.

"But the material is huge," Daniel interjects. "The group can be used to push ourselves."

Gail can't deny what he has said.

"We know we have to focus," Nate adds. "We need to work on things."

Daniel sums up their predicament. "What else is there to do? We have to live a life."

The group falls into silence. A magnitude has fallen upon them.

Ronnie directs attention back to Gail. "Do you think you could work with the group if things were different?"

Gail is almost dismissive. "I don't know what I think."

"We could decide on things to work on," Ronnie exclaims, pushing the issue. "We could work together."

Gail reacts against the attempt to draw her in. "I don't even know where all of you are at with this stuff. There's a whole lot more to it than just the flyers. The whole challenge of a warrior is to re-vamp their lives."

The others agree, but act almost offended.

"We know it's huge," Nate responds, a bit defensive. "We've all read the books. We know it's a matter of going forward."

Gail concedes his sentiment, but isn't willing to go any further.

"And the material is divided into *dreaming* and *stalking*. Those are the two topics that everything falls under." Nate has made an effort to push his point; he does understand something about the books.

Gail agrees with him.

"You could lead us in *dreaming*," Ronnie says. "It's what you're focused on." Her attempt to include Gail in the group is blatant, almost desperate.

Gail is being pressed. The focus on her is intense, but she isn't willing to budge. What she says next is more of a deflection. "There isn't much to *dreaming*. It's all in the books. It just takes time to practice."

"But you have experience," Ronnie responds. "We'd listen to you." She then adds. "And it wouldn't interfere with what you're doing. You could guide us."

Gail can't deny the rationale of what has been said.

"It could be a challenge for you," Ronnie concludes.

Yes, it could be a challenge. Gail lets the idea sink in. It obviously has her attention. The idea of a challenge is always what drives a warrior.

"I could be willing to be involved with *dreaming*," she finally offers. "But that's it. You're on your own with *stalking*."

A wave of relief moves through everyone. They couldn't imagine going forward as a group without Gail.

As for *stalking*, the other main area of focus for their practice, it is understood that Les would be best to lead, but he isn't available now.

Owen has watched the group's drama unfold while leaning against the wall at the entrance to the hallway. He had been invited to be part of what was going on with Les, but the group's dynamic remained separate from him. But it has been interesting. A group of warriors struggling to state their positions against the magnitude of what they are facing. It was like currents of energy flowing back and forth. Now that energy has coalesced, it almost isn't a surprise when he feels it turn toward him.

"So where are you at with all this?" Gail then asks, turning to look at him. They all shift their attention. He has become the focus. "Would you be interested in being involved?"

Owen doesn't move. He feels their attention gather.

"You have experience," Ronnie adds.

"You practice *stalking*," Nate says. "You're really into this stuff."

Owen remains motionless. What he does next will determine everything.

"You could give direction," Nate continues.

He waits until a pressure gathers. His answer becomes undeniable. An equilibrium is crossed. "Makes sense."

Elation and relief erupt amongst them.

"We have a group!" Daniel exclaims, throwing up his hands.

Owen remains leaning against the wall. The magnitude of what has happened is overwhelming. He is part of a group. How the hell did that happen?

CHAPTER TWENTY-SIX

"We should get started!" Nate exclaims after the group's initial enthusiasm settles. "We're all here anyway. We might as well do something."

Everyone agrees.

With his decision to join the group made, Owen steps forward. They make space for him, and he sits at the end of the couch next to Nate.

Gail takes the lead. It feels like her natural place.

"As the two main areas of focus for the practice, *dreaming* and *stalking* are like the two sides of a coin. *Dreaming* deals directly with the second attention, the expanded facet of awareness, while *stalking* deals with the first attention, the world of everyday life."

"It's where we get our energy," Nate injects. "The energy from *stalking* is used for *dreaming*."

"Absolutely," Gail answers. "The energy gained is redirected toward exploring the second attention."

They all take in what she has said. It's big stuff.

"And that's about it," Gail then says, throwing up her arms. "*Dreaming* is simple."

They all know she is joking. The scope of *dreaming* is huge. But the concepts and techniques are fairly basic. Still, they want Gail to talk more. The goal is to have a shared understanding.

"*Dreaming* is the art of attention," Gail says, then starts again. "The same attention used to hold the ordinary world together. In *dreaming* we focus our attention on a different facet of awareness, the second attention, an awareness available to everyone, but only as warriors are we conscious of it and choose to explore it. The ancient practitioners discovered that during sleep, the assemblage point relaxes its position and shifts naturally. The focus of dreaming is to extend that natural shift and fixate the assemblage point on new positions."

The group reacts with excitement at being reminded of the concepts and possibilities of *dreaming*. They decide they want to start the practice as soon as possible. The question then is whether they are all able to stay the night. None of them has any plans. When Les called the meeting, they didn't know how long it would take, so they planned to stay a while. So, they can start practicing *dreaming* tonight!

The attention then turns back to Gail for further comment and review. She smiles, appreciating their willingness, but hesitates, saying it might be best to discuss *dreaming* when they are ready to practice, so that it's fresh in their minds.

The others understand.

But what are they going to do for now? It's not even noon. They should do something. The obvious idea is to do something with *stalking*. All eyes turn to Owen.

Owen takes a deep breath. He knew the focus would be on him eventually; he just didn't think it would be so soon.

Gail has taken the lead in discussing a few preliminaries of *dreaming,* and he decides to follow her lead in dealing with *stalking*. The idea is to give the group a shared understanding.

Owen takes a moment to focus. Stalking is a huge topic, but there are some basics. What makes it easier is that he is sure they have read it all before in the books.

"*Stalking* is a systematic approach to dealing with the everyday world. It is a strategy for defeating self-importance which requires almost all of our available energy to be used to maintain our notions of ourselves and everything around us."

He looks around to see everyone watching him intently.

"So *stalking* is a strategy for gaining and redeploying energy…"

"And recapitulation is the best technique for freeing up energy," Nate suddenly interjects. "It's what you practice."

Owen nods. Yes, recapitulation is the most expedient way to free up energy.

"So we should do recapitulation," Daniel states.

Owen laughs. They're getting ahead of themselves. Recapitulation isn't so simple. The obvious obstacle is that they don't have crates, which are essential to the practice.

"Well, we could make them," Daniels says, undeterred.

Yes, they could make them, but where would they get the material?

It's decided there's a home improvement store not far.

"OK. But where would you put them?"

Daniel is quick to answer. "In the garage, I'm sure Les wouldn't mind. We'd have to move his car."

All eyes shift to Gail. She agrees Les wouldn't mind. She'd be sure to ask him.

The basic obstacles to proceeding with recapitulation have been eliminated. Their attention turns back to Owen. He's not sure they know all they're getting into. "That's a bunch of crates to build."

They understand. If recapitulation is essential to their practice, they'll have to build them anyway. They might as well get started.

Owen continues to hesitate, but can't think of a good reason not to go forward.

"Yeah, I guess so."

Once again, elation washes through the group.

"Let's have a crate-building party!" Daniel exclaims.

They all stand, ready to begin. After another moment, they move as a group to the garage.

Nate and Jessie both have building experience. Les has some basic tools in the garage.

The crates are simple to make, just four walls big enough for someone to sit inside, a door, and a lattice top for ventilation.

A materials list is put together. Dan then jumps in Nate's truck along with Jessie, and they're off.

Gail, Ronnie, and Owen move to the kitchen and begin getting something ready to eat. Suddenly, Les appears from the hallway, looking a bit disheveled and still out of sorts. He absently walks to the refrigerator, pulls out a carton of juice, and pours a glass. Gail takes the opportunity to inform him of their plans. Les lazily lifts a hand above his head, telling her to do whatever they want, and wanders back toward his bedroom. Gail says she will bring him some lunch when it is ready.

When the guys return, and after a quick bite to eat, the crate building begins. Sheets of plywood are spread out on the driveway, and some overturned milk crates from the garage are used as sawhorses. The guys get to work sawing and screwing things together. The women decide to have fun and break into a cheerleading routine. Soon, four crates are built. Both Owen and Gail have crates at home, so they don't need one. Folding chairs from inside the house can be brought for them.

The group stands back, admiring the results of their effort

"So we going to give them a try?" Daniel asks.

Everyone is willing. There is no reason not to. Even Owen

hardly hesitates. The whole thing of recapitulation has taken on a momentum of its own.

With Les's car out of the way and some of the other items in the garage moved aside, there is plenty of room to place the crates with some space between them. It is then time to outline the details of what they plan to do. The others stand facing him.

"The ancient practitioners discovered that every encounter we have with another person that involves emotion is an exchange of energy. With that as their understanding, they devised a way to reclaim both the energy expended in the encounter and expel the energy left in them."

Owen looks at each of them to be sure they are following.

"The procedure is quite simple, actually. The key is breath. For a warrior, breath is magical. In the beginning phase of recapitulation, start with the first encounter that comes to mind. With your chin on your shoulder, slowly inhale in an arc to your left shoulder. This retrieves all the energy you expended in the event. Then repeat the arc in the other direction while slowly exhaling. This ejects the filaments of energy left in you by the other person. Continue the process until you feel you have captured and released all the available energy. This is called 'fanning the event'. After completing it, move on to the next event that comes to mind."

Owen lets his words sink in. When he says no more, the others realize he has finished his instruction.

"Sounds easy enough," Nate says.

Owen says it is at least simple. The ancient practitioners were endlessly pragmatic.

With nothing else needed, they all move into the garage and enter their crates. Owen waits until everyone is settled, then presses the button, and the door closes to complete darkness.

. . .

After nearly an hour, Owen raises the garage door. The group emerges from their crates and stands in the driveway, letting their eyes adjust to the light.

"Well, that was sure something," Daniel offers.

They all agree they can sense the potential.

"How long we supposed to stay in there?"

Owen says for as long as they can. The amount of energy available is unlimited.

"Remember, in the books, people could stay in their crates for up to six hours at a time, for weeks, months, and even years. The goal is to completely remake yourself. Relieved of the debilitating effects of past experience, a warrior can become as light as air."

Everyone is greatly impressed. The potential of human beings is truly unfathomable.

The group then returns to the house. Some of them get something to eat, so they all gather in the kitchen.

Nate has a sudden idea.

"Hey, we should go through the books again, as a group."

Everyone likes the idea. It will give them a chance to better understand the material. Reading the books together will give them a chance to discuss the material and motivate them to keep reading.

They decide to start with the first book in the series and try to have it read for the next time they meet.

The day is moving on toward evening. They have nothing else to do. It is decided they should spend some time with *dreaming*. It is still too early to go to bed, but Gail can talk more about *dreaming* in preparation. They all take seats in the greater area. Gail sits in a chair facing everyone.

"*Dreaming* is the practical way of putting ordinary dreams to use. It is the direct involvement with the second attention. The goal of *dreaming* is to impart order to the non-ordinary world of dreams. *Dreaming* is the art of displacing the assemblage point at will from its habitual position in order to enhance and enlarge the scope of what can be perceived."

She looks to see that everyone is with her, then continues.

"We have to break the barrier that prevents us from bringing dreams to our conscious attention. The second attention is like a muscle that has atrophied from nonuse."

Gail is struggling to find words to communicate. She gazes into the space above her, choosing her words carefully.

"*Dreaming* is like walking and talking. It took a great amount of effort for us as children to learn to walk and talk, but they were within our ability. The most important thing is to believe it is possible."

Gail pauses to let her words sink in.

"The first step in activating the second attention in our dreams is to fixate our attention on a specific item. It is the first step in gaining control. The ancient practitioners suggested we look for our hands because they are something familiar and always available."

"Gail has found her hands!" Ronnie suddenly blurts.

A shock of incredulity moves through the group. Ronnie sits with her hands to her face, mortified by her outburst, as if she couldn't help herself, as if she just revealed a great secret.

Everyone wants to know if it is true. Gail admits that it is.

"How come you never said anything?" Jessie asks in a tone of recrimination.

Gail hesitates. "Obviously, I told someone. I just didn't know where you all were at with this stuff."

The focus stays on her. The group continues to be amazed.

"Hey, I've been at this a while," Gails says. "You'd think I'd come up with something." Her tone is light, as if her attempt is to be joking. But she knows what she has said is serious. "And I've only been able to find my hands a couple of times. I'm just getting started."

The group remains greatly impressed. What Gail has said is

monumental in advancing something theoretical into something that can actually happen.

Everyone waits to see what comes next, but Gail has nothing more to add. She says she has given them a basic understanding of dreaming, and the only thing left for them is to practice. In an attempt at levity, they joke that it's too early to go to bed. But everyone wants to try dreaming. They all eventually retreat to different rooms and parts of the house, ready for sleep.

After waking up the next morning, they all gather to meet in the kitchen and share breakfast. None of them has anything interesting to report as a result of their *dreaming* last night. Gail laughs.

"It takes time. Remember, it took some warriors years to find their hands. The key is persistence. The mind and all its rational defenses can't cope with persistence. And treat your dreaming as entertainment. Don't pressure yourself. Dreaming has to be done with integrity and seriousness, but in the midst of laughter and with the confidence of someone who doesn't have a worry in the world."

That works for everyone. They know they are just getting started.

After breakfast, it is suggested they spend some time gazing in the backyard. There aren't enough posts for everyone, so some sit in patio chairs. The sun is only partially available, but they do their best. Afterward, they have another session of recapitulation. After that, lunch is available, and then everyone needs to return home. They agree to meet the following weekend. They all commit to reading the first book. Spirits are high. They leave each other in a feeling of shared adventure.

CHAPTER TWENTY-SEVEN

When the weekend comes, the group looks forward to getting together. It isn't until Friday evening that they can all meet at the house after their workweek. The conversation is light and almost festive, and it isn't until later that they refocus on the material. With the night ahead, another session of dreaming is available. They talk in general terms about the second attention's amazing magnitude and the availability of a whole new area of awareness to explore, then retreat to different areas of the house to retire for the night, going to sleep with the focus of looking for their hands in their dreams.

In the morning, they are all up early and have another session of gazing. Afterward, they have breakfast, then move on to practice recapitulation again. They stay as long as they can in their crates. When Owen senses the group has had enough, he calls the session by opening the garage door. It's important that as a group, they don't force the issue. Everything in a warrior's world is done gradually but with consistent effort. They are in it for the long haul.

After lunch, the group decides to gather outside in the nice weather and sit on the patio, discussing the first book in the

Carlos series. They all have to laugh. Carlos, the anthropology student, thought his involvement with don Juan was a scientific study of the use of hallucinogenic plants in South American indigenous culture. But what he entered was a whole new world. The situations he got himself involved in were absolutely hilarious. Carlos tried to approach his experiences from a rational perspective. But what he encountered shattered those notions and catapulted him into experiences he could never have imagined. And having don Juan as his guide not only supplied Carlos with what he considered to be outrageous concepts that confronted his very notion of reality, but also supplied a different way of thinking that challenged his very idea of what it meant to be alive.

What captures the group's attention is that Carlos, the narrator, relates his experiences and how they affect him, yet he really has no idea of the underlying foundation of what is going on. Only in later books is the nature of don Juan's world revealed, and what his motives were in involving Carlos and dealing with him the way he did. It presents a massive, unimaginable view of the world and reality, staggering in its scope and implications. The hilarity of the books is that Carlos struggles with every fiber of his being to hold on to his notions and rationale for his understanding of the world, yet don Juan continues to prove to him with his own expansive reasoning and perpetrated actions that reveal a view of the world far beyond what Carlos has ever encountered, that there is little doubt his inherited interpretation of reality is severely limited.

The group's discussion of the books becomes a frolic and continues with great intrigue and a strong desire to express not only understanding and impressions, but absolute awe at what they have encountered and what it means to them, and what they feel has been made available. Their lives have changed. The scope of the material is huge. They no longer have any idea where their lives are leading them. All they can follow is a path with heart. But just having people as intrigued as they are is a great start. Working with a group is a definite advantage.

When it is time to sleep, they all prepare for another attempt at finding their hands in their dreams, with the understanding that they can't expect any immediate success. The goal is simply to focus on the possibility that, as the second attention, another facet of awareness is available to them. Gail reminds them that engaging the second attention requires a boost of energy they don't necessarily have, but they are gaining by redeploying the energy used to maintain the fixation of the first attention in their everyday life. It is then a matter of intending that energy in a new direction. It takes time and is a process of degrees, but as their energy is disengaged from self-importance and from an emphasis on self-reflection as the source for interpreting the world, changes will occur and be noticeable. As that develops, they need to continue their *dreaming* in a spirit of entertainment. What else do they have to do? It is better than just going to bed with nothing in mind. They might as well have fun with it.

In the morning, the day starts with what will become a weekend routine. They practice gazing, have breakfast, have a recapitulation session they intend to make longer each time, take time to eat a bite before discussing the next book in the series, and then retire for the night with another focus on *dreaming*. In the morning, most of them have to get up early, some well before daylight, to get back to their everyday lives. They look forward to seeing each other again next Friday.

Their time getting together continues. But the gap between their meetings can seem large. The elements of their daily world can easily dominate them, and their focus on the material easily overwhelmed. They know this is the challenge of the first attention, and their daily world is where they battle to gain power, but they just aren't fully capable yet and are easily distracted. There is also the challenge of scheduling. They can't all make it every weekend, and because of the distance they need to travel, they can't always stay the full weekend. Just being a part of the group is helpful in their personal practice, but it can feel like it isn't always enough.

Owen proposes a solution, at least in theory. It might be far-fetched and surely is a thing of the future but it is worth considering. It is how don Juan's party, working with his benefactor, the nagual Julian, solved the same issue. They all lived together and worked together in a business that the nagual Julian created. It gave them unlimited access to each other, and they were free to be completely absorbed, individually and collectively, in the life and focus of being a warrior. Owen suggests they consider starting a business together. None of them is committed to long-term careers, so it wouldn't be much to shift away from the work they are doing now. He admits that part of his interest is that, since the dissolution of his business with his partners, he has had enough money not to be concerned with making a living, but that time will end; he needs to think about his next step. If they are serious about pursuing their practice as a group and see working together as a viable next step, he would be willing to explore some options and let them know what he comes up with. The others see the value and agree it is something to look into.

It soon becomes obvious that the group is losing energy. It is in part, understandable after their strong start. A long continuation requires a different kind of energy and focus. They do their best. Working with the material is difficult. The concerns of the daily world are relentless. The power of the first attention is truly formidable.

It is no surprise when word reaches the group that Jessie is dropping out. Jessie hadn't been around much lately, and it was difficult for him because he had to travel the farthest to the house. He had a steady job and hadn't been putting in much effort on his own. Still, it is disappointing. Everyone liked Jessie.

He was a good guy, earnest and sincere. They hope for the best for him. It confirms the difficulty they face.

The real blow to the group, however, is learning that Nate is leaving. He hadn't been coming around as much either, and it was understood that he and Ronnie, as a couple, were going through a tough time on top of everything else. There is hope that Nate's departure might be temporary. Still, it is hard to think that Nate might be dropping out, because he really did seem to be into working with the material. He had enthusiasm and a lively energy, and maybe even some natural talent. He had also experienced things that should have kept him motivated. Les is irreverent enough to make the crass statement that he suspected Nate was only hanging around to stay in Ronnie's pants. But the group still feels the shock of losing someone they felt close to.

So, when Owen gets an email from Nate asking to meet, he is surprised but pleased, and when he mentions it to Gail and Les, they are only pleased as well. Nate is at least keeping in contact with the group. It does seem a little odd that Owen would be the person he would ask to meet, but they had some remarkable encounters and always had a good relationship. Of course, Owen will meet him, though again he is surprised when Nate emails back to suggest they meet at the same café where the group pulled their prank on him. There are surely places that are closer to them, but the cafe is a place they are both familiar with. The thought does run through Owen's mind that maybe the group is setting him up again for something because the idea of Nate leaving the group would surely be serious enough to guarantee that he would agree to meet with him. But meeting at the same location seems way too obvious for the group if they were planning on pulling something. To be sure, Owen decides to ask Les directly if something is up, because if something is going on, Les would surely be in the middle of it. Les assures him that nothing is happening and is openly flattered that Owen would be so suspicious.

Owen spends some time thinking about how he wants to approach his meeting with Nate. It is not his place to intervene and try to convince him to return. But he is not interested in being passive either. This opportunity has presented itself. He is reminded of the story of don Juan and his grandson, when don Juan made a play to present his knowledge to his grandson by having Carlos buy tequila for him and some friends as a chance to gather them for a conversation. Don Juan had no luck in interesting his grandson, as suspected, but said it was important to insist, "even though we know what we're doing is useless. But we must first know that our acts are useless, and yet we must proceed as if we didn't know it. That's a warrior's controlled folly." That's the way Owen feels about meeting with Nate. He can't care in the least about the result. The encounter has to be his bid for power. The challenge is to do his best, open himself to the designs of spirit, and follow his connection.

CHAPTER TWENTY-EIGHT

When the time comes to meet Nate, Owen arrives a little early, as always. Immediately, the eatery feels different: smaller than he remembered and a bit dull and ordinary. It is not peak business hours, but it wasn't when he was here before; there is hardly anyone in the place. To avoid recognition if he is seen by the same manager who chased them out, he wears a ball cap, believing it is enough of a disguise. Owen is aware of how easily details escape people, and sure enough, when the same manager is in the area, he doesn't give him a second glance. Then, as a not-doing, Owen orders the same sickly-sweet fruit drink he ordered for himself and the two women the first time he was here. Every time he takes a sip, he will be reminded of the craziness of what the group put him through. It will be a good point of reference for keeping his focus on controlled folly when dealing with Nate. Just for kicks, he sits at the same table where he, Nate, and the two women sat before.

It isn't long before Nate walks through the front door, and right away, there is a difference about him; he seems rough. His hair is longer than Owen remembers and a bit mussed, and there is a heaviness to his demeanor instead of his usual energetic bounce. Over jeans, he wears a light blue and gray plaid shirt with sleeves rolled up, open in front over a dark-colored T-shirt.

As he gets closer, Nate looks even worse. Dark circles under his eyes and a gaunt face make him look even worse. Owen's surprise makes him laugh, then exclaim, "What the hell?"

When he reaches the table, Nate slides into the chair across from him and lowers his head. He shakes it in amazement. When he looks up, he smiles in an effort to be cordial. "Thanks for coming."

Owen acknowledges the gesture with a nod, but remains focused on his shock at Nate's condition. He makes an effort to express his concern. "So what's going on?"

Nate looks down again. "I don't know," he says, and continues to shake his head.

Owen is direct in his reaction. "You look rough as hell."

Yet in the next instant, Owen experiences a very different response to Nate's condition. It is a bodily reaction, like a jolt. He suddenly remembers how Ronnie looked when he first met her. She had the same look of dishevelment; the same tone of despair, used to disarm and draw him in. And they are in the same place at the same table! The volume of coincidence suddenly piles up on him until he instinctively looks around but doesn't see anyone, and for the moment dismisses his suspicion. In the next moment, as a way to get Nate talking, he asks, "You OK?"

Nate leans forward over his arms crossed on the table. "I'm a mess," he admits, lowering his head and shaking it again. His look of amazement seems to have deteriorated into being overwhelmed and maybe even further into despair. "This sucks."

Owen is a bit unnerved and laughs. "You look like someone beat you up." He is reaching for a way to lighten the mood between them.

Owen also makes an effort to stay aware of what is happening around him. The similarity between Nate's appearance and demeanor and his experience with Ronnie in this place remains striking. He's not about to let his guard down.

What he really needs is for Nate to explain himself. It's his way of controlling the battlefield. He needs to gauge Nate's response. "So how much of this has to do with Ronnie?" he asks, forcing the issue, almost to the point of being affronting. He knows from what the others have told him that Nate's relationship with Ronnie is a factor in his leaving.

Nate reacts as if he has been punched in the chest. "Ah geez," he says, slumping back in his chair. A pained expression crosses his face. Then, in the next instant, he seems to follow the recoil of the blow forward and leans back over his arms. "This sucks. It really does."

Nate's reaction appears genuine. He doesn't believe Nate could be capable of that kind of acting. Owen still wonders if anything could be brewing behind the scenes, but refuses to be trapped in any suspicion. He feels for Nate. Great forces of emotion seem to be surging inside him. Owen has felt the pain of heartbreak before. But he isn't going to be dominated by any force of sympathy. There isn't much he can say. "Sorry to hear that."

Nate remains in the throes of misery. What is most telling is the grimace on his face. Words push out of him. "I mean, we've been together almost two years. Something like that doesn't just end. We were good together. I was in love with that girl!"

Owen is surprised that Nate is so forthcoming. He has mostly been in the dark about Nate and Ronnie; he wasn't even sure they were a couple until he heard they were separating. He knew they hung out a lot and lived close to each other, and that was all he needed to know. He feels the need to ask something to keep the dynamic going.

"So you broke up?"

Nate's response is to push back in his chair again. "I don't know. Nothing makes sense." He is uncomfortable talking about

Ronnie, but the issue dominates him. "She's just so damn into the books." Nate catches himself. "I mean, I'm into the books too, but there can be other things, right? I mean, you can be with someone while being involved with the material."

Owen agrees with him, though he doesn't know to what extent. What has mostly caught his attention, however, is Nate saying he is still into the books; it makes him think there might still be a future.

"I mean, there are instances of warriors being a couple," Nate says, adding weight to his argument. "I just don't think it has to be all or nothing. I mean, we're still human beings."

Nate is looking to him for support, but Owen doesn't have much to offer. Yes, it is true; there were references to warriors being romantically involved in the books, but not many. Romantic interest definitely fades as a warrior develops a deeper understanding of knowledge. But being in love wasn't banned or anything.

"Maybe at some point, things between us would have changed," Nate says. The pain in his face and voice is evident. "But I don't think there's any need to force the issue. There was a lot of good between us. We were good together."

Nate seems to want to convince him, and it's not what Owen is here for. He wants to keep the conversation focused on the core issue of why they are meeting. "So is that why you're leaving the group?"

Nate's emotions seem to rush in a new direction, and he leans to one side as if being pushed. His pained expression remains the same. "Naw," he says, looking away. "I'm not leaving. I believe in this stuff too much. It makes too much sense. I just need a break."

Owen is surprised at what he is hearing. The impression he got was that Nate was quitting.

"And I can't blame Ronnie," Nate continues. He then tries to explain. "It's not her fault. I need to be clear about that. I mean, this thing with Ronnie has really screwed me around, but I take full responsibility. That's why I wanted to meet with you. I know I have to fully commit to the material, but I'm just not in that space right now."

Owen doesn't know whether there is a right space, but he can see Nate's point. On the surface, Nate makes sense.

"And there are plenty of examples in the books, right?" Nate continues. He seems to be on a roll, presenting his case. "I mean, it seems like what every warrior goes through. Carlos went through it, and so did don Juan. They both walked away from the practice for a while. You have to walk away to know it is something you really want."

What Nate is saying again has an element of truth. Both don Juan and Carlos, as apprentices, stepped back from the material before fully crossing the line and fully committing to the path, but there is a big difference between Nate and the warriors he is referring to. The awareness develops until Owen is clear about what he is saying. "But remember, Carlos and don Juan had no choice but to return because they were already hooked by *power* through their involvement with a nagual. They just needed time to realize it. But you haven't come to the material through being hooked, so there is no guarantee you will come back."

Nate winces at having a hole poked in his argument. "But this stuff is so powerful. You can't ignore it. It explains the world. It's worthy of a life. To just walk away would be absurd!"

Owen understands but doesn't think Nate is considering the full picture. "But without being hooked, you'll be vulnerable to the power of the everyday world," he says, continuing in the direction he started. "And it's nothing to take lightly. Remember the flyer's mind and its ability to convince itself? You'll have no shields, nothing to protect yourself. You will get caught up in the doings of everyday life." Owen feels the strength of his reaction and pushes to make his point. "You could be setting yourself up." He then thinks of something that strengthens his argument.

"Remember, spirit travels in a straight line and doesn't circle back for anyone."

Nate sits back in his chair with his eyes lowered, taking in the brunt of what Owen has presented.

Owen's interest is to keep up the pressure. He realizes this might be his one chance to make an impression. He wants to use everything available and decides to use Nate's own words against him by referring to something Nate said during their initial interview. "So what does your death say about all this?" he asks. "I thought you were using death as an advisor?"

It's another strong blow that strikes Nate squarely, causing him to shift uneasily in his chair.

"Remember, we are all on our way to dying," Owen states and smiles, pushing his point hard. "There are no survivors. Death is the great equalizer."

Nate seems pinned down by the weight of his own words, used against him. Owen then has a choice about how to proceed. He is reminded again of the story of don Juan and his grandson, and of how, when you like someone, you should insist properly even when you know it is useless. Owen doesn't know if it is useless, but he can't care. The challenge is his. His feeling is still that this is his last chance to impress upon Nate what he is really up against, and Owen is willing to be ruthless.

"Hey, you're a young guy," Owen says, sensing an angle to pursue. He decides to be light and jovial. "You'll find another girlfriend." Owen feels a direction opening. "You'll get wrapped up in your jobs. You'll be making money, probably save up, and buy a new truck. Maybe you'll get more involved with your music." He remembers Nate telling him that one of the things he really wanted to do was become a musician. "Your involvement with the material will begin to fade." An alternative scenario is emerging, and he believes it is more likely. "At some point, this will all seem like a crazy dream. You will look back and remember a time when you got involved with some strange people, thinking some wild stuff. You can even blame it on being under the spell of a woman. Heck, you might even think of us as some crazy cult you almost got caught up with." It's a funny image that makes him laugh.

Nate doesn't even smile. He is taking the full force of Owen's pressure.

Owen continues pursuing his opportunity. He has Nate cornered and wants to make an impression. Nate is at a crossroads. If he is going to make a decision, he might as well have everything in front of him. "Don't think you have a lot of time, Nate. Remember, you can only choose once. A warrior treats everything as a battle for his life. Because you're on the menu, dude. It's the flyer's mind that is licking its chops."

Owen laughs again at his choice of words. He realizes he is being a bit ridiculous, but he is having fun with it.

"Look closely at the world," he says, continuing to press forward. "Stare into the lives of those around you. See the madness. Look beneath the surface. There are no survivors. You have only one life to live. You know you're connected to spirit, so you have to find a way to live that connection."

When Owen finishes, Nate is unable to lift his head.

Owen has nothing more to say. He has reached the end. He has done his best. In response to his conclusion, he stands, recognizing that this might be the last time he will ever see Nate. His involvement with Nate has benefited him. They have shared warrior gestures. For that, he is grateful. He only wishes good for Nate and feels the need to tell him. "From my warrior's spirit, I wish you well."

Owen turns to leave.

Something else comes to him, however, from his belief that he could never see Nate again, and from his commitment to folly as a warrior's only relief from the relentless pursuit of infinity; there is the feeling of unfinished business, something left dangling. The idea offers a tone of lightness, even a chance for humor, something to leave Nate with, but also the chance to satisfy his curiosity. "So…what was all that yelling about the first time we met?"

Nate is surprised. His reaction is to sit back in his chair. He remains looking down. It takes him a moment to shift his focus, but he seems obligated. He takes a deep breath.

"Something Les had me do."

Owen laughs. It is about what he expected, but there is still something more. Again, motivated by his understanding that this could be the last time he will ever see Nate, he wants to push the issue all the way through.

"So what was the point?"

Nate slumps back in his chair. He seems devastated and completely exhausted. He barely seems able to muster the energy to respond.

"He said if I chased you away, I wouldn't have to do the round." There it is! The picture is complete! Laughter rolls from him.

It seems the perfect place to end their encounter. Owen wishes Nate well and would like to see him again, but against the backdrop of infinity, it can't matter in the least. Owen turns again and walks out of the restaurant.

CHAPTER TWENTY-NINE

Returning to the house, everyone is eager to hear about his meeting with Nate. Owen gives his account, making sure everyone knows that Nate doesn't consider himself to have quit the group; he's just taking a break. Ronnie is especially anxious to hear about the meeting and is clearly affected by their breakup as well. The others seem concerned but offer little comment beyond wishing Nate the best. It is understood that Nate is on his own.

But Nate's loss again underscores the power of what they are up against when working with the material. It clarifies their challenges. They must stay clear in their focus. Any progress they make with the material must be repeated to the point of exhaustion before their lives fully open to it. The mind and all its rational defenses cannot cope with persistence. The two basic qualities warriors must cultivate are sustained effort and unbending intent. If one is to succeed at anything, success must come gently, with great effort but without stress or obsession.

They believe they are on the right path and continue to expand their understanding of the books while keeping up with their practice. Their focus is on impeccability, gaining energy, and living a disciplined life. But the group can't be a way to remove themselves from the world. They need to use it properly, as the world is still their hunting ground. They come across a section in the books in which Don Juan admonishes Carlos for his vanity in believing that he lives in two worlds and can choose. "The only world available to you is the world of men, and that world you cannot choose to leave."

A nice surprise for the group has been the continuing return of Les. After time away, and then time when he seemed to remain on the fringe, he has come to recognize more and more the value of the group. But his relationship with the group is different from before. He enjoys the interaction and needs it to boost his own effort. Les is fine with not being the leader. Yet the group does decide they have a special position for him, one that only he is eminently qualified for, a job of utmost importance to the survival of the group because they know that proceeding forward with lightness and play is their best strategy against the immensity of what so easily promotes heaviness and lethargy and self-reflection and indulgence. The only way to counteract the devastating effect of the warrior's world is to laugh at it. So, they promote Les to chief folly maker and even have a ceremony of dedication that results in Les being presented with a crown of colored feathers. Les accepts their designation with all the false humility he can muster. Everyone laughs and has a great time.

Otherwise, the group stays focused on their work. Owen has continued living almost full-time at the house, and Daniel has found ways to spend more time there as well. After separating from Nate, Ronnie at first had trouble getting a vehicle, but she finally did. Yet the drive out to the house remained a challenge because of her work schedule. Gail found driving back and forth to work from Les's house too much, so she decided to stay home more. As a result, Ronnie moved in with her, and the two have become an inseparable team. Their focus has remained on *dreaming* as their natural proclivity, and they have continued to make progress, but without any major breakthroughs. The guys have stayed focused on working with the recapitulation crates, but they have continued to work on *dreaming*, while the women have kept up with their *stalking*. For his sake, Owen feels his greatest progress with the material has been the steady freeing up of his energy, and as evidence, he has noticed a lightness in his overall demeanor and a great increase in the vividness of his dreams. Each night, he goes to sleep with the assignment of finding his hands, and he hasn't, but the scope and clarity of his dreams have him waking in amazement.

Still, the situation with the group is not ideal; they all agree there is much more they could do together, and meeting only on weekends is far from optimal. The biggest obstacle has continued to be the need to make a living, and it is becoming an urgent issue for Owen; there just isn't much time left before he runs out of money. He could sell his house if he is going to continue living with Les, but he is not convinced he wants the arrangement to be permanent. The sale of his house would not make all that much money anyway, after all the expenses incurred and the mortgage paid off. He could rent out the house, but the idea of renters and all that entails is hardly appealing. What he really needs is a steady source of income. He has enjoyed having so much time to dedicate to the material, outside of the need to make a living, but knows that extending into the world is also a direction needed for his practice. And when he goes out into the world, he would like to create a good opportunity. He continues to think of don Juan's situation with his teacher, the house where all the members of his party lived and worked together in the nagual Julian's business.

The best opportunity to work with the material and make a living still seems to be starting a business. From that thinking comes the idea of sales. Owen presents his thinking to the group. The idea of sales would satisfy the group's needs on a couple of levels. It wouldn't require much money if they weren't purchasing product to sell. And the challenges of sales can be intense on a personal level. Nothing is as challenging as sales because it involves dealing with people. Sales can be an absolute assault on one's self-importance and a great opportunity for stalking oneself. It would offer the challenge of overcoming natural shyness by forcing them to interact with people and not on their own terms, as the safety of a storefront would offer. Owen reminds the group of don Juan, who, in the books, says that people are the most ruthless and relentless of adversaries, and that, compared to dealing with people, facing infinity is a cinch, not the other way around, as one would expect.

So, when Gail comes to him saying she has found a building she wants him to look at for a potential site for their business, Owen is surprised. He hadn't even thought of a building. The whole appeal of sales is that they wouldn't need the expense of a physical location. But Gail has a different idea. If they decided to represent products, they would need storage and distribution, and maybe a small storefront to maintain direct contact with customers. And the place she wants them to look at is perfect for that. It is small and inexpensive, but in a great location in the town where she already works. And the idea of having a place to work from would also force them to come together and actively do the business. It would remove the distractions inherent in working from home. Owen still isn't interested in the cost of inventory, but is mostly pleased that Gail is at least showing an interest in what he has been proposing. If only to encourage her, he's willing to check out a building. It is decided that Les will go along as well; they can all use a little outing. Owen and Les will meet Gail on her lunch break.

The next day, Les and Owen are on their way to Plainfield. The appointment is for one o'clock. It is a nice, sunny day, a bit cool, with the feeling of the change of seasons in the air. Les is in good spirits and is looking forward to their small adventure. They have packed his oxygen tank, though with the low humidity, he doubts he will need it. Their conversation is light and focuses on the passing landscape. Les comments on the suburban growth and all the changes that have taken place over the past several years.

Owen has never been to Plainfield and is looking forward to visiting a new town to check out a possible location for starting a business. He asks Les a few general questions about Plainfield and receives general answers. Les guesses the population to be around ten thousand and notes that, like most towns in the area, it grew up as the center of an agriculture-based community.

After reaching Plainfield, Les directs him to a parking lot on the edge of town. After leaving the vehicle, they walk to a small park to find a bench to sit on and wait for Gail. Owen's first impression is that Plainfield is a good-sized town; he can see two-story buildings that line Main Street beyond where they are sitting.

Les and Owen both enjoy sitting and watching people pass by. It is lunch hour, and there is plenty of activity. A woman walking her three dogs is completely engrossed in keeping the leashes untangled and in keeping her packages from dropping.

Gail soon walks up and greets them. She is bright and cheery as usual and looks very professional in her chocolatier uniform: a brown dress with white buttons down the center and a white-winged collar. She is the manager of a candy company. Owen would like to see where she works, and she promises to show him later.

Leaving the bench, they step onto the sidewalk and turn toward downtown. As they enter the main business district, buildings crowd the street, and parking meters staggered along the curb further narrow the sidewalk, making it impossible to walk three abreast. Gail links her arm in Les's and walks ahead, and Owen is fine following behind. What he is most interested in is deciding whether the town would be a good place to start a business. Is there enough population for retail? Is there a good diversity of businesses? Are there enough other businesses that they could blend in without being conspicuous? Owen has always been leery of small towns and their fishbowl atmospheres, and at first glance, Plainfield is encouraging because it isn't as small as he thought it might be. From what he can see, Main Street stretches a good way ahead of them and is lined on both sides with shops and businesses. Owen doesn't notice any vacancies. He is encouraged to see that the old stone building fronts look well cared for, and the sidewalks are clean and look updated. There is a nice, balanced feel to Plainfield, a balance of old-time small-town flavor and an obvious effort to upgrade and progress.

As they cross a side street, Owen looks down the block and sees that the business district extends beyond Main Street; he notices what appear to be office buildings or professional buildings a block over. It means the town is more than just shopkeepers. It is a sign of a strong tax base and an opportunity for broad-based networking. The town has an upbeat energy and seems to be bustling. Owen realizes that it is still lunchtime and that the people walking around aren't a true indication of overall activity, but at least something is happening.

A jarring collision suddenly jolts him!

He has collided with someone!

As Owen regains his balance, he looks down and is even further shocked to see a woman bent over, hanging onto a parking meter! "Oh gosh!" he exclaims, immediately reaching to help.

But the woman whips herself upright and confronts him with a sneering and angry face. "What the hell is wrong with you?" she nearly spits at him. "You trying to kill me?"

Owen's reaction is to jerk back in astonishment and immediately apologize. But the woman is having none of it.

"You frickin' jerk," she hisses at him through glaring and

squinted eyes, red lipstick, and exaggerated makeup. "You think you own the place? You think you can just run people over?"

Owen assures her that he doesn't think anything of the kind, but the woman races on in her rant.

"Why don't you look where you're going, you big galoot." Owen again is quick to apologize. "Not everyone is as big as an ox, you know," the woman hurls at him. "You could have killed me!" Owen assures her again that it wasn't his intent.

He suddenly finds himself in a nasty situation. What is appalling is not only the woman's furious tone but also the sight of what is in front of him. The woman is hideous-looking, with wildly messy hair, a dirty face, and a nasty sneer. Her clothes are old and torn; she is obviously a street person. His reaction is to look to Gail and Les for support, but all he sees are their backs as they walk away, seemingly unaware.

"Where are you going?" the woman accuses, catching him looking beyond her. "You gonna run off?" She even grabs him by his shirt at his waist and holds on with both hands. "You're not going anywhere."

The woman is now attached to him! Owen assures her that he isn't going anywhere, but the woman doesn't relax her grip. He fights back a rising panic. But his next instinct is to try to calm her. "Now take it easy."

But the woman immediately takes offense. "Don't tell me what to do," she says, staring up at him. "You're the asshole who ran me over!"

Owen is aware of another issue; people around him have stopped and are looking at him. The situation is escalating. He finds himself struggling against a rising sense of embarrassment. The back of his neck tingles and feels electric. Owen's reaction is to at least let the people know he didn't mean any harm to the woman by offering a more sincere apology. "Listen, I know it's my fault. I wasn't looking. I'm very sorry."

But the woman refuses to be placated, and her response

seems determined to portray him as some awful brute. "Oh, big tough guy, running over an old lady!"

Owen feels forced to defend himself. "It was an accident. I didn't see you. I apologize."

"Oh, so that's supposed to make it all better?" the woman retorts, matching his determined effort. "Just because you're sorry?"

Owen's composure is starting to fade; he feels the back of his neck continue to inflame, his ears are beginning to burn. What dominates his attention is a strong need to compete with the woman for the crowd's attention. If the people think he really is an uncaring jerk, they could turn on him. Owen has to hang in there and try to appease the woman, but more importantly, convince the crowd that he only wants to help resolve the situation. "So what can I do to make this better?"

But the woman completely dismisses his attempt. "You can go jump in a lake!" she suddenly yells, calling for someone to call the police. Owen is shocked. The last thing he wants is for the police to be involved. Owen is now desperate to appear reasonable. If the police come, the people around them will be the ones asked to explain what happened. It was an accident. He has been forced into a confrontation with a crazy woman. It is the story he needs everyone around him to believe.

Owen's strategy is to give in to the woman at all costs, no matter what she does to him, to establish a disparity between them, to identify her as the aggressor. He is determined to wait the woman out and resigns himself to her holding on to him. It is just an indignity he will have to suffer. It is a strategy straight from his martial arts practice: by yielding to the woman, he is actually connecting to her and controlling the situation. All she can truly hurt is his pride, and he doesn't give a fig about that. But he also needs to engage the woman, to give the impression that he is truly working toward peaceful resolve. She is upset, and from her perspective, rightfully so.

He needs to acknowledge that. "Are you sure you're all right?" he politely asks.

"Of course I'm not all right, you asshole! You ran me over!" Owen is undaunted. "Listen, I'm truly sorry."

"What's 'sorry' got to do with it, you big jerk?" Owen continues, "I know I should be more careful." "You're damn right!"

But the woman's vehemence is losing steam. She seems to be repeating her indignation. It has become obvious that she is the one extending the confrontation, and the woman seems to notice. Owen senses her measuring the situation, deciding how to proceed.

"So what are you going to do about it?" the woman asks in the next moment.

It is a change of direction for their encounter. Owen is willing to follow along and asks her what she would like to see happen. The woman still glares at him, then leans into him, staring up at him from beneath his chin. "Give me fifty bucks."

What! Owen is shocked. His reaction is to rebel against her request; giving the woman money would be paying her off, and he didn't do anything intentionally. The bottom line is he doesn't have fifty bucks, and he tells the woman as much.

"Give me twenty," the woman counters in the same undertone, so no one else can hear.

Owen does have twenty dollars, and he knows how much he would like the situation to go away, but what has his attention is how quickly the woman has changed her tone. Before, she seemed lost in a storm of righteous fury, and now she seems able to focus on getting money from him. It makes him wonder what is really going on. Is the woman trying to shake him down? He feels the need to look closer at her, but when he tries to step back, the woman moves forward, staying against him. Owen doesn't want to get too vehement, but he is able to keep her at arm's length.

The woman stands before him. He looks at her closely. Her nasty sneer remains, but what first strikes him is that she isn't as old as he thought. She looks severely unkempt from living on the streets, but her clothes are more torn than tattered. She doesn't smell. When Owen makes the conscious effort to fully open to his impressions of the woman, he expects to notice the smell of body odor and maybe urine, as the smells of a madwoman living on the streets. There are grime marks on her face, but they look like they could have been put there. The woman's eyeliner is exaggerated, and her lipstick is uneven.

What is going on? Owen is looking at a woman pretending to be crazy! And the woman is aware that he recognizes her. Her stare suddenly falters, her eyes flutter. But it doesn't take her long to regain her composure. In an even, quiet voice, she says it again, just for him to hear. "Why don't you buy me lunch?"

Owen is appalled. It's true! The woman before him is pretending to be someone else! He jerks back, but she moves forward again, remaining attached to him. His next instinct is to announce his discovery to everyone around, but he catches himself; she will surely deny everything. It will be her word against his.

But he has no intention of giving in to the woman. She is probably a con artist. It is Owen who will now benefit if the police come, if he can get anyone to believe what he knows about her. That is his predicament. And she hasn't really done anything. As much as Owen thinks she is trying to shake him down, she hasn't committed any crime. He can almost predict what will happen. The police will come, he will accuse the woman, she will deny it, and the crowd will be involved. And maybe the result will be that it is proven that the woman is impersonating a woman living on the streets. But so what? Where will that get him?

Owen needs to end this; he has to find a way to get out of the situation. The woman has actually given him an opportunity. He could agree to buy her lunch. Of course, he won't, and when he gets her alone, he'll turn the tables on her, confront her, and try to figure out what she is really up to. But at least they will be separated from the crowd, which is his main objective.

Owen agrees to take the woman to lunch. For the crowd's benefit, he makes it official in a tone everyone around them can hear. "Ma'am, for the trouble I have caused you, how 'bout I take you to lunch?"

CHAPTER THIRTY

The woman lets him go, takes a step back, and even gives a slight bow of appreciation as she accepts his invitation to take her to lunch.

Applause breaks out among the crowd. Everyone is relieved, and people seem genuinely thrilled by their peaceful resolution. "Way to go!" is even shouted at the two of them. The woman takes in the attention as if she were a ham actor. She smiles, bows to the crowd, and even links her arm with his, turning the two of them to face their admirers. Owen does his best to follow her lead and even feels obligated to bow his head.

Just then, he turns to see Gail and Les standing with the rest of the crowd, grinning broadly and clapping. Owen is surprised. They must have returned when they realized he wasn't behind them. He wonders how long they have been standing there and how much of the confrontation they have seen.

But by the direction of their eyes, he realizes they are clapping for the woman as well. He looks at the woman, and she smiles at them; there is a shared look of recognition and a shared glow of accomplishment. They all look at him in unison.

Owen's mind shifts, then cartwheels as he tries to comprehend. The realization hits him full force: they know each other! He was set up! He is the victim of another prank! The look of surprise on his face is obvious; the three of them suddenly bend over laughing.

Owen is appalled! They are having fun at his expense! The volume of confusion and embarrassment he feels quickly escalates into a rush of indignation that threatens to explode into blind fury.

The onslaught continues. Any attempt to resist it is futile. Whatever he is experiencing is beyond his control. Dark spots suddenly appear before his eyes, his vision begins to blur, his consciousness begins to waver.

Suddenly, he is above the scene, looking down from about a dozen feet. He can see himself collapsed into a sitting position. The other three huddle around him, clearly concerned.

He is experiencing a split perception. He has some awareness of what is happening. His assemblage point has shifted to a new position. This is mentioned in the books. Owen watches as a passive observer. He is absorbed in the scene unfolding. Gail says she is going to get water and quickly leaves. Les puts a hand on his shoulder to steady him.

"What do you think is happening?" the other woman asks, alarmed but anxious to understand.

"I'm sure his assemblage point is shifting again," Les answers.

The woman is both surprised and impressed.

"He can do that?"

"It's been happening lately."

Gail suddenly reappears, carrying a paper cup. She splashes water on his face and the back of his neck.

He feels the wetness of the water from both positions: the one where he hovers above the scene and the one where he is in the scene itself. It causes a jolting shiver, and he becomes aware of himself sitting on the ground.

Owen jumps up. A flush of embarrassment and anger continues to surge through him. The strange woman is in front of him, and he directs his full attention to her.

"So who the hell are you?"

The woman takes a step back to separate herself and gain her composure. She straightens herself up. Then, facing him directly and beaming with a most exaggerated smile, she says, "My name is Reena Yankovich." She then gives a quick bow before standing straight again. "And I am at your service."

She has given the warrior's greeting; of course, she is a warrior.

Her statement, however, offers little explanation. Owen's only interest is in grasping the situation. But the flash of annoyance he felt after learning what they did to him is offset by having to admit that what they did was within the bounds of how warriors behave with one another. They treated him as a challenge. They exercised their folly and used him as an opportunity to enjoy themselves.

"So what are you doing here?"

"I wanted to meet you," the woman proclaims, maintaining her official demeanor.

There's that "meet you" thing again, the same explanation given for the first prank when the group jumped on him.

Before he can think of something else to ask, Reena turns to Les as if seeing him for the first time. "Hello, sweet man," she says, stepping toward him with open arms. They hug and kiss, a great display of affection. "So good to see you," Reena coos in greeting.

Owen is shocked by the sudden change in circumstances and feels a flare of annoyance at being abruptly dismissed. He wonders if they are trying to disarm him, but their reunion scene seems genuine. Les beams with delight. It is truly as if they haven't seen each other in years.

After Les and Reena's shared moment of greeting, the group

suddenly realizes they are blocking the sidewalk and moves aside to let people pass. To get out of the way, they turn and start walking back in the direction they originally came. Owen walks next to Gail and behind Les and Reena, as the two of them walk arm-in-arm, leading the way. They continue to thoroughly enjoy each other's company.

Owen is left awash in his feelings of annoyance and curiosity. He realizes any questions he has won't be answered soon. Instead, he watches Reena closely. What is most surprising is that he ever fully believed she was a bag lady. Having the chance to look at her more closely, he sees that she looks much younger than he initially thought. Her tattered costume seems contrived, and her makeup is veritably smeared on her face. It was surely her nasty attitude and play-acting that pulled the character together. But why all the effort? Wanting to meet him is hardly much of an answer. He thinks of her unusual name and her accent, which he expected to fall away with her sneer, as another detail of her bag-lady character. Owen guesses she is of Eastern European descent. She has dark hair, a roundish face, and brilliant dark eyes. There is an intensity about her, a strong and forceful energy.

As a group, they walk down Main Street. Reena suddenly starts panhandling, saying she might never have such an opportunity again. She looks to be showing off, or it could be another demonstration of her *controlled folly*. The look on people's faces when they encounter her is quite remarkable. Some people make no attempt to hide their disdain, while others are torn between helping her and wanting to get away. Finally, Reena gets an older man to give her money, and she is absolutely delighted. "Pretty good," she says, showing off her couple of dollar bills.

As a group, they agree to meet back at the house. Gail has taken the afternoon off from work, and Reena will ride with her. The two of them start walking back down Main Street toward where Gail parked her car.

For the moment, Les and Owen watch the two women walk away. "So what the hell was that?" Owen asks as soon as the two women are out of earshot.

Les only smiles. "Ah yes, the return of Reena."

Owen isn't willing to have his intrigue deflected any longer. "So what's goin' on?"

"I'm not sure," Les says without altering his gaze.

"So who is she?"

"Someone we have known."

"How long ago was that?"

"Oh, three, four years."

Les's answers to his questions don't seem as cryptic as they might, given the lack of any real effort to explain anything. Owen hopes to have Les fill him in on the details, but Les seems lost in his own thinking.

"So what is she doing here?" Owen asks, trying again for information.

"I understand she's here to work on d*reaming* with Gail."

What? Now there's something of real interest. Yet what most surprises him is that this is the first time he has heard about it. "So how come I was never told?"

Les only shrugs. "All I know is I was instructed not to give you any information."

Owen is taken aback; his sense of being toyed with again threatens to turn to indignation. But what most interests him is the intrigue of knowing that Reena planned their meeting. "So what's that all about?"

"It seems Reena wanted to meet you on her terms," Les answers directly, then adds, "You have to admit, it's a good warrior strategy. It's very hard to overcome what people think of us."

CHAPTER THIRTY-ONE

Making the drive back to the house, they arrive before the two women and find Ronnie there. It soon becomes apparent that Ronnie is also waiting to meet Reena. She seems nervous, a bit unsettled.

Soon, Gail and Reena come walking through the door. Reena immediately gushes over being back in the house. She actually twirls around with open arms as she takes in everything around her.

Gail introduces Reena to Ronnie. Ronnie is openly pleased to meet her but seems shy as if she were meeting someone important.

Reena has changed clothes. She is dressed in nice jeans, a white cotton button-down blouse, and shiny black pumps. She seems overdressed for the occasion, though Owen isn't interested in making any judgment. She is wearing hardly any makeup now, which allows Owen to get a good look at her. What strikes him most after looking at her closely is that he has no new impressions; he expected that shedding her façade would be revealing. Her face is still bright and open, but with her dark eyes and eyebrows, there is the same dominating intensity. Her dark hair is cut just below her ears. She is neither pretty nor unattractive. Her body is fit but not slim. Seen together, Reena and Gail are about the same height and shape, but they are very different. Reena's energy is much more bombastic and aggressive.

As Reena moves farther into the house, she remains effusive about being back and seems content to let herself be swept up in a whirlwind of nostalgia. She then turns her attention back to Les and resumes her show of affection. "Oh, my dear Les, it really is so good to see you."

Les repeats his delight at seeing her again as well, but he doesn't come close to matching Reena's exuberance. Gail stands off to the side, smiling as an amused onlooker.

"And here's Owen, my new friend," she says, turning to him and grabbing his arm as she passes by. She then turns them both to face Ronnie. "Did he tell you about our introduction?"

Ronnie assures her that she knows nothing about what happened. "Oh, it was wonderful," Reena says, turning to him to gauge his reaction. "We had a marvelous first meeting."

She then launches into a recap of their encounter, saying she was looking forward to meeting the new guy. "I heard he was quite good but a little stiff and on the serious side." She acknowledges him with a quick wink and a teasing smile. Owen looks at Gail, who gives him a surprised look and shrugs to communicate that she never said anything of the kind. "So I wanted to test him," Reena says. She then tells of the prank she decided on and how she put together her costume. She says being penniless and living on the streets has always been a fear of hers, so she could tap into it. She says she waited at a determined spot, and as soon as Gail and Les walked past, she stepped in front of him. But she was not prepared for how hard he hit her. "This guy could have been a linebacker!" she states emphatically. She swears she saw stars. Her hanging onto the parking meter wasn't an act; she was hanging on for dear life!

"And he looked so shocked," she says, imitating his look of dismay.

Everyone openly laughs. Ronnie is amazed.

Reena continues her blow-by-blow description, telling how she thought Owen was going to run off on her, so she had to grab hold of him by his shirt with both hands. At that point, she actually grabs onto him again, and for a second time, he is forced to deal with having this woman attached to him. She tells how she threatened to call the police, and even imitates him looking in both directions to see if the police were coming.

Owen is well aware that her account of their meeting is dominating the group. He has to believe she is aware of what she is doing and that her actions are either another display of controlled folly or a reaction to being genuinely nervous about being in a new situation and being the center of attention. Either way, he is willing to go along with her, but when she says the crowd was becoming furious with him and would have jumped on him if he tried to move against her, he feels the need to clarify. "The crowd was just as much on my side," he says, pushing back against her embellishment. "They felt sorry for me for having to deal with such a lunatic."

Reena laughs and doesn't dispute his version. "I was good, wasn't I?" she says, not fishing for a compliment but asking for an exclamation point.

Owen gives in to her and agrees. Why not? Her performance was impressive. "Yes, you were very good."

Reena chortles over his confirmation and seems to take his agreement as permission to proceed; she takes off again, giving her account. Owen feels the need to jump in again to correct her when she says she had him in the palm of her hand. She even has the outlandish audacity to say she thought he was going to pee his pants.

"C'mon," Owen rebukes. "I had you as much as you had me. I knew something was up."

"You wouldn't have if I hadn't asked you for fifty bucks," she replies. She goes on to admit to everyone that she overplayed her hand. "I got greedy," she confesses.

Her admission has taken away the power of his rebuttal, leaving Owen to reinforce his position. "I could tell you were someone else."

Reena agrees with him while facing the others. "Yes, yes, he had spotted me. I could feel the tables turn, and I couldn't shake him."

She imitates Owen shifting his head from side to side, trying to peer beyond her facade. It is very funny.

Reena ends her story by noting that the crowd applauded when they reached the resolution of going to lunch together. Ronnie is delighted. And it was amazing. There were so many twists and turns in such a short period.

"Well, at least we put on a good show," Reena offers, and as a gesture of camaraderie, she squeezes his arm.

Reena turns him and steers him to the couch, suggesting they sit. Owen is aware of being caught in her undertow. Reena is relentless; her desire to control the situation is unabashed, but Owen doesn't feel put upon enough to resist. Les and Gail follow and sit in the chairs on either side of them, and Ronnie sits on the floor. "So how's Nevada these days?" Les asks Reena after everyone has settled in.

Reena reacts as if completely surprised by the question. "Oh, hot, dry, with plenty of sunshine," she manages to say, then laughs at her own glibness.

Les smiles at her. "And how's the group?"

Reena turns her upper body to face him. She seems to be openly studying him. "The group is good."

The idea of another group of practitioners instantly captures Owen's attention, and he is eager to hear more, but Les moves on to ask something else. "So what have you been working on lately?"

"Wow, nothing like skipping preliminaries," Reena says, laughing and unable to contain her amazement. She then looks around at the rest of them, drawing attention to her sense that Les is being so forward.

Owen is only pleased. He had been wanting to learn more about Reena and had been wondering how to steer the conversation toward getting information. He is surprised and glad that Les has taken the initiative.

Les's question is still pressed against her, and Reena is obligated to answer. "Well, as you know, it's all about *dreaming* with me."

"So how's your progress?" Les asks after Reena has hesitated and doesn't seem willing to say anything more.

Reena laughs and acts shocked at Les's blatant directness. "Geez, Mr. Twenty Questions!"

Les smiles but remains undeterred. "We haven't seen you for a while."

Owen is surprised by Les's boldness. He seems intent on pressing her, and there is little doubt he has his own agenda. Les seems genuinely curious about Reena, but there is also a hint of suspicion.

And Reena doesn't seem to be able to deny him, maybe out of respect or from not wanting to appear dismissive. "Oh well, a warrior has nothing to hide," she says with resolve, quoting from the books. "I'm up against the second gate of *dreaming*."

A wave of surprise spreads through the group. The second gate of *dreaming* is a big deal. Owen notices that Gail is the only one who isn't surprised, but of course, she already knows.

"So you're able to wake up from one dream into another?" Les asks, unabashedly intrigued.

"I think it's better to say my interest is to change dreams in an orderly manner," Reena answers, in a tone of feeling that it is necessary to correct him.

"And you're able to do that?" Les asks, both amazed and determined to be sure of what she is saying.

"Not as much as I'd like," Reena replies. "The challenge is to control a dream and make it cohesive."

The magnitude of what Reena is saying looms large amongst them. What Owen understands is that when a dreamer isolates an element in a dream, it stays fixed, and by taking short glances rather than staring at it, they can move from item to item.

"And then move from one dream to another?" Les adds.

"As many dreams as possible. But in an orderly and precise manner. The goal is to exercise the dreaming attention."

Owen finds himself needing to confirm something important, the thing he and the others strive for every night when they go to sleep. The question jumps out of him so that he almost blurts it. "So you can find your hands whenever you want?"

Reena looks at him and laughs. "Don't get so focused on your hands, though the hands are a good place to start. Remember, focusing on any item in your dreams will do. Once isolated and controlled, the item becomes a point of departure. From there, you wake up into another dream."

The group stares at her in silence.

"So how is working with Gail going to help?" Les then asks.

Reena feigns shock as she looks at him. She seems to think Les's questions are over, but the pattern that developed between them has continued. "My dear Les," she says. "You are just incorrigible." Is she actually feigning a coy southern belle's accent?

But Reena has their undivided attention. "I'm sure it's no surprise to you, but my energy can be a bit chaotic." A high laugh punctuates her attempt at understatement. "But it's also my saving grace. I am able to abandon myself, which is necessary for my task, but I can also get carried away. As you might remember, female warriors in particular fall prey to the lure of the second attention. They are nimble enough to go into it with no effort at all, often too soon for their own good. And that's where I'm at. The truth is, I can scare myself. A dreamer needs to be a paragon of sobriety, which is where Gail comes in. She is much more sober and rational, but not as daring. We're hoping to balance each other. Remember, the paradox of dreamers is that they need to let go but not lose their marbles."

Reena laughs at her statement, then looks to Gail for confirmation. Gail smiles back at her.

"So you are going to dream together?" Les asks, greatly interested.

Reena smiles. "That would be great, but it's not our intent. At least, we're not at that point yet. I need Gail as a safety net, and she needs me as a boost."

Owen is left reeling. The magnitude of what is being proposed is far beyond what he has ever encountered.

"So how exactly are you going to help each other?" Les asks.

"We're not entirely clear on that," Reena answers. "We definitely have some things to work out. But we've put ourselves in the hands of *spirit*. *Spirit* will give the indications. We have to trust. Both of us feel strongly that this is the way. Maybe it will be enough for us to just be there for each other."

Reena then adds, "And I understand you folks are doing some great work with recapitulation. I could use more of that. As you know, controlling the *dreaming attention* still depends on gaining and redeploying energy."

From there, the conversation doesn't go any further, and they are left to bask in the magnitude of what has been revealed and proposed. After another moment, Gail suggests they eat something. Reena says she is starving. The women move to the kitchen, and after another moment, Les and Owen follow. The conversation continues while food is prepared, though it stays light and festive. They are a bunch of friends who have gotten together.

After eating, the women decide to go back to Gail's place to get settled. They promise to come back in a couple of days. Reena says she will need a recapitulation crate, and Owen says they inherited a couple extra, so it won't be a problem. Ronnie leaves with them.

When Owen is alone with Les, he addresses the situation directly. "So what do you make of all this?"

"I'm not sure," Les says, thinking to himself. There is an undertone of apprehension in his voice.

"Is Reena dangerous?" Owen hears himself ask. He is surprised by his choice of words.

"Of course," Les answers. "She has to be."

CHAPTER THIRTY-TWO

The addition of Reena changes the dynamics of the group. The women become more separate, and their focus remains on the practice of *dreaming*. Even the men, who are very interested and motivated by what the women are doing, concentrate more on *dreaming*. When members of the group are together, it can lead to long discussions about *dreaming*, the use of dreaming attention, and all the procedures associated with setting it up and exploring it. They search through the books to clarify issues and gain understanding. At night, they follow the techniques prescribed in the books and go to bed with smooth rocks or crystals pressed between their fingers to activate the dreaming attention and direct it toward the particular tasks they have chosen. Dreaming is an adventure. They are standing before the door to the unknown.

But the dynamic of the group changes again when Reena asks to stay at Les's house. The issue is that Gail and Ronnie are at work most days, leaving Reena alone. She has always functioned better when involved with others, and besides, for most of their *dreaming* work together, they don't need to be in the same house. By staying at Les's place, Reena hopes to take advantage of the group energy of working with the guys in the recapitulation crates. Reena strongly believes in the power of recapitulation as a great way to free up energy, and energy is what she needs most for everything she hopes to accomplish in her *dreaming* with Gail. Les offers her a room.

It is very different having Reena around, and an interesting dynamic develops between her and Owen. It seems to be a carry-over from their first encounter, when Reena posed as a street person, and they became locked in a competitive struggle. For some reason, they can't be in the same room without turning on each other. Just the sight of the other will set them off. It is a verbal jousting that they immediately get into.

"Oh, here he is, the big tough guy," Reena might throw at him. "Ah, yes, my lunatic friend, "Owen might answer.

"You're so stiff you squeak when you walk," Reena could counter. "If I give you a dollar, will you spin your head around?" Owen might retort.

It becomes a battle of wills, a battle of folly. And it's not just about who can antagonize the other the most or be the most ridiculous or condescending. Their banter and game of one-upmanship can go in any direction. They can push each other to extremes. At one point, Owen is actually cutting up vegetables on Reena's plate and feeding her like a child.

What they are experiencing is a release of energy. It is something they cause in the other and is best described as a kind of polarity that activates between them and then escalates. But where does it come from? There is a sense of precedence, of a source, from a previous connection. "I think we've known each other," Reena blurts. It feels true, as if they were feeding off some past involvement, continuing a relationship that feels recondite, otherworldly yet palpable. Could they have known each other before? When? Where? It hardly matters. Any experience they had with each other would have had to originate in the second attention, and details would be unavailable, because of the barrier of perception, as any experience in the second attention is inaccessible to normal awareness. They might recover it in the future if they develop their abilities. At their current level of proficiency, their challenge is to release and cultivate energy.

They try to catch each other off balance, aiming to do so when they are most open and available, when the energy rises most, and when the chance to release is greatest. The emotion generated in their exchange can incline them to defend themselves and turn the attack back against the other. If the two of them can stay detached from the process, they can almost watch their person expand. The amount of energy generated and released is incredible. It becomes the perfect counterbalance to the long periods of physical inactivity spent in the recapitulation crates and the perfect antidote to the rigors, innate fears, and doubts caused by dreaming and the unworldly nature of focusing on the second attention.

Yet after a while, the energy generated by their exchange begins to wane, and they risk falling into a pattern of repeating themselves. But they are committed to taking advantage of what is between them and can find a new source of energy by combining their efforts and focusing in the same direction. A very different dynamic develops. They become peaceful with each other, restrained and serene. The solace they experience in each other's company stems from their activated polarity, which can best be described as an emotion of union and longing. In each other's company, they are more than they could be by themselves and are quick to get lost in a kind of blending. They begin taking long walks together, first through the neighborhood, then in parks and in forests.

But it is not enough to be contained within themselves. They need to extend their awareness and connect with other energies. So they visit art galleries and museums and take a day trip to the zoo. They even take a trip to the woods where Owen first met Nate and spend a night gazing at flames and shadows. It is all part of a focus they have found for their lives. Against the immensity of the world, they bolster themselves and support each other. The two of them go to movies, the theater, and sporting events. There is no real reason for what they do beyond wanting to open themselves and be moved by the volume and particularity of what they experience.

That energy also eventually diminishes, as if reaching toward an end, exhausting a direction. They are surprised but determined to keep going, convinced there is still something for them. It feels too good, too right. They are just so complete and comfortable with each other. They are overcome by the joy of having a partner, someone to validate them, give them permission, as if in a blissful oblivion, a stasis of basking. But they begin to experience a strange loss of energy; they lose weight, and dark circles appear under their eyes. They are not sure what to think, but they are unable to muster any great alarm. They could spend the whole day sitting around as if they had been smoking weed.

"Are we in love?" Reena suddenly asks.

They sit stretched out on the couch, their feet facing each other from opposite ends.

His first reaction is to laugh at the absurdity. There has been a strong attraction between them, and the idea of being in love could explain their affinity, but on the level of being warriors, their romance is with knowledge, first, foremost, and always.

But Reena is a serious person. Beyond all the crazy things she says and does, there is always a serious interest in exercising and understanding. She deserves an answer. Owen fully takes in her question.

Reena continues to stare at him intently. He senses a measure of desperation. Owen takes another moment to gather himself.

"I think maybe we have just reached a new level of indulgence."

They look at each other. The effort is to fully connect.

Suddenly, they burst out laughing. It is an outburst neither of them expected. They laugh until they are uproarious. Something has released inside them, as if a dam has broken.

They continue laughing.

They are completely amazed.

They shake their heads

When their laughter subsides, they experience a deep sense of release. Finally, they both stand. They are still together, but never in the same way again.

They walk to the hallway, then leave the house through the back door. They walk along the pathway to the courtyard and find the others sitting at the patio table. As they walk through the entrance to the shrubbery, Les, Gail, and Daniel turn to them. There is an immediate recognition of their change. They all grin broadly.

"They're baaack!" Les exclaims, throwing up his arms.

Yes, they are back. Laughter breaks out amongst everyone.

"We were getting ready to stage an intervention," Les jokes, as they walk closer. Owen and Reena sit in open chairs.

"You guys were scaring us," Gail adds.

Owen and Reena can only imagine. They shake their heads in amazement and disbelief.

"It's not like we didn't try," Gail adds, laughing.

It's true, they did try. At different times, both Les and Gail had voiced their concern, but Owen and Reena easily dismissed them.

"So what the heck was going on?" Gail asks, voicing the others' huge interest.

Reena and Owen both make an effort to explain, as much as to clarify for themselves.

"It just happened," Reena offers. "We were just following along."

Somehow, their energies combined to boost them. Where it

took them was beyond what they could have imagined. They were sure they were following a path with heart.

But they took it too far. "Being in love would have been the easy explanation," Owen states, giving Reena's conclusion.

They all laugh loudly, hearing the assessment.

"Hey, we've all had our crazy experiences," Les comments.

"Love would sure do it," Gail agrees.

"Or maybe hate," Daniel adds. It is the first time he has spoken since they all gathered. The others notice his effort to contribute to the conversation and congratulate him.

But the relating of their experience is a testament to the nature of the assemblage point. "It's crazy to think that how we behave and feel as human beings is a matter of the position of the assemblage point," Les comments.

They all agree. And it can shift so easily. It's what happened to them. "It's like a light switch turned on and off," Reena says.

Because as warriors, their focus has been on loosening the assemblage point, and now that it has loosened, it doesn't take much for it to shift. The challenge is to control and direct that movement.

But it's so daunting. If they allow themselves to think about it, what they focus on is a crazy proposition; they are actively trying to control their perception. The idea hardly makes sense if they approach it only rationally, from anything close to their normal everyday perspective. Their only hope is to continue viewing the world through the lens of expanding awareness.

But it's so difficult. Even after years of study, the practice barely makes sense from where they are. They can feel so inept at times. Their ability to relate to and interact with the world as a warrior can so easily elude them. They often feel as if they are starting from square one.

They are quick to remind themselves that a warrior spends years in a kind of limbo, neither yet a man of knowledge nor still an average man. It's like learning to walk for the first time, or maybe first starting to crawl.

They are worse off than average men. The books talk about it: average men have their shields to protect them against the unknown; their beliefs and notions of the world, and the confidence and dedication they have to pursue and perpetuate a view of themselves and the world around them that goes unchallenged. Average men are insulated from the unknown and have no idea it even exists. As warriors, they are convinced that the world is so much more than what meets the eye, but they have no way to reach out and connect to it. They are left completely vulnerable. They have their training and belief in the Warrior's Way, but that can feel like sand that slips so easily through their hands.

They are in a terrible spot. They can see how warriors must struggle against the tendency to become morose and morbid. Awareness of the unknown can be such a pressure. Their only hope, as the directive of their training, is to laugh at their situation and at themselves. Against the finality of death, nothing can be more important; as warriors, they must consider themselves already dead. The premise of controlled folly is what they have to lean on. But even that can seem like a pie-in-the-sky concept.

It feels as if a cloud has descended upon them. They are pinned down by the debilitating and untenable magnitude of the paradox. They have to go forward, yet they have so little to start with.

They need to snap out of it, yes, but they also understand that the attitude of a warrior is not to deny themselves anything and to express themselves fully in what they are feeling, as a strategy for release.

With that in mind, the idea comes to have a pity party. Why not? They feel pressured and overwhelmed, so why not express their misery together? It can be an attempt at group energy. They can have fun with it.

They decide to celebrate themselves by heaping great gobs of sentimentality on each other and offer odes of lament.

"We are nothing."

"We are worse than lost."

"We could spend our lives wandering in circles."

"What if we are only fooling ourselves?"

"Whose idea was this anyway?"

"Damn these books."

"I could have been a plumber."

"I could have been a housewife."

When Ronnie returns from work and finds the group in high spirits and a bit unhinged, she quickly understands what is going on and welcomes the chance to join in, admitting she feels the same kind of pressure.

The feeling of levity and camaraderie continues. The hell with it! They're going all the way. They decide to make dinner and even have some wine. They pull things out of the cupboard and refrigerator and make crazy concoctions. Ronnie ends up pouring cereal over her salad.

Afterward, they do the flyer dance. It is the first time Reena has heard of it, and of course, she performs with abandon and gusto. How big and bloated can they all be? They are up against the forces of infinity. The odds against them are great. When the words to the music come around, they are quick to sing in full: "Would you like to dance with me? We're doing the cosmic slop!" They have big fun.

When thoroughly exhausted, they collapse into the chairs and couch and laugh. Of course, they will eventually have to get serious, at least a little. They know they will have to focus again. To set that direction, Les decides to rally the group and read a few quotes from the books that have become their cornerstones. He goes to his room and returns with a couple of sheets of paper. He stands before the group as an orator, raising an arm and pointing a finger to the heavens, dramatically delivering great words of knowledge.

"Man's possibilities are so vast and mysterious that warriors, rather than thinking about them, choose to explore them, with no hope of understanding them....Choice, for warrior-travelers then, is not really the act of choosing, but rather acquiescing elegantly to the solicitations of *spirit*....The ultimate accomplishment of a warrior is joy....The art of being human is to balance the terror of being human against the wonder of being human."

CHAPTER THIRTY-THREE

Owen is in the courtyard, practicing the tai chi form. It is something he does most mornings to start his day. It is his way of awakening his energy, of connecting his body and extending his awareness throughout himself and out to the world around him. He moves slowly through the movements, relaxing his energy down through his body and feeling it sink into a gentle compression against the ground, then gathering to cross an equilibrium of pressure that expands and returns through his body, extending out through his hands and fingers. The energy generated by the movements extends out from him like water washing up on shore, reaching its full expression before falling back through his body to the ground, then gathering and expanding out from him again. The movements are connected to the inhaling and exhaling of his breathing. The shapes and movements express the ebb and flow of energy. The energy created directs his body.

At some point, he notices Gail has entered the courtyard. He expects Gail to start gazing or work on her morning yoga practice, but she doesn't and stands off to the side, watching him. It makes him a little self-conscious to have someone watch him but he accepts the added dynamic as a challenge. He stays contained in himself, letting the energy move through him as freely and fully as possible.

After a while, he realizes that Gail is waiting to talk. He is toward the end of his workout anyway, and after finishing the form, he covers his fist with his palm and bows slightly, acknowledging the great "All" of everything he is connected to.

When he turns toward Gail, he is aware that something is different about her. As he approaches, he notices an agitation on her face.

Something is going on. As he draws near, they exchange greetings. He is already preparing himself, and Gail waits until he is directly in front of her. "There is something I need to tell you," she says, meeting his gaze with a look of resolve. "Reena is going back to Nevada, and I've decided to go with her."

Owen feels the words as a volume that keeps coming until the path the words travel is wide enough to barely fit inside him. Gail is leaving, and Reena is leaving as well! In response to trying to control the volume, he takes a quick stab at understanding. "What's going on?" He listens as Gail explains that Reena has reached a dangerous place in her dreaming and needs to return to people more experienced than she is. She says she needs to go forward with dreaming, and working with Reena is her best opportunity. It is not what she wanted, but the direction of spirit is clear. Ronnie will be going with them.

Owen struggles to withstand the volume, with no hope of stopping what expands inside him. It will be the end of the group. It will be the end of his practice as he knows it. His life is changing. It is too much to give credence to everything at once, and he holds back against the power by keeping the ramifications separate from him and hovering in space so that when Gail finishes her explanation and falls silent, he has nothing else to say. Gail lowers her head. She remains a moment, then turns and walks away.

Owen stands alone. He is devastated. Pure magnitude dominates him.

To relieve some of the pressure, he focuses on understanding. What could have happened? It seems so drastic. Nothing was mentioned. Why wasn't there any indication? And why did Gail feel it necessary to tell him herself? Since he and Reena have been spending so much time together, he would have thought she would be the one to inform him.

That last thought takes another direction. What has happened with Gail's announcement feels contrived. He hesitates, letting the thought expand, but it does offer an alternative. Having Gail tell him they are leaving would definitely capture his attention. He was just thinking the other day that things have been pretty quiet among the group. Maybe they are pulling another prank on him. The prank would be devious enough to be worth their effort.

Owen becomes a swarm of conflict. He can't deny that these people are dedicated tricksters. And Gail would be the perfect front person because she is so straightforward and reliable. She was the front person in their initial prank, getting him to believe that she and Ronnie were being pursued by other warrior teams. But maybe it is true and they are leaving. He can't deny the possibility. It would be the end of the group.

Owen remains awash in surges of emotion. He has to find out. What convinces him is the sudden awareness of himself standing alone in the courtyard, feeling completely neutralized by what Gail has said. He has to do something. Because of the bombshell Gail has dropped on him and the sketchy explanation, he will demand more information. They must be expecting him to follow her back to the house, and that is exactly what he feels he needs to do. If they have intentionally led him to this point, it is brilliant, and his only course of action is to acknowledge their success and deal with what happens next head-on. It means he has no choice but to go to the house. He needs this to be decided. He is going to confront someone.

Owen walks with determination. Entering the house, he doesn't immediately encounter anyone and walks straight down the hallway past the closed doors to the living area. There, he finds Les and Gail on the couch, embraced. Owen is shocked and manages to step back into the hallway before he is noticed. He sees Les turned toward him, a pained look on his face. Gail is consoling him, telling him how much he means to her and how grateful she is for having him in her life.

Owen is caught in a terrible situation. He suddenly finds himself eavesdropping on a most intimate moment, yet he is also aware that his momentum of resolve and determination has been completely thwarted. It would be just what they wanted. The timing of their show of affection has stopped him dead in his tracks. Did they know he was coming? But there is no way he can force himself into their situation. If they have set this up, he can't help but yield to their direction; they have staged the scene right down to the angle and anguish on Les's face! Owen waits to see if Les glances over to try to catch him watching.

From farther down the hallway, a door opens, and Reena emerges from what he knows to be the bathroom. Giving him no more than a glance, she continues into a bedroom across the hall and closes the door behind her. Was that staged as well? To divert his attention from Les and Gail? To neutralize him? Again, the timing appears perfect. His attention is now split between wanting to hear more of what Gail and Les will say to each other and pursuing Reena. But Reena is more available, and there is no front for her to hide behind. He starts down the hall. Reaching the room, he knocks once to announce himself before opening the door.

Reena's reaction is to whip herself around in surprise. Her eyes flash at him. "What are you doing?" she says, facing him from the other side of the bed.

Owen won't be denied. "What is going on?" "What did Gail tell you?"

"That you're leaving." "Yes, it's true."

"Why didn't you tell me?" "Gail felt it was her place." "Why all of a sudden?" "There's no time to wait."

"But you've never said anything about what was going on."

"It's not the relationship we have with each other."

Owen has exhausted his initial thrust of questioning and gained little understanding. He is desperate to know whether they are truly leaving.

Reena continues to hold his gaze. "Owen, I need you to know that nothing was planned." Her demeanor shifts to become earnest. "And this is nothing I want, but I am at my wits' end. I have reached a barrier in my dreaming that I am unable to cross."

Owen is interested in what she has to say but is also wary of being placated.

"I am at the mercy of forces that are threatening my progress."

"We all are."

"You know the only direction is to go forward."

Confirmation of everything she says is reflected in the complexity of Reena's expression. After her initial reaction to him, her face has changed, revealing a depth of uncertainty, maybe even true fear. It is as if the determination he expected, along with the confidence and resolve he has come to know from her, has been stripped away, leaving her vulnerable and exposed. Owen can only imagine what she is up against.

"The life of a warrior is endless struggle," Reena continues. "I have come to accept that. We are forever pitted against the forces of the unknown. I can't deny my heritage any more than you can."

Owen feels caught up in what she is saying and is willing to let her words determine his response.

"I feel we entered a realm together beyond what either of us can control," she says, still staring at him. "What you have offered me has taken me beyond where I have ever been. For that, I am grateful."

The direction of her talk has shifted to a more personal tone. "I wish you well as I need you to wish me well."

She is stating her truth, and as he takes in her words, he feels a building inside, a matching of her sentiment. Something is opening inside him. His initial reaction is to resist, but the expansion creates a space, full and definite. As soon as he is forced to acknowledge its existence, he experiences a release, as an equilibrium is crossed, as a wave of kinship bursts out from some recondite corner of himself.

"The path forward is our connection. It is all we have, but all we will ever need."

The sound of her voice seems to act as a conduit to another space, another kind of time. It is as if blood is rushing through his body with unusual pressure. She steps forward, and he steps toward her, confirming that both enhance and accelerate, until they meet in an embrace. A flow of words builds until they are both speaking at such a volume and speed that the only thing discernible is an expansion of release that explodes over them, in such a rush that there is no hope but to be swept away. There is only expanse and going forward. His vision begins to blur; there is a swirling inside as he gives himself over as the only thing possible.

CHAPTER THIRTY-FOUR

Owen awakes to find himself lying across the bed. The thoughts that come to him are vague remnants and impressions of what happened and how long he has been there. At some point, he realizes Reena is lying next to him in the opposite direction. She is not moving, and Owen is not interested in moving either. He lies feeling spread out but aware of the space around him.

After a while, Reena gets up and sits on the edge of the bed. It doesn't change how Owen feels; he feels dominated by the space beyond. After another moment, Reena gets up and leaves the room. He lies in a particular space, a place where something has happened. For the moment, he is open to wondering but knows he is not capable of understanding, so he remains available to just lie there. The world is huge. But the realization is nothing new to him and offers nothing that will take him any further, and what he is left with is the awareness that he cannot stay in the room forever. He then feels forced to focus on possibility. His life will proceed from this moment. Eventually, lying there makes him uncomfortable, and he sits up. After another moment, he rises and walks out of the room.

He walks down the hallway. Entering the great area, he sees Gail and Les on the couch and Reena in one of the chairs. Owen walks over and sits in the other chair. No one moves or speaks. There is a connection between them that Owen is willing to be a part of. The feeling is that a volume has been created. A space has been reached. They could live their lives in this space if that was intended.

They continue to sit. For his part, Owen sees the time together as a kind of gathering, a gathering of focus and strength. Their journey will be long. They need to use everything available to them. For now, he feels they are in the best possible place.

Eventually, Les gets up and goes to the back rooms, and after a while, Reena does the same. Owen gets up and goes to the kitchen for a glass of water. When he returns to where he was sitting, Gail hasn't moved. They eventually strike up a conversation. He asks when they plan to leave, and she says as soon as possible. It will take them at least a couple of days to pack up their things and settle their affairs. When he asks how long they plan to be gone, he already knows the answer, but he listens as Gail says she has no idea, that everything in a warrior's world needs to be treated as permanent.

Over the next day, Owen encounters each member of the group, unfolding as a series of tableaux. Between the scenes, a common theme of resolve and acquiescence emerges.

The first scene is with Ronnie, who returns to the house and finds that Owen and Les have been told about their departure. She is first determined to make sure everyone is all right. She is openly concerned about Les and quick to thank him for everything he has done for her. It is then that the magnitude of her situation takes over, and she becomes distraught over the drastic change her life is about to undergo. She never meant for anything like this to happen. She only ever saw her life as something developing. For a moment, she is inconsolable, and the others rally to support her. Finally, she admits that pursuing the material is the only thing that has meaning for her anymore; she desires to live a full life of exploration and is only grateful to have a direction and a chance to live the depth of her possibilities.

A similar scene repeats with Daniel when he returns home from work and is told by Les about the latest developments. He is shocked and dismayed, overcome by a sense of loss and devastated that life as he has known it is coming to an end. What he holds onto is the feeling that there must be a mistake, that the women can't be so certain about needing to leave. But he comes to understand that what is happening is beyond his control, that he can only trust that the women are serious practitioners and that their actions are guided by *spirit*. He has no idea what will happen but that is the condition of his life. He ends up only being amazed. He is sure he has a lifetime of wonderment ahead of him.

Owen's next encounter is with Gail. But it is more a discussion of particulars, and Gail asks for his help in returning the house she rents back to the owners, arranging the sale and distribution of her furniture and other contents she won't be able to take with her. Owen faces the residual effects of her leaving and abandoning them, which mostly manifest as resentment toward her for hurting Les. But he is able to get beyond his feelings by recognizing that Gail is the consummate warrior, whose only focus is serving her connection to power and the great unknown. In this understanding, he takes his lead from Daniel and the response he demonstrated by giving himself over to trust and amazement. He only wishes Gail well and expresses his gratitude for all she has done for him. They share a genuine embrace. Of course, Owen will help her in any way he can. It will be his honor to give service to a fellow warrior-traveler. They talk over details and plot strategy.

The next morning, Owen finds himself alone with Les in the

courtyard. They both shake their heads and laugh at the predicament they have found themselves in. It feels good to let go, to give in to folly, to know they can't change one iota of what is happening, though Les admits to feeling overwhelmed, saying that just when you think there isn't anything else the material can strip from you, it will find something. But immediately he laughs again and admits to his feelings as an old pattern of indulgence and self-pity. They both know that emptying themselves is endless. The real key is what fills the space made available.

His last conversation is with Reena. When they find themselves alone, they feel the need to talk. There is much between them. They decide to walk together through the neighborhood, as they have many times before. Their mood is nostalgic, and there is a strong sense of affinity and kinship. They have no explanation for what has happened between them, except that in their involvement they have offered each other a boost, both as a release of energy and as an opening to a new direction. They are grateful to each other. They spend time talking about their experience in the room the last time they were together. Both admit to feeling the room waver, then lift and swirl. It was as if something picked them up, or as if some space opened to them. They both feel a great sense of movement, as if they had traveled some distance together, though neither remembers anything specific. They can only conclude that they entered the second attention and were moved by the force of their combined energy. They admit that what they experienced is staggering, and against that magnitude they hold themselves up to the power of what it means to be alive. What they experienced together is something they will have to struggle to remember, just as anything experienced in the second attention is available to be remembered only after the barrier of their perception has been broken and they bridge their two awarenesses and gain the totality of themselves.

Reena goes on to discuss what she has encountered in dreams and why she has to return to Nevada. Owen is surprised to hear her say this, since he didn't ask, but he realizes that her willingness to be open and talkative is another attempt to abandon her personhood, a warrior strategy. Reena starts by talking about the second attention. "As you know, an element of the second attention is its unbending fixation on detail; the smallest detail that would go thoroughly unnoticed by the attention of everyday life can be a world of interest in the second attention."

Owen is following her.

"The challenge of dreaming is not to get caught up in the almost invincible pull of the second attention. One must give only cursory glances to everything and be satisfied with the briefest possible views. As soon as one focuses on anything, one loses control."

They continue walking through the neighborhood. The sky is heavily overcast. The houses are set back from the road and separated by enough space that each seems like its own world. The scene is static, as if they are walking through a poised landscape.

"Imagine the outlandish joy of examining your dreams' contents," Reena continues. "Then imagine yourself going from dream to dream, examining every detail."

Owen can only imagine the challenge.

"It's easy to realize that one can get carried away and sink to mortal depths. Especially if one is given to indulging. And that's where I am at. I have a strange possessiveness that I have to admit speaks to my bent of character." She gives a strange laugh, a mixture of desperation and amazement. "I'm a compulsive maniac, and it pains me to say that I'm completely boring myself."

Owen is fascinated. "But I thought you reach the second gate of *dreaming* when you wake up from one dream into another?"

"Yes, but it requires a control of my *dreaming attention* that I just don't have. Remember, one has to change dreams in an orderly and precise manner."

What Reena says has taken him to the edge of his understanding of *dreaming,* and he feels compelled to take her at her word. "So what are you going to do?"

"I don't know. I feel I've reached an impasse I'm unable to get beyond. My fear is in letting go. Maybe it's what every dreamer has to face, and what we all as warriors will have to face for the rest of our lives if we want to progress. The thing I can attest to is a lack of sobriety and, consequently, a lack of available energy. I thought I had accomplished some things with my energy, but obviously, I haven't."

"Are you afraid you won't be able to get back?" Owen asks, suddenly reflecting on a fear he has always had, a fear that seems natural. The understanding from the books is that if dreamers aren't the paragon of sobriety, they can be stranded in other worlds.

"I won't deny it is possible to get lost in the second attention," Reena continues. "The words of don Juan that warrior-travelers only enter the second attention under the strictest of conditions are clear in my mind, and once the assemblage point breaks away from its normal position, it can become fixed at other positions, by other alignments. But remember, the natural inclination of the assemblage point is to return to its natural position when the dreaming energy is exhausted."

Owen continues to follow her line of thinking. What she is saying is remarkable.

"Remember, in *dreaming,* there is no way of directing the movement of the assemblage point," Reena then says. She seems to be talking as much for herself as for him. "All we can direct is its fixation. In that sense, dreamers are like fishermen equipped with a line that casts itself wherever it may, and the only thing we can do is keep the line anchored at the place where it sinks."

"So why do you need to go back to Nevada?"

"The balancing act a dreamer needs to maintain is too delicate, too subtle for me to accomplish on my own. I need the guidance of someone more experienced. Maybe I only need support, but there's a husband-and-wife team of dreamers, that I have worked with, and they're the reason I came here in the first place. I thought I needed to separate from them. I thought they were too demanding, too arbitrary. But I realize they were right. I have to be more ruthless with myself. Remember, women need to be contained, men have to be hooked and led. And it's being contained, I fought against. I made the mistake of judging the people I needed most. Now I am afraid I will have to beg them to take me back."

They have reached a favorite setting, a special place at the edge of a lake. There is a bench to the side where they have spent hours in the serenity of each other's presence, gazing out over the spreading water's peace and calm. They remain standing, letting the force of eternity gather. Reena then turns to him, and he turns to face her. Her eyes are dark liquid pools reflecting an immensity. "Look for me in your dreams, Owen. I will look for you in mine." He understands her remark as admitting their connection, but offering him a beacon, a guidepost, a calling out, a chance to release and direct himself forward.

CHAPTER THIRTY-FIVE

The activity over the next few days focuses on the women getting ready for their trip. Gail and Ronnie are the ones who have to wrap up their affairs. Notices are given that they were leaving their jobs. There are friends and even family members who have to be contacted. It is a very challenging and emotional time. As support and maybe as their last focused effort as a group, they struggle to maintain a conscious attitude of lightness and folly. They only want to celebrate and stand before the great mystery.

With preparations for the trip complete, it is time for the women to leave. The day is sunny with blue skies, perfect for traveling. To keep the mood light, they have decided to make it a festive occasion. Everyone has put on their better clothes. It feels like a send-off for close relatives. Daniel operates a camera and takes dozens of pictures, of course, without recording anything. As a group, they pose for prosperity in front of the house. They take pictures in pairs and of the car being loaded.

"Geez, you'd think you'd have more than that to show for a life," Les jokes, looking at the few articles inside the trunk of her vehicle before Gail closes the lid.

Everyone laughs and enjoys the moments of levity.

Then it is time to go. Goodbyes are said. Another round of hugs is exchanged, and best wishes are given.

But before getting into the car, Gail performs the warrior's maneuver for leaving a place of great meaning and consequence, probably forever. Facing the house, she clasps her hands with great speed to produce a clapping sound, imprisoning the feelings she does not wish to leave behind. Then, with her hands clasped and with great force, she takes the captured feelings to the middle of her stomach and stabs herself, as if holding the dagger with both hands. The emotion of the moment is almost too much to bear. A sob comes from Ronnie, and Les has to turn away. But nothing can be done. A warrior's attitude has to be that all the sentimentality in the world can't move them one iota from the direction of their fate.

Just as swiftly as the excruciating moment comes over them, it passes, and as a group, they return to joviality as the women get into the car. From their fierce determination to make the best of the situation, they wave goodbye, laugh, and wish each other luck.

Then the women are off.

The three men stand at the side of the road, watching the car drive away until it turns the corner.

It is Les who breaks the silence. "Well, gentlemen," he says, turning to them and hiking himself up to face the moment. "It looks like our women have left us."

Owen and Daniel only agree.

"But you two look pretty good all dressed up," Les continues, looking each of them up and down in their collared shirts and dress slacks. "And it would be a shame not to take advantage of this momentous occasion. How about we go get something to eat? I know a place with great steaks. I'm buying."

Owen and Daniel look at each other, then shrug. A steak

would be nice. "And maybe some big-ass beers," Owen says, feeling the chance to extend the mood of enjoyment.

"Hey, we could stop at a hardware store and buy you a bucket," Les suggests. "Then you can just belly up to the bar."

The image strikes them as funny. They enjoy a good laugh.

www.ingramcontent.com/pod-product-compliance
Lightning Source LLC
Chambersburg PA
CBHW070139100426
42743CB00013B/2768